PRAISE FOR
PAUL ROGAT LOEB

"*Soul of a Citizen* helps us find the faith we need to act on our deepest beliefs—and keep on. As Paul Loeb eloquently shows through a chorus of diverse voices, when we connect with others it makes each of us more whole. If you care about a just future for all our children, read this book."
— Marian Wright Edelman, president of the Children's Defense Fund

" 'We must be the youngest species on Earth,' as Harlem environmental activist Bernadette Cozart puts it, 'because everything else seems to know what to do.' *Soul of a Citizen* helps teach us what to do."
— David Brower, former executive director of the Sierra Club, founder of Friends of the Earth, Earth Island Action group

"*Soul of a Citizen* is hopeful, compassionate, and powerfully written. In a time of cynicism and anxiety, it's important to hear about the work being done by courageous, active, everyday Americans."
— Grace Paley

"If you are ready to serve as a wounded warrior in order to bring peace and healing to our planet, read this book and then join the battle."
— Bernie Siegel, M.D., author of *Love, Medicine, & Miracles*

"Paul Loeb has been doing wonderfully patient work for some years now, exploring the American conscience from the inside. I regard Loeb as something of a national treasure."
— Susan Sontag

"Loeb's extensive personal interviews give his work authenticity. The style of his writing makes his discoveries accessible."
— Henry Louis Gates, Chairman of African American Studies, Harvard University, on Paul Loeb's *Generation at the Crossroads*

"Hopeful, fascinating, and admirable."
— Robert McAfee Brown, chaplain emeritus of Stanford University

"This wonderful book teaches us the value of taking chances and not being afraid to fail. It reminds us that the more we help others build productive lives, the better our own lives will be."
— Bob Chase, president of the National Education Association

"Loeb tells a variety of personal stories, and of unknown people, which is encouraging to all those who are accustomed to being given famous heroes and heroines to emulate. The book will inspire people new to activism, and deals with cynicism and burnout in a good way for movement veterans. Altogether, Loeb has done a wonderful job, producing a work that's rich with specific experience, not abstract theorizing."
— Howard Zinn, author of
A People's History of the United States: 1492–Present

ALSO BY PAUL ROGAT LOEB

Generation at the Crossroads:
Apathy and Action on the American Campus

Hope in Hard Times:
America's Peace Movement and the Reagan Era

Nuclear Culture:
Living and Working in the World's Largest Atomic Complex

Soul of a Citizen

LIVING WITH CONVICTION
IN A CYNICAL TIME

PAUL ROGAT LOEB

St. Martin's Griffin **M** *New York*

Excerpt from "A Walk" as submitted from *Selected Poems of Rainer Maria Rilke*, edited and translated by Robert Bly. Copyright © 1981 by Robert Bly. Reprinted by permission of HarperCollins Publishers, Inc.

Ken Kesey quote courtesy of *Whole Earth* magazine.

Book Design by Jane Adele Regina

Library of Congress Cataloging-in-Publication Data

Loeb, Paul Rogat
    Soul of a citizen: living with conviction in a cynical time /
Paul Rogat Loeb.
    p.   cm.
    Includes bibliographical references (p.).
    ISBN 0-312-20435-3
    1. Social action—United States. 2. Social participation—United
States. 3. Community organization—United States. I. Title.
HN65.L58 1999
361.2'0973–dc21   99-14058
                                            CIP

First St. Martin's Griffin Edition: May 1999

10 9 8 7 6 5 4 3 2 1

Contents

Introduction

If I am not for myself, who will be for me? And if I am only for myself, what am I?

—RABBI HILLEL

We can never predict the impact of our actions. When she was two months pregnant, Rebecca Hughes worried about how she'd find time to continue her work as a freelance science and health writer, and also be a good mother to her first child. On the spur of the moment, she approached a woman in the elevator of their large Boston apartment building. The other woman was about eight months pregnant. Although they'd never spoken, Rebecca introduced herself and blurted, "I see you're pregnant. I am, too. What if we exchanged baby-sitting?" Scrawling her phone number on a scrap of paper, she placed it in the other woman's hand.

The woman looked alarmed, but took the note and hurried off the elevator. Rebecca felt embarrassed, but a week later the woman called her. "I've been thinking about it," she said. "Would you like to start exchanging even before your baby is born?" Rebecca accepted the offer. She and her new friend invited several others they'd met in the neighborhood to participate, including a nun who took care of the baby of a single surgical intern. The group soon became a close-knit extended family, baby-sitting each other's children daily, holding a weekly play group, sharing emotional support, volunteering together at a local community help line, and exchanging tips on raising children, staying healthy, and managing crowded lives.

In time, twenty families were involved, and the co-op had become permanently woven into the fabric of their neighborhood. "It just seems like a more hopeful way to live," Rebecca recalls years later, after she and I met—and eventually married. "Finding group solutions to individual problems, I felt a lot less alone."

In both intent and outcome, Rebecca's effort was modest. It resolved an everyday personal dilemma, while helping nurture an old-fashioned sense of community in an urban setting. Yet it also had a powerful emotional and spiritual impact on her life. It helped replace isolation with connection.

We can take the lesson of Rebecca's story—that our problems can often best be solved through common effort—and apply it on a larger stage as well, addressing the major issues of our time.  When we open ourselves up to those around us, asking for and offering help and support, we discover strengths and passions we never knew we had. We begin to reconnect with our fellow human beings, with our wisest and most humane instincts, and with the core of who we are, which we call our soul.

A More Hopeful Way to Live

In the personal realm, most Americans are thoughtful, caring, generous. We try to do our best by family and friends. At times we'll even stop to help another driver stranded with a roadside breakdown, or give some spare change to a stranger. But increasingly, a wall now separates each of us from the world outside, and from others who've likewise taken refuge in their own private sanctuaries. We've all but forgotten that public participation is the very soul of democratic citizenship, and how much it can enrich our lives.

However, the reason for our wholesale retreat from social involvement is not, I believe, that most of us feel all is well with the world. I live in Seattle, a city with a seemingly unstoppable economy. Yet every time I go downtown I see men and women with signs saying "I'll work for food," or "Homeless vet. Please help." Their suffering diminishes me as a human being. I also travel extensively, doing research and giving lectures throughout the country. Except in the wealthiest of enclaves, people everywhere say, "Things are hard here." America's economic boom has passed many of us by. We struggle to live on meager paychecks. We worry about layoffs, random violence, the rising cost of health care, and the miseducation of our kids. Too stretched to save, uncertain about Social Security, many of us wonder just how we'll survive when we get old. We feel overwhelmed, we say, and helpless to change things.

Even those of us who are economically comfortable seem stressed. We spend hours commuting on crowded freeways, and hours more at jobs whose demands never end. We complain that we don't have enough time left for families and friends. We worry about the kind of world we'll pass on to our grandchildren. Then we also shrug and say there's nothing we can do.

To be sure, the issues we now face are complex perhaps more so than in the past. How can we comprehend the moral implications of a world in which Nike pays Michael Jordan more to appear in its ads than it pays all the workers at its Indonesian shoe factories combined? Today the five hundred richest people on the planet control more wealth than the bottom three billion, half of the human population. Is it possible even to grasp the process that led to this most extraordinary imbalance? More important, how do we even begin to redress it?

Yet what leaves too many of us sitting on the sidelines is not only a lack of understanding of the complexities of our world. It's not only an absence of readily apparent ways to begin or resume public involvement. Certainly we need to decide for ourselves whether particular causes are wise or foolish—be they the politics of campaign finance reform, attempts to address the growing gap between rich and poor, or efforts to safeguard water, air, and wilderness. We need to identify and connect with worthy groups that take on these issues, whether locally or globally. But first we need to believe that our individual involvement is worthwhile, that what we might do in the public sphere will not be in vain.

This means we face a challenge that is as much psychological as political. As the Ethiopian proverb says, "He who conceals his disease cannot be cured." We need to understand our cultural diseases of callousness, shortsightedness, and denial, and learn what it will take to heal our society and heal our souls. How did so many of us become convinced that we can do nothing to affect our common future? And how have some other Americans managed to remove the cataracts from their vision and work powerfully for change?

When we do take a stand, we grow psychologically and spiritually. Pete Knutson is one of my oldest friends. During his twenty-five years as a commercial fisherman in Washington and Alaska, he's been forced, time and again, to respond to the steady degradation of salmon spawning grounds. "You'd have a hard time spawning, too, if you had a bulldozer in your bedroom," he says, explaining the destruction of once-rich salmon habitat by commercial development and timber industry clear-cutting. Pete could have simply accepted this degradation as fate, focusing on getting a maximum share of the dwindling fish populations. Instead, he's gradually built an alliance between Washington State fishermen, environmentalists, and Native American tribes, persuading them to work collectively to demand that the habitat be preserved and restored.

The cooperation Pete created didn't come easy: Washington's fishermen were historically individualistic and politically mistrustful, more inclined, in Pete's judgment, "to grumble or blame the Indians than to act." Now, with their new allies, they began to push for cleaner spawning streams, preservation of the Endangered Species Act, and an increased flow of water over major regional dams to help boost salmon runs. But large industrial interests, such as the aluminum companies, feared that these measures would raise their electricity costs or restrict their opportunities for development. So a few years ago they bankrolled a statewide initiative to regulate fishing nets in a way that would eliminate small family fishing operations.

"I think we may be toast," said Pete, when Initiative 640 first surfaced. In an Orwellian twist, its backers even presented the initiative as environmentally friendly, to mislead casual voters. It was called "Save Our Sealife," although fishermen soon rechristened it "Save Our Smelters." At first, those opposing 640 thought they had no chance of success: They were outspent, outstaffed, outgunned. Similar initiatives had already passed in Florida, Louisiana, and Texas, backed by similar industrial interests. I remember Pete sitting in a Seattle tavern with two fisherman friends, laughing bitterly and saying, "The three of us are going to take on the aluminum companies? We're going to beat Reynolds and Kaiser?"

But they refused to give up. Instead, Pete and his coworkers systematically enlisted the region's major environmental groups to campaign against the initiative. They worked with the media to explain the larger issues at stake. And they focused public attention on the measure's powerful financial backers, and their interest in its outcome. On election night, November 1995, Initiative 640 was defeated throughout the state. White fishermen, Native American activists, and Friends of the Earth staffers threw their arms around each other in victory. "I'm really proud of you, Dad," Pete's twelve-year-old son kept repeating. Pete was stunned.

"Everyone felt it was hopeless," Pete said, looking back. "But if we were going to lose, I wanted at least to put up a good fight. And we won because of all the earlier work we'd done, year after year, to build up our environmental relationships, get some credibility, and show that we weren't just in it for ourselves."

We often think of social involvement as noble but impractical. Yet as Pete's story attests, it can serve enlightened self-interest and the interests of others simultaneously, while giving us a sense of connection and purpose nearly impossible to find in purely private life. "It takes energy to act," said Pete. "But it's more draining to bury your anger, convince yourself you're powerless, and swallow whatever's handed to you. The times I've compromised my integrity and accepted something I shouldn't, the ghosts of my choices have haunted me. When you get involved in something meaningful, you make your life count. What you do makes a difference. It blows my mind that we beat 640 starting out with just a small group of people who felt it was wrong to tell lies."

In fighting to save the environment and his economic livelihood, Pete strengthened his own soul. How the rest of us might achieve something similar is not always clear. We often don't know where to start. Most of us would like to see people treated more justly, to have the earth accorded the respect it deserves, and to feel less pressure in our lives. But we find it hard to imagine having much of a role in this process. We mistrust our own ability to make a difference. The magnitude of the issues at hand, coupled with this sense of powerlessness, has led far too many of us to conclude that social involvement isn't worth the cost.

Such resignation isn't an innate response, or the creation of some inevitable fate. Rather, it's what psychologists call learned helplessness. Society has systematically taught us to ignore the ills we see, and leave them to others to handle. Understandably, we find it unsettling even to think about crises as huge and profound in their implications as the extinction of species, depletion of the ozone layer, and destruction of the rainforests. Or the desperate poverty that blights entire neighborhoods in our nation's largest cities. We're led to believe that if we can't solve every one of these kinds of problems, we shouldn't bother to become socially active at all. We're also taught to doubt our voice—to feel we lack either the time to properly learn and articulate the issues we care about, or the standing to speak out and be heard. To get socially involved, we believe, requires almost saintlike judgment, confidence, and character—a standard we can never meet. Whatever impulses toward involvement we might have, they're dampened by a culture that demeans idealism, enshrines cynicism, and makes us feel naive for caring about our fellow human beings or the planet we inhabit.

THE DREAM OF PRIVATE SANCTUARY

When I came of age, during the Vietnam War, peace and justice activists worked tremendously hard to convince their fellow citizens that our leaders were lying. Back then, most of us grew up believing our government. It took massive betrayals of trust, and much patient work, before large numbers of Americans decided that this confidence was often unwarranted, and that they needed to challenge official policies. After Vietnam, Watergate, and a parade of other government abuses and scandals, however, people began assuming that all politicians lie; indeed, in this cynical era, lying is considered their defining characteristic. And we consider it normal for wealthy interests to buy and sell our elected officials like so many trading cards. But as singer Bruce Cockburn says, "The trouble with normal is it always gets worse." By allowing others to set the standards that debase the public realm, we risk passing on a world that's meaner, more polarized, more desperate, and unquestionably more corrupt. Working to change things doesn't guarantee that our lives or our society will improve. But hopelessness becomes a self-fulfilling prophecy.

In the chapters to follow, I'm going to try to convince you that our most serious problems, both the public ones and those that seem most personal, are in large part common problems, which can be solved only through common efforts. The dream of private sanctuary is an illusion. It erodes our souls by eroding our sense of larger connection, whether to our fellow human beings or to that force many of us call God. The walls we're building around ourselves, around those closest to us, and ultimately around our hearts may provide a temporary feeling of security. But they can't prevent the world from affecting us. Quite the opposite. The more we construct such barriers, the more private life, for most of us, will grow steadily more insecure.

Think about why we spend more and more time at work, and why most families need two incomes to get by. There are various reasons, of course, but none more relevant than the fact that average wages buy less than they did in the early 1970s. Would such pressures be as acute if we hadn't enshrined "Greed is good" as a core cultural ethic, justifying all manner of destructive economic and political decisions? We worry much about paying the bills when we or our children get sick. We wouldn't if the United States joined every other advanced industrial nation in providing universal health care coverage. If public support for our schools were adequate, and we didn't pay our teachers less than in all comparable nations, we wouldn't have to devote so much time and energy to making sure our kids get a decent education. We used to hope for solid pensions funded by our employers. Now we rely on anything-but-solid IRAs, Keoghs, and 401(k)s, and spend hours trying to figure out how to make the right gambles in a casino economy, so our investments will increase enough to support us in our old age. Surely, as Rebecca says, there's a more hopeful way to live.

AN ANTIDOTE TO POWERLESSNESS

I've written *Soul of a Citizen* because I'm certain this more hopeful way is possible. I'm certain because I've witnessed it—again and again, under every imaginable set of circumstances, and among people as diverse as America itself. For much of the past thirty years, I've watched ordinary citizens get involved, find their voice, take a stand. I've seen them embark on that passage from a purely private life, in which we leave the destiny of our communities to others, to one that joins private and public. I've also explored why so many other people, including once passionately involved individuals, find it hard to act on their beliefs—why they get caught in doubt and hesitation or burn out in despair.

My experience leads me to believe that the main distinction between those who participate fully in their communities and those who withdraw into private life doesn't rest in the active citizens' grasp of complex issues, or their innate moral strength. Instead, those who get involved view their place in the world very differently. They have learned specific lessons about approaching social change: that they don't need to wait for the perfect circumstances, the perfect cause, or the perfect level of knowledge to take a stand; that they can proceed step by step, so that they don't get overwhelmed before they start. They savor the journey of engagement and draw strength from its challenges. Taking the long view, they come to trust that the fruits of their efforts will ripple outward, in ways they can rarely anticipate.

Useful books exist on the nuts and bolts of social involvement: lobbying Congress, pulling a rally together, coordinating a mailing list, running an effective meeting, and generally mobilizing our communities. I've listed some in my Resource Guide. But *Soul of a Citizen* is less about these important strategies and tactics than about the equally critical question of how we, as individuals, can learn to heed our deepest convictions, to act—together with others—toward shaping a better world, and to continue doing so throughout our lives. In particular, I'd like this book to be an antidote to the sense of powerlessness that pervades our culture, a meditation on what it means to fight for more humane social and economic conditions in a sometimes discouraging time.

Along the way, I hope to dispel the idea that people who take social stands and those who don't represent different species, separated by impassable barriers: A marginal few leap from the womb holding protest signs; the rest of us are more "normal," so rarely concern ourselves with issues we can't control. We begin to think of our political withdrawal as almost a genetic trait which can't be modified. I'll look at both the barriers we face and how to overcome them.

Community involvement, like any challenging personal path, offers no instant miracle cures: "Save the earth in thirty days. Ask me how." But when I talk with people who've been active for years, few regret their decisions, for all the difficult tasks they've taken on. In addition to the satisfaction they may derive from succeeding in their causes, they say that they've enriched their personal lives as well. Social activism gives them a sense of purpose, pride, and service; teaches them new skills; shows them how to confront daunting obstacles; lets them experience new worlds. It offers a sense of camaraderie and helps them build powerful friendships, partnerships, and sometimes even romances. Even many who've withdrawn from the public arena and now watch from the sidelines wistfully recall feelings of commitment and common purpose. There's no greater antidote to powerlessness than joining with others in common cause.

You may wonder whether this book covers all forms of community involvement, or only those congruent with my own particular perspective, shaped by the peace, justice, and environmental movements of recent years. I considered including citizens associated with the political right. Their movements are important subjects of inquiry. Their rank-and-file participants are sincere, and sometimes seem more motivated than activists who take stands closer to my heart.

But this isn't an encyclopedia of social activism. Rather, it's the testament of one human being, about what gives me hope. So I've drawn my examples from people who inspire me. Not all consider themselves driven by explicit political visions—left, right, or whatever. Many are just trying to help their communities. If you, my reader, are a political conservative, I suspect you'll find significant parallels with your own dilemmas and decisions, and that you'll respect many of the people whose stories I describe, even if their convictions differ from yours. You may even find unexpected common ground.

Who are these individuals? What qualities unite them? A Maine housewife helped lead a pathbreaking campaign finance reform initiative "so my kids won't grow up in a cynical world." A Seattle environmental activist who had just celebrated her hundredth birthday concluded, after speaking out all her life, "You do what you can. And then you do some more." After an elderly neighbor died of cold because no one would repair her house, a Latina with an eighth-grade education got involved in a local community organization in San Antonio. She eventually testified before the U.S. Senate on an innovative job program she helped design. An African American man who had served seventeen years in the California prison system initiated a pioneering drug rehabilitation effort based on trying to give people, as he says, "the support they need, in a language they can understand."

The causes that stir our hearts will inevitably differ. So will our approaches. Our conscience and judgment may lead us to widely differing positions. But activists seem to take parallel routes to involvement, whatever their goals.

Those of us who hold back seem to encounter similar obstacles. Whatever our passions and commitments may be, we all face similar questions about how to cross the threshold from passivity to participation, make our voices heard and make our actions count, and reawaken and sustain our faith in the future.

In keeping with my belief that common solutions emerge best from common discussion, I've woven the voices and perspectives of dozens of people into this book—individuals from diverse backgrounds, situations, and belief systems, whose efforts to heal the world have given me hope. You might want to envision this book as a walk in the woods with this varied group, a chance to engage them in a passionate conversation about the state of the world, the state of our souls, our role as citizens, and the legacies we'll leave to our children.

WORTHY OF OUR CONVICTIONS

None of us has the final answers to such questions. But as you listen to this wide-ranging conversation, keep in mind that we're talking about the common problems of our society, and their potential common solutions. No individual citizen is solely to blame for homelessness, toxic waste, the collapse of family farms, or the growing divide between rich and poor. But at the same time, we can remember that institutions and societies consist of individuals. And that anything done on behalf of a group is also done on behalf of its members. As Rabbi Abraham Heschel said, "In regard to cruelties committed in the name of a free society, some are guilty, while all are responsible."

I'd like this book to speak to that part of ourselves that isn't apathetic or uncaring, but feels overwhelmed and wonders whether our actions can matter. Many of us are already involved in worthy public concerns. Because we feel our causes are urgent, we assume others will join once they get the information they need. But people are spurred to action not so much by knowing the right facts and numbers as by hearing stories and developing a worldview that make sense of the confusion and contradiction in their lives. When we get lost in what Trappist monk Thomas Merton once called "the contagion of [our] own obsessions," we forget this basic lesson. We need to know why people resist even the most urgent social causes, if we are to be able to change their minds.

Those of us who've made social activism a focus of our lives also need to develop the steadfastness that will enable us to persist in the face of the inevitable frustrations. In spite of our passionate engagement, we all hit moments of bleakness. I'd like to offer some perspectives to sustain our spirits for the long haul, to help us savor the journey, and to help us find hope when progress seems elusive.

Many of us have joined various movements over the past thirty years, then burned out and left. We may have spoken out against dubious military interventions from Vietnam to El Salvador or worked to protect the environment, to secure equal dignity for women, or to improve the future of our communities. Then we hit walls of indifference, became overloaded, felt let down by our fellow activists or the visions we pursued. After a while, we concluded sadly that meaningful action was impossible.

Most of us who've withdrawn in this fashion remain concerned about the future, uneasy about our silence. With our political voice grown rusty, guilt about our inaction and memories of frustrated hopes may actually make it harder to recommit ourselves than it would be to get started if we had never gotten involved to begin with. We find it easier to stay disgruntled spectators. Turning our attention toward easier tasks, we become what political theorist Hannah Arendt once called "inner immigrants," privately outraged at our society's directions, but publicly silent.

I hope this book will help those of us with this history to re-
kindle our concern and rediscover the visions of human dignity
that stirred our passions in the first place. I want to challenge the
notion that if we don't find the perfect solution, the approach that
will instantly change the world, our efforts are worthless. If we can
reconnect with our conscience and regain a sense of hope, our
voices can be powerful once more.

Finally, many of us would like to be involved but have never
taken the first steps. Maybe we've been too psychologically intim-
idated, or have focused on other priorities, such as family responsibilities, workplace survival, or internal spiritual growth. Maybe
the time and circumstances never seemed right. Without any previous experience, we may feel even more overwhelmed at the
thought of beginning, more uncertain of our voice, more doubtful
that our choices can matter. Working for social change may indeed
take us into a new country, expose us to new vulnerabilities, demand strengths that we never knew we had. Yet there are ways to
avoid exhaustion and overload. There are ways to learn as we go,
from the people we'll meet and from the impact we'll have, ways
to make our journey of commitment less daunting. If we're just
beginning to consider social involvement seriously, I'd suggest we
think about how much it can give back, both to ourselves and to
the world.

For all of us engaged in this journey, I hope *Soul of a Citizen*
will strengthen our vision. I hope it will give us ways to keep commitment alive, tap wellsprings of creativity and optimism, and remind us all of the potential power of our actions. As Rabbi Hillel
asked two thousand years ago, "If I am not for myself, who will
be for me? And if I am only for myself, what am I?" Whoever we
are, and whatever our paths, we can all lead lives worthy of our
convictions.

Chapter One

Making Our Lives Count

Souls are like athletes that need opponents worthy of them if they are to be tried and extended and pushed to the full use of their powers.
—*THOMAS MERTON*

We're often taught to view social involvement as a zero-sum game. With all our life pressures and the stress that comes with them, we barely have time for family and friends. How could we possibly take on some demanding cause?

Yet for all the frustration we expect, when we do get involved, we get a lot back: new relationships, fresh skills, a sense of empowerment, pride in accomplishment. "A rich life," writes philosopher and theologian Cornel West, is fundamentally a life of serving others, "trying to leave the world a little better than you found it. . . . This is true at the personal level . . . [but there's also] a political version of this. It has to do with what you see when you get up in the morning and look in the mirror and ask yourself whether you are simply wasting time on the planet or spending time in an enriching manner."

Again and again, I've heard active citizens say that what motivates them the most is the desire to respect what they see in the mirror. The exercise isn't about vanity, but about values, about taking stock of ourselves and comparing the convictions we say we hold with the lives we actually lead. It's about seeing ourselves from the viewpoint of our communities, the earth, maybe even God. If eyes are windows to the soul, and faces reflections of character, looking in the mirror lets us step back from the flux of our lives and hold ourselves accountable.

Sound a bit daunting? It can be. As the saying goes, not one among us is without fault. But such self-examination also can be enormously rewarding. For it's equally true that not one among us lacks a heart, which is the wellspring of courage (the word is derived from *coeur,* French for heart). At the core of our being lie resources many of us never dream we possess, much less imagine we can draw upon.

"I NEVER KNEW I HAD IT"

Virginia Ramirez, of San Antonio, Texas, could easily have lived out her days without ever discovering her hidden inner strength. She left school after eighth grade to get married. "That was what most Hispanic women in my generation did. My husband went to work after sixth grade." Although dropping out seemed normal at the time, she felt frustrated when she couldn't help her children with their homework, and dreamed of resuming her education someday. Virginia wasn't completely detached from her community: She was active in the PTA, "not running the meetings, but making the cookies and punch, carrying out the tasks." She'd baby-sit for her neighbors, help in whatever ways she could, "doing basic community work without realizing it." Mostly, though, she focused on private life, raising her five children while her husband worked for a taxi company.

When Virginia was forty-five, she realized that an elderly neighbor was getting sick every winter. The neighbor was a widow who lived in a house so dilapidated that it couldn't retain heat. "She was one of those people who always paid her taxes on time, always faithfully making out her little money orders. But she couldn't afford to repair her house, and everyone around here was just as poor. So I went with her to city agencies trying to get help. They kept sending us from place to place, from department to department. Finally she died of pneumonia. The paramedics said she'd never have died if her house hadn't been so freezing cold.

"I was very angry," Virginia recalls. "I'd never been so angry in my life. This woman had done everything she was supposed to, and now she was dead because no one could help her fix her house. Someone said there's this community organization called COPS, and maybe they could help. I'd heard of them before, but thought they were too radical, a bunch of nuts."

At that time, in the early 1980s, the largely volunteer-based COPS (Communities Organized for Public Service) had been around for eight years. Growing out of a network established by the late Saul Alinsky, the godfather of modern community organizing, COPS began by working through churches to organize San Antonio's desperately poor Latino population. The group successfully pushed for municipal investments in storm sewers, parks, and schools in the town's long-neglected barrios, and got major downtown businesses to hire their residents. COPS eventually secured over a billion dollars of public and private resources for their community through a combination of grassroots organizing and innovative protests. During one series of protests, lines of COPS members endlessly exchanged pennies to tie up traffic at local banks, and sympathetic nuns tried on bridal gowns at local department stores to put pressure on their staff. But Virginia had paid them little heed.

So it was with some hesitation that she attended a COPS meeting at her church, Immaculate Conception, where she raised her hand and said, "I have this problem. This neighbor lady of mine died because it was cold and they wouldn't fix her house. I want someone to do something about it."

"What are *you* going to do about it?" the COPS organizer asked. But Virginia didn't know what to do. That was why she'd come to the meeting in the first place. "I thought you people were supposed to be able to help," she said, and walked out of the meeting in anger.

A few days later, a COPS organizer knocked on Virginia's door. She was a nun, which was the only reason Virginia let her in. "All I want to know is why you were so angry," asked the nun. Virginia was angry, she said, because she'd tried to help the old lady and failed. But that wasn't all. She also was upset because her kids weren't getting properly educated in school. Because she'd given up on her own education and dreams. Because she'd had to watch her father, whom she'd adored, be humiliated again and again by police and store owners when they drove from state to state to pick crops. She was upset because no one seemed to care about her community.

The nun didn't advise Virginia to do anything in particular. She just asked if they could talk again. When she returned she suggested Virginia hold a house meeting, to see if her neighbors had concerns as well.

Nine people came. Virginia had never conducted a meeting. Her stomach felt hollow and clenched. Her legs shook so much she almost fell over. But gradually people began to talk of their problems and experiences. Their neighborhood had been thrown together at the cheapest possible cost, built for workers at the nearby slaughterhouses, which were now closed down. It lacked sidewalks and adequate sewers. Most of the houses were crumbling. As she listened, Virginia realized that more was at stake than the sad death of a lonely widow; this was about the future of her community.

Convinced that the neighborhood hadn't received its share of public funds, Virginia and other COPS members painstakingly researched documents at city hall. And they were right: The city had built a street in a more affluent area with money actually earmarked to repair homes in their barrio. The next step—testifying before the city council—took even more courage. When Virginia walked to the podium to protest the diversion of funds, she was so nervous she forgot what she was going to say. "I didn't remember my speech. I barely remembered my name. Then I turned around, saw the sixty people who'd come with me, and realized I was just telling the story of our community. So I told it and we got our money back.

"It was hard to stand up to politicians and tell them what we wanted, because it's been imbedded in my mind to be nice to everybody. It seemed rude at first. But I began to understand the importance of holding people accountable for what they promise."

As they did with other newly energized community members, COPS trainers encouraged Virginia to continue learning, so as to make her involvement in social causes more effective. They helped her to reflect on each step she took in every campaign, and to acquire the skills to research, negotiate, articulate a point of view, analyze people's needs, and channel her anger. They also introduced Virginia to a new community of people who were similarly involved. One of these new colleagues, a sixty-eight-year-old widow, became her inspiration. "Even though she didn't know English and couldn't read or write," Virginia recalls, "she spoke out and stood up for her beliefs. She talked to other families. And she keep telling me, 'Go back to school.' She always said, 'You have to represent us.' "

Even with this support and inspiration, Virginia's journey into public life wasn't easy. She often prayed over whether her new-found path was right, asking God for guidance, "like what am I doing with these crazy people and where is it going to lead." Yet her involvement also strengthened her faith, giving new meaning to biblical lessons that had once seemed more remote and abstract. "Suddenly you read these stories about injustice from thousands of years ago," Virginia says, "and it seems like they're talking about today. You feel like you have a chance to be one of God's instruments, to do His work by helping your community. You feel closer to Him in the process."

Yet Virginia's choices still raised difficult tensions, particularly in her family. At first her husband was critical of her involvement, saying "That's not your role" and telling her she was neglecting her household. "My kids were mostly grown, but Hispanic women weren't supposed to do these things. It was hard for him to understand that I was becoming a totally different person—going out of the house, going to meetings, wanting to talk about the things I was doing. Then my mother would call every day and say, 'This is not for you. What are you doing to your family?' It was like twenty-four-hour guilt. You're torn between your home and your desire to grow as a person. For a while I thought my family was going to break up."

Eventually, Virginia returned to school and acquired her GED. Then she enrolled at a community college. Studying for a college test—her first test in over forty years—Virginia was sitting with books spread across the kitchen table, and no supper ready, when her husband came home. He ran his finger over the furniture to show her the accumulated dust. "Look at this house!" he yelled. "It's going to ruin. You're not taking care of anything."

"I'm preparing my future," she responded, her voice trembling. "If you don't like it, that's too bad, because I'm going to do it."

She'd never talked to him that way, and he was shocked. "I'm sorry," Virginia said, "but this is a priority." It took her husband a long time to get used to her new attitude and concerns, "to realize," as Virginia says, "that I was going to keep on going to school and to my meetings." But he slowly accepted Virginia's transformation and even took pride in it. "I'd begun to think of myself as a person. I'm Virginia Ramirez, not just someone's wife, mother, or daughter. My husband realized I was getting involved for both of us."

College gave Virginia the credentials to secure a new job, training and supervising over three hundred volunteers who do health education outreach in low-income neighborhoods. During her fifteen years with COPS, she's moved up in the organization, first training people in her parish, then working with other local churches to develop their members' leadership skills as well. She's focused particularly on women like herself—working to inspire them, as others had spurred her to action. Using her own unexpected journey as an example, she's taught them to find their own voice and speak out for their communities, despite any doubts or hesitations they might have, and even over the initial resistance of their husbands. "At first all the men in the neighborhood said they had a lot of respect for me, 'but just don't get my wife involved.' After a while they began to come around."

Virginia's also negotiated with the mayor and bank presidents on major community development projects, pressured local corporations for decent jobs, pulled together after-school literacy projects. "You should see our neighborhood now," she says. "It's just so pretty."

She realized how far she'd come when she went to Washington, D.C., to testify before the U.S. Senate on an innovative job-training program that she and other COPS members had helped develop. "I stood there getting an award from Clinton and Gore," she recalls. "I thought about how you can't do anything by yourself, but with other people you can change things. I also thought about how this process has changed me, developed potential I'd never have dreamed of. Fourteen years ago I was a stay-at-home mother. That was my world. Never in my wildest imagination could I have thought that I'd be here. Now I tell people I learned all my talents and confidence at the University of COPS. The people there found some spark in me. I never knew I had it."

Entire communities can similarly grow when challenged. When Cherokee leader Wilma Mankiller visited the impoverished three-hundred-family town of Bell, Oklahoma, she asked the residents what would most help improve things. She expected them to suggest projects that addressed alcoholism, unemployment, or kids dropping out of school. Instead people wanted something simpler, something most of us take for granted: a clean water supply connected to every house, so their kids wouldn't have to bathe in polluted streams or drink from a single spigot at the schoolhouse. Mankiller responded by challenging each family to lay a mile of pipe and also help with fund-raising and other tasks. Soon families were racing to complete their sections the fastest. Inspired by its own success, the formerly passive and demoralized community tackled other projects, such as building better housing and making an organized effort to preserve the Cherokee language and culture. The town became a model of hope. Just as COPS had called forth the "spark" of strength and vision in Virginia Ramirez, so

Mankiller helped revive the collective spirit of Bell. She went on to be elected chief of the Cherokee nation.

STRETCHING THE SOUL

"Heart," "spark," "spirit"—whatever word we use for the mysterious force that animates us, its full potential cannot be realized in isolation. Indeed, according to developmental psychologists, individual growth is possible only through interaction with the human and natural world, and through experiences that challenge us. "Souls are like athletes," wrote the Trappist monk Thomas Merton, "that need opponents worthy of them if they are to be tried and extended and pushed to the full use of their powers."

Many of us may already know the value of stretching our souls in personal life. We know the virtue of learning to voice our needs, fight for our choices, recover from psychological intimidation. This process may require acknowledging painful truths, withstanding conflict, standing firm on what seems like shaky ground. We may need to question familiar habits, overcome self-doubt, and begin to separate who we really are from the roles we've been taught. Jungian analysts like James Hillman would say that by taking these steps we reconnect with what the Greeks called the *daimon*, the "acorn" of character at the core of our being. The psychiatrist M. Scott Peck describes spiritual healing as "an ongoing process of becoming increasingly conscious."

We are slower to attempt such transformations in the public sphere. Self-assertion there requires us not only to modify our outlook and behavior but also to confront a bewildering and often disorienting maze of institutions and individuals, powers and principalities. So we stay silent in the face of actions we know are unwise or morally troubling. We keep our opinions to ourselves, because we doubt our voices will be heard, mistrust our right to speak, or fear the consequences if we do speak out. We feel we

lack essential political skills. Like Virginia before she attended her
first COPS meeting, we simply do not know we have it in us.

Yet coming out of one's cocoon in the public sphere is just as
necessary to self-realization as it is in the private. I once told a
young Puerto Rican activist about the notion, common among
many of his fellow students, that they'd lose their identity by getting involved—find themselves "swallowed up" by the movements
they joined. He laughed and said the reverse was true. "You learn
things you never knew about yourself. You get pushed to your
limits. You meet people who make you think and push you further.
You don't lose your identity. You begin to find out who you really
are. I feel sad for people who will never have this experience."

You begin to find out who you really are. The implication is
clear enough: We become human only in the company of other
human beings. And this involves both opening our hearts and giving voice to our deepest convictions. The biblical vision of *shalom*
describes this process with its concept of "right relationships" with
our fellow humans, and with all of God's creation. The turning
point for the Buddha, writes James Hillman, came only "when he
left his protected palace gardens to enter the street. There the sick,
the dead, the poor, and the old drew his soul down into the question of how to live life in the world." As Hillman stresses, the
Buddha became who he was precisely by leaving the cloistered life.
A doctor I know works in a low-income clinic because, she says,
"seeing the struggles of others helps me be true to myself. It helps
me find out how people in very different circumstances live out
their humanity." Community involvement, in other words, is the
mirror that best reflects our individual choices, our strengths and
weaknesses, our accomplishments and failures. It allows our lives
to count for something.

THE COSTS OF SILENCE

Twenty years after Harvard Law School hired him as its first full-
time black professor, scholar and author Derrick Bell took an un-

paid protest leave, refusing to teach until the school hired a minority woman. It was not a decision made in haste. Bell had long campaigned for diversification. But each time a new position opened, Harvard somehow could find not a single minority female candidate in the world who was worthy enough to hire. The school's resistance continued despite Bell's stand. After three years, he was forced to resign. His conscience had cost him a tenured job at the most prestigious law school in America.

Yet Bell didn't feel defeated. Quite the opposite. His public stance had preserved his core identity and integrity. "It is the determination to protect our sense of who we are," he writes, "that leads us to risk criticism, alienation, and serious loss while most others, similarly harmed, remain silent."

What Bell means is that silence is more costly than speaking out, because it requires the ultimate sacrifice—the erosion of our spirit. The toll we pay for stifling our emotions in personal life is fairly obvious. Swallowed words act like caustic acids, eating at our gut. If the condition persists and the sentiments are sufficiently intense, we grow numb, detached, dead to the world around us. When, however, we take steps to redress our private losses and sorrows, we often feel a renewed sense of strength and joy, of reconnecting with life.

A similar process occurs when we want to address public issues but stay silent. It takes energy to mute our voices while the environment is ravaged, greed runs rampant, and families sleep in the streets. It takes energy to distort our words and actions because we fear the consequences. It takes energy, in other words, to sustain what the psychiatrist Robert Jay Lifton calls "the broken connection," splitting our lives from our values. Like autistic children, we can blank out the voices of our fellow human beings, feeling overwhelmed. But if we do, we risk the decay of our humanity. When we shrink from the world, our souls shrink, too.

Social involvement reverses this process, releasing our choked-off energy, overcoming the psychic paralysis so many of us feel, reintegrating mind and heart, body and soul, so that we can speak in one voice—our own—and mean what we say. There's even a physical corollary to this integration. In *The Healing Power of Doing Good*, Allan Luks describes a variety of studies that confirm what he calls the "helper's high": People who volunteer in their communities experience significantly greater physical pleasure and well-being in the process of their work, a general sense of increased energy, and in some cases an easing of chronic pain. A recent Harvard School of Public Health study found that African Americans who challenged repeated discrimination had lower blood pressure than those who did not. So taking stands for what we believe may help us save more than our souls.

Philosopher Parker Palmer describes the resulting unleashing of truth, vision, and strength in the lives of people like Rosa Parks, Václav Havel, Nelson Mandela, and Dorothy Day, who've acted on their deepest beliefs. "These people," he wrote, "have understood that no punishment could be worse than the one we inflict on ourselves by living a divided life." And nothing could be more powerful than the decision to heal that rift, "to stop acting differently on the outside from what they knew to be true inside."

LEARNED HELPLESSNESS

America's prevailing culture of cynicism insists that nothing we do can matter. It teaches us not to get involved in shaping the world we'll pass on to our children. It encourages us to leave such important decisions to others—whether they be corporate and government leaders, or social activists whose lifestyles seem impossibly selfless or foreign. Sadly, and ironically, in a country born of a democratic political revolution, to be American today is to be apolitical. Civic withdrawal has become our norm. To challenge this requires courage. It also requires creating a renewed definition of ourselves as citizens—something closer to the nation of active stakeholders that leaders like Thomas Jefferson had in mind.

The importance of citizens' direct participation in a democracy was expressed thousands of years ago, by the ancient Greeks. In fact, they used the word "idiot" for people incapable of involving themselves in civic life. Now, the very word "political" has become so debased in our culture that we use it to describe either trivial office power plays or the inherently corrupt world of elected leaders. We've lost sight of its original roots in the Greek notion of the polis: the democratic sphere in which citizens, acting in concert, determine the character and direction of their society. "All persons alike," wrote Aristotle, should share "in the government to the utmost."

Reclaiming this political voice requires more than just identifying problems, which itself can feed our sense of overload. I think of an Arthur Miller play, *Broken Glass,* whose heroine obsesses over Hitler. From the untroubled environs of Brooklyn, she reads newspaper articles about *Kristallnacht*: synagogues smashed and looted; old men forced to scrub streets with toothbrushes while storm troopers laugh at them; and finally, children shipped off to the camps in cattle cars. Her concern contrasts with the approach of her family and friends, who insist, despite the mounting evidence, that such horrors are exaggerated. Yet she does nothing to address the situation publicly, except to grow more anxious. Eventually she becomes psychosomatically paralyzed.

The approach Miller's protagonist takes toward the horrors of Nazism resembles the condition psychologist Martin Seligman calls learned helplessness. People who suffer from severe depression, he found, do so less as a result of particular unpleasant experiences than because of their "explanatory style"—the story they tell themselves about how the world works. Depressed people have become convinced that the causes of their difficulties are permanent and pervasive, inextricably linked to their personal failings. There's nothing to be done because nothing can be done. This master narrative of their lives excuses inaction; it provides a rationale for remaining helpless. In contrast, individuals who function with high effectiveness tend to believe that the problems they face result from factors that are specific and temporary, and therefore changeable. The story they live by empowers them.

This is not to say that change is easy, nor that everyone is in an equal position to bring it about. Some individuals and groups in America possess far more material and organizational resources than others. This reflects our deep social and economic inequities. But as social theorist and *Tikkun* magazine founder Michael Lerner has observed, we often fail to use the resources we do have, which may be of a different kind. "Most of us," Lerner says, "have been subjected to a set of experiences in our childhood and adult lives that makes us feel that we do not deserve to have power." Consequently, we can't imagine changing the direction of our society. We decide that things are worse than they actually are—a condition Lerner refers to as "surplus powerlessness." Think again of Virginia Ramirez's accomplishments, when she joined forces with other once-powerless people in fighting for their community.

The illusion of powerlessness can just as easily afflict the fortunate among us. I know many people who are confident and successful in their work and have loving personal relationships, yet can hardly conceive of trying to work toward a more humane society. Materially comfortable and professionally accomplished, they could make important social contributions. Instead they restrict their search for meaning and integrity to their personal lives. Their sense of shared fate extends only to their immediate families and friends. Despite their many advantages, they, too, have been taught an "explanatory style" that precludes participation in public life, except to promote the most narrow self-interest.

Whatever our situations, we all face a choice. We can ignore the problems that lie just beyond our front doors; we can allow decisions to be made in our name that lead to a meaner and more desperate world. We can yell at the TV newscasters and complain about how bad things are, using our bitterness as a hedge against involvement. Or we can work, as well as we can, to shape a more generous common future.

THE MEANING OF INTEGRITY

Paradoxically, one effect of overcoming learned helplessness is recognizing the extent to which others have helped us, and the extent to which our lives are bound together. Despite the myth of the rugged individualist, none of our lives is entirely of our own making. Small wonder, then, that those who participate in public life talk so much about the need to repay the blessings they've received. For some, this stems from a specific sense of good fortune, of living in comfort while others are hungry and desperate. But I've heard the same sentiment expressed by people from the poorest of surroundings, recalling key friends, relatives, or mentors who offered them inspiration, hope, or a helping hand. As Marian Wright Edelman writes, social involvement may simply be "the rent we pay for living."

Often this rent turns into a down payment on a new and more powerful sense of ourselves. Take the case of massage therapist Corrine Kelly, who participated in a series of New Age self-actualization groups because, she says, she felt that it's important for everyone to "pay attention to their muscles, their breath, and their emotions. I like seeing them reconnect with their bodies. That's why I went into massage." But sadly, she found the New Age emphasis on one's own internal healing to the exclusion of other concerns "just fostered personal aggrandizement, like all people wanted to do was get their own lives perfect and not worry about anyone else." When Corrine read the paper or watched the TV news she "found it very depressing, even though I was doing okay professionally and economically. I cared and wanted to help, but just didn't know how to act. There's a process of dying that happens when you shut yourself off to the inequalities and injustices in front of you. I felt I was living happily in my own small nucleus while the rest of the world decayed around me."

Corrine began attending a local Unitarian church, "because I wanted a spiritual base. They combined different traditions, and their members seemed to really live their beliefs. I was raised in the Pentecostal tradition. There's a lot from that I've let go of, like the more intolerant judgments. But there are lots of themes that really touched me, like the importance of love and compassion."

Corrine's new Unitarian minister spoke powerfully to these same themes, "calling forth the basic sense of caring I grew up with." The congregation continually linked personal spiritual development and visions of social justice. Through a church committee, Corrine joined a grassroots network, Promise the Children, whose members tutored kids, educated voters, and spoke out for children's access to decent education, housing, and health care. She got involved slowly at first, then ended up on the network's statewide board.

Corrine still took pride in her massage work, "because personal and social healing should be parallel, and I like helping to heal people." Her political efforts drew on her self-help group experience, "like trying to create win-win situations and encouraging people to listen to their bodies. But I felt more empowered, with less of a sense of despair about everything that's wrong. At one point I looked up all the different meanings of the word 'integrity.' It's more than just being honest. It has something to do with the wholeness and interconnectedness of the world, and how essential it is to being human. My spiritual path shouldn't just be about me as an individual. It should be about what I give back to the community."

By expanding her definition of healing, Corrine described the powerful effects of working shoulder to shoulder with others for a greater common good. We see this phenomenon in other contexts all the time. People become inspired and expansive when they pull together to face a storm, flooded river, or other natural disaster. Though the U.S. armed forces have often fought for problematic causes, a similar feeling makes soldiers look back to their war experiences as a time of profound meaning and unparalleled camaraderie.

Rarely does social involvement place us in the path of destructive natural forces or armed opponents, but it does involve risk. At the very least, it requires us to make ourselves psychologically vulnerable. It impels us to overcome distracting habits and petty concerns, to challenge internal fears, and to face criticism from those who will call our efforts fruitless, foolish, or a waste of scarce time.

In return, social involvement converts us from detached spectators into active participants. We develop new competencies and strengths. We form strong bonds with coworkers of courage and vision. Our lives become charged with purpose. Yvon Chouinard, the founder of the Patagonia outdoor clothing company, once told me about the challenges he faced while mountaineering, surfing, and building a successful corporation. By the tone of his voice, he communicated the sense of accomplishment these activities had given him. But his enthusiasm grew even stronger when he described helping organize Japanese surfers to clean up their beaches and switching Patagonia's buying patterns to phase out environmentally destructive nonorganic cottons. Chouinard's participation in environmental activism was even more deeply gratifying than his corporate success, because it produced results well beyond what he could achieve personally.

Whatever propels us beyond the merely personal—be it awe at the power and mystery of nature, religious belief, outrage at the sight of another person suffering, or simply a sense that we can do better than we have—we each need to take that all-important step of bringing our private convictions into the larger public arena. Because that's where we'll find our common humanity. As my friend the fisherman Pete Knutson says, "You get a lot back when you're with a good group of people taking a stand on something that matters."

Again and again, I've seen people transformed when they begin to voice their beliefs. "One day during Pride Week," said a gay student from Penn State, "I wore my 'Love knows no gender' T-shirt all around campus. I never had so much bounce in my legs.

I felt wonderful and proud to be gay. I was full of positive energy. I was happy and people were looking at me like 'What is that?' I didn't even feel nervous—it was unbelievable."

Religious traditions stress the importance of listening to the spirit within, to guide our personal choices. This same voice can guide our public action. In fact, the connection between soul and acting rightly in the world lies at the core of these traditions. The ancient Jews spoke of *ruah,* the spark of life or breath of God, which gave insight, understanding, and physical sustenance. The obligation to love others and love God was the essence of right living, they said, of being truly human, as opposed to pursuing false gods and living a life of estrangement. As Thomas Moore writes, soul "is not a thing, but a quality or a dimension of ex-periencing life and ourselves. It has to do with depth, value, relat-edness, heart, and personal substance." In other words, we achieve redemption through engagement, not isolation. The more we ex-ercise compassion for our fellow human beings, the closer we get to God.

Whether we frame the world in religious or secular terms, we don't have to be passive creatures of our circumstances, con-demned to watch from the sidelines. The psychologist Jean Houston urges us to overcome detachment and ineffectiveness by joining "local life to great life." Cornel West talks of redeeming "life's epic significance." And we do both when, like Corrine Kelly, we extend the caring and generosity that characterize healthy in-timate relationships to a larger social domain.

Mary Oliver describes the resulting gain in her poem "When Death Comes":

> When it's over, I don't want to wonder
> if I have made of my life something particular, and real.
> I don't want to find myself sighing and frightened,
> or full of argument.
>
> I don't want to end up simply having visited this world.

Oliver's images go to the heart of the matter. Will we remain mere visitors, planetary tourists? Or will we recognize that the earth is our home, and that we'll create its future with our fellow inhabitants? Only by choosing the latter course will we realize, in the words of a young Atlanta activist, Sonya Vetra Tinsley, "that you can shape the world as much as it shapes you."

HOLDING TO THE DIFFICULT

Social involvement isn't Candyland. I won't pretend that successes come easily and instantly. It often feels hard just to raise public issues. Unless our acquaintances, colleagues, or friends already define themselves as socially involved, it's awkward to ask them to act or even care about homelessness, global warming, or Bosnia. It feels as if we're intruding on their private liberty, their right to be left alone by the claims and the afflictions of the world. Our culture makes us feel that raising our beliefs in public is like parading some disreputable personal passion. "Are you talking about politics again?" our acquaintances may moan, as if the whole subject is just too strange to mention.

The more we challenge institutional power, the more heat we'll take. As Sister Helen Prejean writes in *Dead Man Walking*, her memoir of working with death-row inmates, "Get involved with poor people, and controversy follows you like a hungry dog." When Martin Luther King, Jr. challenged the Vietnam War, he found himself attacked by *The New York Times, The Washington Post*, even the NAACP. "Many who have listened to him with respect will never again accord him the same confidence," wrote the *Post*. "He has diminished his usefulness to his cause, to his country, and to his people."

Participation in public life often requires us to confront greed and bigotry, blindness and shortsightedness, and the will to dominion that theologians call evil. Taking on larger causes sets us up for repeated heartbreak, and for feeling angry and frustrated when people spurn the most basic appeals to human solidarity. Like any true path of psychological or spiritual inquiry, social involvement invites us to confront issues and forces we'd just as soon leave undisturbed. It sometimes brings us face to face with more cruelty and suffering than we ever thought possible.

Yet even the hardships teach valuable lessons. Someone once asked the Dalai Lama how he responded to the continued brutal occupation of his country by the Chinese. "Because of the difficult situation," he explained, "this Dalai Lama became more realistic, closer to reality. If things are good, it's easy to pretend. When things become desperate, we cannot pretend. We have to accept the reality." The poet Rainer Maria Rilke explained: "We must always hold to the difficult; then that which now still seems to us the most alien will become what we most trust and find most faithful."

I Enjoyed That Day

As Rilke and the Dalai Lama suggest, satisfaction can be found even amid the most testing of situations. Muhammad Ali recalls how good it felt to decide finally to resist the Vietnam-era draft. He lost his boxing championship title, was publicly reviled, and was sentenced to five years in prison (though the sentence was finally overturned on a technicality). If he quietly submitted, Ali was assured, he'd never face combat. But he could not live with supporting a war he felt was morally wrong and "leading more boys to death."

"That day in Houston in '67 when I went to the induction center, I felt happy," he says, "because people didn't think I had the nerve to buck the draft board of the government. And I almost ran there, hurried. . . . The world was watching, the blacks mainly, looking to see if I had the nerve to buck Uncle Sam, and I just couldn't wait for the man to call my name, so I wouldn't step forward. I enjoyed that day."

In *Revolution from Within*, Gloria Steinem describes a test of her own spirit. Steinem grew up in East Toledo, Ohio, the poor side of town. At a Toledo women's conference where she was speaking years later, she met contemporaries from her working-class high school; gutsy, highly vocal women who'd brought sex discrimination suits in their factory jobs, organized battered women's programs, and defeated an antiabortion ordinance in their heavily Catholic communities.

As always, Steinem was a political lightning rod. During a local TV interview, she described some of the women's stories that she'd heard. A man called in to denounce the conference as "antifamily" and Steinem in particular as "a slut from East Toledo." When she was growing up, the label would have devastated her. Instead, Steinem and the other women laughed. They turned an apparent insult into a tribute to their hard-won independence, their willingness to challenge prescribed roles and rules, and the sense of solidarity they'd built. "As we toasted each other as 'the sluts from East Toledo' with coffee and beer after the interview, I thought: Not a bad thing to be. Maybe I'll put it on my tombstone."

Chapter Two

We Don't Have to Be Saints

We can make ourselves whole only by accepting our partiality, by living within our limits, by being human——not by trying to be gods.

——WENDELL BERRY

I believe many of us feel uneasy about America's fragmentation and relentless self-interest—what Thomas Moore calls "a national persona of hype, ambition, narcissism, and materialism." We would like to find ways to connect with each other and express our compassion, experiencing a sense of purpose impossible to attain through private pursuits alone. When we don't find ways to voice this larger self, our most generous impulses have nowhere to go.

Chief among the obstacles to acting on these impulses is the mistaken belief that anyone who takes a committed public stand, or at least an effective one, has to be a larger-than-life figure— someone with more time, energy, courage, vision, or knowledge than a normal person could ever possess. This belief pervades our society, in part because the media tends not to represent heroism as the work of ordinary human beings, which it almost always is. A few years ago, on Martin Luther King Day, I was interviewed on CNN. So was Rosa Parks, by phone from Los Angeles. "We're very honored to have her," said the host. "Rosa Parks was the woman who wouldn't go to the back of the bus. She wouldn't get up and give her seat in the white section to a white person. That set in motion the year-long bus boycott in Montgomery. It earned Rosa Parks the title of 'mother of the civil rights movement.' "

I was excited to hear Parks's voice and to be part of the same show. Then it occurred to me that the host's description—the story's standard rendition—stripped the Montgomery boycott of all its context. Before the day she refused to give up her bus seat,

Parks had spent twelve years helping lead the local NAACP chapter, along with the union activist E. D. Nixon from the Brotherhood of Sleeping Car Porters, teachers from the local Negro college, and a variety of ordinary members of Montgomery's African American community. The summer before, Parks had attended a ten-day training session at Tennessee's labor and civil rights organizing school, the Highlander Center, where she'd met an older generation of civil rights activists and discussed the Supreme Court's recent decision in *Brown* v. *Board of Education* banning "separate but equal" schools. During this period of involvement and education, Parks had become familiar with previous challenges to segregation: Another Montgomery bus boycott, fifty years earlier, successfully eased some restrictions; a bus boycott in Baton Rouge had won limited gains two years before Parks was arrested; and the previous spring, a young Montgomery woman had also refused to move to the back of the bus, causing the NAACP to consider a legal challenge until it turned out that she was unmarried and pregnant, and therefore a poor symbol for a campaign. In short, Parks's decision didn't come out of nowhere. And she didn't single-handedly give birth to the civil rights movement. Rather, she was part of an existing broader effort to create change, at a time when success was far from certain. This in no way diminishes the power and historical importance of her refusal to give up her seat. But it does remind us that this tremendously consequential act might never have taken place without an immense amount of humble and frustrating work that she and others did earlier on.

I often ask students what words they associate with social activists. "Fanatical," they'll say. "Crazy." "Troublemakers." "Angry." "Extremists." Then I'll ask where Martin Luther King, Jr. fits in, and after a pause, they'll characterize him as someone morally superhuman, who stood above or apart from life, a man so rare that nothing he did could be replicated, even on a smaller scale. These judgments, they acknowledge, come not from direct experience but from cultural images. Their high school textbooks, they say, "only mention the conclusions," omitting accounts of how ordinary citizens have repeatedly shaped America. Today, activist stories rarely make the news. Apart from a few pictures, a three-minute feature on a "person of the week," or a brief sound bite here and there, most of us have encountered little that conveys the actual process of social change, with all its passion, frustration, difficult perseverance, and sense of consequence and purpose.

The students' superficial understanding of key events in American history is not unusual. For most of us, the past is a foreign country. The very stories that might remind us of our potential impact and strength are too often forgotten, caricatured, or ignored altogether. Apart from obvious times of armed conflict, or the legends of those few people we've elevated to the status of "hero," most of us know next to nothing of the many battles ordinary men and women have fought to preserve freedom, expand the sphere of democracy, and create a more just society. Of the abolitionist and civil rights movements, we at best recall a few key leaders— and often, as with Rosa Parks, we don't know their actual stories. We know even less about the turn-of-the-century populists who challenged entrenched economic interests and fought for a "cooperative commonwealth." Who these days can describe the union movements that ended eighty-hour workweeks at near-starvation wages? Who knows about the citizen efforts that first pushed through Social Security? How did the women's suffrage movement spread to hundreds of communities, and gather enough strength to prevail?

Many have remarked on America's historical amnesia, but its implications are hard to appreciate without recognizing how much identity dissolves in the absence of memory. In our collective amnesia, we lose the mechanisms through which grassroots social movements of the past successfully shifted public sentiment and challenged entrenched institutional power. Equally lost are the means by which their participants managed to keep on, sustaining their hope, and eventually prevailing in circumstances at least as difficult as those we face today. As the novelist Milan Kundera writes, "The struggle of man against power is the struggle of memory against forgetting."

Think about the different ways one can frame Rosa Parks's historic action. In the prevailing myth, Parks decides to act almost on a whim, in isolation. She's a virgin to politics, a holy innocent. The lesson seems to be that if any of us suddenly got the urge to do something equally heroic, that would be great. Of course most of us don't, so we wait our entire lives to find the ideal moment.

The real story conveys a far more empowering moral. It suggests that change is the product of deliberate, incremental action, whereby we join together to try to shape a better world. Sometimes our struggles will fail, as did many earlier efforts by Parks, her peers, and her predecessors. Other times they may bear modest fruit. And at times they will trigger a miraculous outpouring of courage and heart—as happened with Parks's arrest and all that followed. We can never know beforehand the consequences of our actions.

"I think it does us all a disservice," says Atlanta activist Sonya Vetra Tinsley, "when people who work for social change are presented as saints—so much more noble than the rest of us. We get a false sense that from the moment they were born they were called to act, never had doubts, were bathed in a circle of light. But I'm much more inspired learning how people succeeded despite their failings and uncertainties. It's a much less intimidating image. It makes me feel like I have a shot at changing things too."

Sonya had previously attended a talk given by one of Martin Luther King, Jr.'s Morehouse professors, in which he mentioned how much King had struggled when he first came to college, getting only a C, for example, in his first philosophy course. "I found that very inspiring, when I heard it," Sonya said, "given all that King achieved."

THE PERFECT STANDARD

Once we enshrine our heroes, it becomes hard for mere mortals to measure up in our eyes. However individuals speak out, we often dismiss their motives, knowledge, and tactics. We fault them for not being in command of every fact and figure, for not being able to answer every question put to them. As Taylor Branch wrote in *Parting the Waters*, the first volume of his epic history of the civil rights movement, we're taught to view social activists as people who shout loudly and rudely in a hushed museum, as grandstanders, as "zealots, people who oversimplify the world into good and evil without room for the murky truth, who lack the quality of self-effacement in their enthusiasm for their own views." We can't imagine how an ordinary human being with ordinary flaws might make a critical difference in a worthy social cause.

As a result of such images, many of us have developed what I call the perfect standard: Before we will allow ourselves to take action on an issue, we must be convinced not only that the issue is the world's most important, but that we have perfect understanding of it, perfect moral consistency in our character, and that we will be able to express our views with perfect eloquence.

The perfect standard assumes many forms. At a small Minnesota college, a half-dozen students were sleeping in makeshift cardboard shelters to dramatize the plight of America's homeless. As one participant recalled, "Lots who passed by treated us like a slumber party. They told us we were cute. But when we kept on for a couple days they began to get annoyed. One girl yelled, 'Homeless people don't have blankets. You're being hypocritical.' I was half asleep but I said, 'Yes they do. They have blankets and friends. They just don't have homes.' She looked like she'd be satisfied only if we got soaked in the freezing rain."

In effect, the activists were ridiculed for not being pious enough. Yet even had they demonstrated their commitment by standing in the rain until they became hypothermic, or by launching a hunger strike, odds are the critics still wouldn't have been satisfied. They would have turned their argument around, and accused the activists of being too holy, of taking things too seriously. Whatever the critique, the approach is the same: Identify a perceived flaw, large or small, then use it to dismiss an entire effort.

To hear others invoke the perfect standard is damaging enough. It's worse to subject ourselves to it. As a result, for instance, we often refrain from tackling environmental issues because they're technically complex. We don't address homelessness because we aren't homeless ourselves. Though outraged when moneyed interests corrupt our political system, we believe we lack the authority to insist campaign financing be reformed. Whatever the issue, whatever the approach, we never feel we have enough knowledge or standing. If we do speak out, someone might challenge us, might find an error in our thinking or an inconsistency—what they might call a hypocrisy—in our lives. As the spiritual writer Marianne Williamson says, "We have insidiously convinced ourselves that our wisdom is not wisdom, our common sense is not common sense, and our conscience is not conscience."

If anything, the proliferation of sources of information makes it more likely that we'll use the perfect standard to justify detachment. Now we can spend our lives in solitude trying to garner ever more information from books, magazines, newspapers, the Internet, satellite cable channels, and radio talk shows. Just as America has no notion of economic sufficiency, so the perfect standard leaves us with a permanent insufficiency of knowledge—and a perpetual mistrust of anyone who dares to voice an opinion or offer an objection. As everything that can be known continues to increase, the effort to know everything grows increasingly doomed. Yet we don't dare speak out unless we feel prepared to debate Henry Kissinger on *Nightline*.

ACT AND THE WORDS WILL FOLLOW

Eloquence is desirable, to be sure, but it's not as important as kindness, concern, and a straightforward declaration of belief, for starters. Dr. Rachel Naomi Remen tells the story of a woman she knew who got cancer. A male psychiatrist who was the woman's longtime running partner began avoiding her, even when she called. Finally the woman beat her cancer back into remission. Shortly afterward, she ran into the psychiatrist, and told him how hurt she was that he hadn't returned her calls. "I'm sorry," he said, "I simply did not know the right thing to say." Remen asked the woman what she would have wanted to hear. She smiled sadly. "Oh, something like, 'I heard it's been a hard year. How are you doing?' Some simple human thing like that."

Trusting our direct emotional responses may give us a way out of the perfect standard's trap. Will Campbell has been a Baptist preacher, a civil rights activist, a farmer, a writer, and a volunteer cook for his friends Waylon Jennings and Willie Nelson. One day he was invited to participate in a student conference on capital punishment at Florida State University. Only at the last minute did he discover that he was supposed to formally debate an erudite scholar whom he personally liked, but whose opinions he disagreed with. Will's opponent delivered a long philosophical argument in favor of the death penalty as a means for buttressing the legitimacy of the state. Then Will got up to present the case against it. Nothing equally weighty came to mind, so he said, slowly and deliberately, "I just think it's tacky," and sat down.

The audience laughed.

"Tacky?" the moderator asked.

"Yessir," Will repeated. "I just think it's tacky."

The moderator asked him to expound, and Campbell repeated his statement.

"Now, come on, Will," the moderator said. " 'Tacky ' is an old Southern word, and it means uncouth, ugly, lack of class."

"Yessir, I know what it means," said Campbell. "And if a thing is ugly, well, ugly means there's no beauty there. And if there is no beauty in it, there is no truth in it. And if there is no truth in it, there is no good in it. Not for the victim of the crime. Certainly not for the one being executed. Not for the executioner, the jury, the judge, the state. For no one. And we were enjoined by a well-known Jewish prophet to love them all."

Not everyone who's committed to justice will agree with Campbell's position on capital punishment, though I personally find it convincing. And I'm not lobbying, nor would Campbell, for disdaining reasoned arguments. But we should never be completely seduced by them into laying aside our core values. Most of us know it's tacky for families to sleep on the street, for children to attend crumbling and underfunded schools, for corporations to clear-cut thousand-year-old forests, and for politicians to sell their favors to the highest bidder. Merely by virtue of its complexity and sophistication, modern society makes moral engagement more difficult. We don't need to compound the problem by demanding perfection of expression. As Campbell's testimony shows, simplicity can still be forceful and eloquent. The larger point is that social change *always* proceeds one way or another in the absence of absolute knowledge, as long as people are willing to follow their convictions, to act despite their doubts, and to speak even at the risk of making mistakes. As the philosopher and poet Rabindranath Tagore once wrote, "If you shut your door to all errors, truth will be shut out."

GOOD-ENOUGH ACTIVISTS

No one is immune to the crippling effects of the perfect standard. In this time of immense technological and economic change, many of us who've been active in social causes before feel daunted by both the size and array of contemporary problems. Though we should know better, we sometimes feel we have to tackle everything at once. If our efforts don't instantly achieve dramatic results, we are quick to criticize ourselves, and doubt that our efforts can matter.

One of my dearest friends, a doctor named Jorge, worked hard during the 1980s to oppose our country's destructive interventions in Central America. Jorge volunteered at a rural clinic in Nicaragua, writing prescriptions on old newsprint and dispensing aspirins one at a time because that was all the clinic could afford. He watched a nine-year-old boy die on his operating table after being shot by Contras who'd ambushed his village. Later, Jorge worked in war-ravaged Mozambique, another country whose violence the U.S. government helped fuel. In both cases, he spoke out extensively on what he'd seen, challenging policies that caused such human devastation.

When the issue of national health insurance surfaced, shortly before Bill Clinton's first term, I asked Jorge why he wasn't more involved in the debate. His political activities had all but ceased when the Central American wars wound down, but he still had a demanding practice working with low-income patients in Seattle, precisely the people who might benefit most from health care reform. The U.S. medical system was deeply flawed, Jorge said, citing needless tests, pressures from drug and insurance companies, greed among high-earning specialists, and the intrinsic limits of Western medicine. It was so flawed that he hesitated to suggest it could be fixed simply by providing patients with greater access to its doctors and institutions. He had come to believe he'd romanticized the Nicaraguan Sandinistas, glossed over their flaws, and "sacrificed some of the truth and complexity of the situation for the sake of the cause." Although he still felt U.S. intervention had been a moral disaster, and that he was right to oppose it, he was wary of being equally simplistic with regard to how he approached future issues.

Yet Jorge still believed passionately that everyone deserved decent health care, and thought the Canadian single-payer model, whatever its limits, was vastly better than ours. By assuming that he needed to address every facet of the question, all at once, he became so overwhelmed he felt unable to take a public stance. Though I know Jorge will reinvolve himself in one cause or another down the line, his humane and thoughtful perspectives would only have enriched this particular debate. More generally, his pained silence exemplifies the predicament many formerly active people find themselves in today. They remain caring and compassionate, but they've lost faith in their voices.

In the 1960s, the psychoanalyst D. W. Winnicott developed the now-accepted concept of "the good-enough mother." Winnicott argued that the goal of errorless child-rearing is a destructive and impossible standard that produces guilt and recrimination. As Jon and Myla Kabat-Zinn explain in their parenting study, *Everyday Blessings,* "There is no question about doing a perfect job, or always 'getting it right.' 'Perfect' is simply not relevant, whatever that would mean. . . . What is important is that we be authentic, and that we honor our children and ourselves as best we can." In this vein, maybe we should also aspire to become "good-enough activists," realizing that although we may never win the Nobel Peace Prize, our contribution can still make a difference.

In *Dead Man Walking,* Sister Helen Prejean stressed the same point: "Better to help ten real hurting people—or nine, or one," she concluded, "than to be overwhelmed and withdraw and do nothing." We can pick one issue or another, this or that tactical style. As long as we act thoughtfully and generously, and don't trample people's lives in the pursuit of our causes, our efforts can help, whether or not we're certain about every facet of each issue. It's like the process that occurs when religious people pray: Even if they don't feel the presence of God with them at every particular moment, the act of praying still has meaning.

If Not Now

According to another version of the perfect standard, we shouldn't begin working for social change until the time is ideal—say, when our kids are grown, when our job is more secure, when we find the most worthy cause, when we retire, or, in Bill Gates–speak, when we "enter philanthropic mode." We wait for when our courage and wisdom will be greatest, the issues clearest, and our supporters and allies most steadfast. Such hesitation is reasonable. We are subject to real pressures and constraints. Yet when in life will we not be subject to pressures, of one kind or another? When will public participation not require a shift from familiar and comfortable habits? What's more, the issues that most need our attention will probably always be complex, forbidding, and difficult to address effectively. As Rachel Naomi Remen reminds us, "Being brave does not mean being unafraid. It often means being afraid and doing it anyway."

If we trust our convictions, we can take stands whether or not we have formal credentials at all. As David Halberstam describes in his wonderful book *The Children,* on the group that led the pivotal Nashville civil rights sit-ins, former Student Nonviolent Coordinating Committee (SNCC) head John Lewis, now a Georgia Congressman, began as the most unsophisticated person imaginable. Lewis was so "country," his friends from the rural South said he made *them* feel like city boys. Stuttering when he talked, preaching to the chickens because he had no other audience (and presiding over chicken births, baptisms, weddings, and funerals), Lewis was the last person one would have expected to change history.

Involvement similarly knows no barriers of age. A young woman named Joby Gelbspan was fourteen when she had a life-changing experience. Her family was on vacation in Ecuador, and a guide was showing them the sights of the rainforest. They came to a series of large, cylindrical holes in the ground, which Joby assumed were made by yet another kind of burrowing animal. But they weren't. They'd been made by an oil company, the guide explained, designed to hold dynamite charges that would blow up the land and buildings of an uncooperative village that was opposing the company's plans for development—the same village where Joby was staying. The villagers had caught the company employees in the act, and driven them off. But they knew they'd be returning soon with the military.

Joby was shocked. She'd never before realized the destructive power of raw economic greed. Soon after, she encountered some petitioners from the citizen group Infact on a Boston street. They were getting people to support a boycott of General Electric for the corporation's prime role in fostering the arms race. Joby signed, began circulating petitions of her own, and at age sixteen, became the youngest-ever member of Infact's national board. She played a major role in their successful campaign to persuade GE to sell off its weapons division and in mobilizing popular support to hold tobacco companies responsible for the health toll of their actions. Most of the Infact board members, Joby says, "were asking my advice on how to deal with their own kids who were my age. But they also respected and listened to me."

While we wait for the ideal time to arrive, weeks, months, and years pass by. We squander repeated opportunities to involve ourselves in the larger community for causes whose justification may be imperfect and whose outcome is far from certain—in other words, causes that are real. The perfect standard promotes endless deferral.

In part, that's because social justice battles always look safer and more clear-cut in retrospect. In the middle of the Iran-Contra hearings, George Bush came to Seattle to deliver a fund-raising speech; I joined a civil disobedience protest, during which several of us were arrested for sitting down in front of the doors where the guests were due to arrive. One of those taken into custody was the head of a local alternative school who'd worked with Martin Luther King, Jr. in the South. The arraigning judge asked him, as he asked all who came before him, whether he'd had any previous arrests.

"I was arrested in Birmingham," my friend explained. "I was arrested in Selma." And he reeled off a succession of civil rights battles. "No," said the judge, getting testy, because those were the "good" arrests, "I mean recently." "Yes," my friend said with an enormous grin. "I have lots of those, too."

Sometimes we're called to take moral stands not only when the time seems less than ideal but also when we're extremely vulnerable. When Alice Walker was a poor and relatively unknown writer, a major magazine commissioned her to write an autobiographical piece about growing up in the Deep South. Over lunch at a fancy New York restaurant, the magazine editors insisted on changes that Walker felt would make the piece more pleasant and sunny, but also wholly inaccurate. She argued and resisted. Finally, one of the editors said, "Listen to us, Alice. If you want us to publish your article, you *have* to make these changes." Walker needed the money and exposure. She was far from being in the perfect situation, where she could begin to call her own shots. But she gathered her manuscript and turned to leave. "Listen to me," she said. "All I *have* to do in life is save my soul."

Contrary to expectation, we're most effective when we realize that there is no perfect time to get involved in social causes, no ideal circumstances for voicing our convictions. What each of us faces instead is a lifelong series of imperfect moments in which we must decide what to stand for. Choices may at times be thrust upon us, as Alice Walker's was on her. More often we'll have to seek them out consciously, in contexts that don't always encourage them and sometimes when we don't feel ready. The wonder is that when we do begin to act, we often gain the knowledge, confidence, and strength that we need to continue.

That Kind of Person

Sonya Vetra Tinsley, whom I mentioned earlier in this chapter, grew up with a sense that change had to come from ordinary people, like those she grew up with in her ten-thousand-person town in rural Georgia. Sonya's grandparents had worked there as sharecroppers. Her father, coprincipal of the local high school, died of cancer when Sonya was six. Her mother taught reading and math, but received only a paraprofessional salary, which left the family economically struggling. "Girl Scouts, the church, and the PTA were different in our African American community than in suburbia," says Sonya. "You weren't doing things just for yourself or for fun. You were also shaping the next generation, trying to prepare kids to swim upstream. You couldn't leave it up to some distant heroes."

When Sonya went off to college at Atlanta's Emory University, it seemed natural for her to start a black women's group, serve on an official committee exploring campus racial issues, and create interracial coalitions to address hunger and homelessness. When she graduated, she ran a youth program in Atlanta's desperately poor Summerhill neighborhood, and started a multiracial circle of young feminists, humorously called Amazon Salon. She also organized a series of concerts in diverse Atlanta neighborhoods that brought together on the same bill hip-hop groups (with their young black audiences), socially concerned rock bands and acoustic musicians (with their mainly white following), and local community activists.

Calling her music project Serious Fun, Sonya hoped it would reduce Atlanta's racial divisions by bringing people together across racial lines, and by offering a broadly inclusive vision of justice.

"So many of the things I believe," says Sonya, "I was taught as a child. Maybe I believed them on a deeper level than anyone intended. But I heard every word about equality and freedom and people having the chance to be who they are. I learned that it is not just bad or lazy people who have hard times. I was also taught to take seriously the biblical message about Jesus Christ living as a human being, with human doubts and frailties. It isn't just a footnote to the story. All of this taught me that your actions could matter even if you weren't famous enough to name a highway after."

Sonya's community involvement led her "to meet so many people who inspired me, people I wouldn't have met in any other way. They were regular people. They didn't have some mythic level of courage or idealism, but they were full of hope and hadn't given up." These encounters, Sonya says, strengthened her homegrown faith "that life doesn't have to be just a series of things that happen to you. And that we're not damned and doomed to the world as it is."

Sonya mistrusts the notion that some individuals are destined for greatness, while the rest of us are not. Her perspective, resulting from direct experience, contrasts sharply with that of countless people who've said to me that they'd like to do more but are just not "the kind of person who gets involved." The suggestion here is that the ability to make a difference in our communities is innate and immutable, either part of our character or not. Given the images of citizenship that dominate our culture, this outlook isn't surprising. As sociologist Richard Flacks explains in his superb book *Making History,* American society teaches us that history is made by others; it's out of our hands.

But if the theories of developmental psychology are right, there are no natural leaders or followers, nor people who by sole virtue of superior genes become activists—only individuals who through happenstance or habit have had their voice and vision sufficiently encouraged. Being able to stand up for our beliefs is a learned behavior, not an inherited disposition. "The essential and democratic finding," writes the essayist Carol Bly, in *Changing the Bully Who Rules the World,* "is that what were once loosely called 'leadership qualities' are part of the formula for every member of the species."

In fact, on some occasions, seemingly powerless people are in a better position to change history than their more fortunate counterparts. At a conference on spirituality and nonviolence convened by the Dalai Lama and his fellow Nobel Peace Prize winners from Guatemala and East Timor, the Dalai Lama commented that small countries like theirs had "taught much to the world." The East Timorese Nobel laureate José Ramos-Horta agreed, speaking of how independent Norwegian organizations brokered key peace accords in Guatemala and between Israel and the Palestinians. More powerful individuals, institutions, and nations, he said, too often are blinded by their strength. It's left to those more vulnerable to promote compassion and justice.

A similar idea underlies what liberation theologians call the "preferential option for the poor." This is the belief that people who apparently occupy the margins of history can transform the world in unexpected, even profound ways. Born in humble circumstances and, as Albert Camus once said, keenly aware that all is not well under the sun, they may offer richer perspectives on suffering and sacrifice, and truer visions of the human condition, than those who from birth are told the world is theirs to command.

The roster of ordinary people who through practice and perseverance have transformed themselves and their communities is long indeed. Consider again Martin Luther King, Jr. early in his career: He was a twenty-six-year-old preacher heading into Montgomery, Alabama, uncertain of what, if anything, he might achieve. Even later on, King's campaigns failed as often as they succeeded, but he didn't let that defeat him. Lech Walesa was a shipyard electrician before events thrust him into the forefront of Poland's Solidarity movement. Wei Jingshen, the long-imprisoned dissident who helped inspire the Tiananmen Square protests, was a technician at the Beijing Zoo who had the audacity to place an essay on a public wall that said China needed more democracy. Lois Gibbs was an ordinary housewife until she organized her neighbors at Love Canal, then founded the Citizens Clearinghouse for Hazardous Waste to assist similarly contaminated communities nationwide. These people were not fulfilling some preordained destiny. They were developing character—their own unique character—by taking the risk of speaking out for what they believed. As the eighteenth-century Hasidic rabbi Susya once put it, "God will not ask me why I was not Moses, He will ask me why I was not Susya."

LEARNING AS WE GO

If participation in public life is not the inevitable realization of intrinsic personality traits but instead a process through which our personalities evolve, then taking action is also an experiment in self-education. The sociologist Todd Gitlin argues that such learning often takes place precisely when we enter "that difficult, rugged, sometimes impassable territory where arguments are made, points weighed, counters considered, contradictions faced, and where honest disputants have to consider the possibility of learning something that might change their minds." Social activism, in other words, is as much a matter of learning how to listen, and especially to those who disagree with us, as of learning how to voice our beliefs.

Viewing our involvement as a process of learning helps us respond to a legitimate question: whether standing up for our beliefs might just make things worse. To be sure, not all grassroots campaigns or acts of conviction are benign. We need to sort out for ourselves the true causes from the false, and the institutional changes that build human dignity from those that erode it. We need to distinguish humane social visions from scapegoating, from projection, from manipulated "reforms" that destroy our communities to save them, and from well-intentioned ideas whose consequences have gone awry.

To begin with, we need to set some limits on our means, so that they're consistent with our ends. It's my belief that bombing abortion clinics, military recruiting centers, or animal research facilities clearly crosses the line by risking human injury. Our political actions may inevitably harm the interests of some individuals and institutions, but we can still be as mindful as possible about what we're doing, and not just dismiss negative consequences.

We can also do our best to be honest in our own political speech. That doesn't mean telling our employer our every thought if we're trying to organize a union, or telegraphing our game plan to a corporation whose toxic dumping we're trying to challenge. It does mean that when we speak for a cause, we represent it, and if we play fast and loose with the facts of the issues we take on, we'll taint those issues in the process. Not knowing every answer is different from manipulating the truth.

But even if we act with all the goodwill and thoughtfulness in the world, how do we know the changes we're promoting will do more good than harm? I'll talk more about this later on, but it helps to constantly test our assumptions, perceptions, and desires against the complex truths we encounter. It matters if we listen to our "opponents," are open-minded about our assumptions, and don't get too self-righteous about our vision. It's also natural for our views to evolve, even while we hold true to basic principles of fairness and justice.

I experienced such an evolution in my own political journey concerning the Vietnam War. In 1964, when I was twelve, I passed out literature for Lyndon Johnson, who said he wasn't going to send American boys to fight in a war that Asian boys should fight for themselves. The next spring, in a debate in my seventh-grade social studies class, I argued that we had to trust our president's decision that the Communist threat in Vietnam was serious, and had to be stopped. My opponent, whose mom would play a major role in an antiwar group called Another Mother for Peace, said we had "a tiger by the tail" and ought to stay out. "If we don't take a stand now," I answered, "they'll be landing on the beaches of California." That dire warning was a commonplace one of the time. Since I was living in West Los Angeles, where kids spent their weekends swimming and body surfing on the beaches, the image hit home. Just about all my classmates backed my position.

Then the myths buttressing the war began to crumble. Exposed to critical perspectives that became steadily more convincing, I joined that small but growing number of Americans who mistrusted the government line. I came to feel that the war was unequivocally wrong and that my previous rationalizations were nothing but official lies. Whereas previously my mother and I would leaf through *Life* magazine, laughing at what she called "those kooky students," I soon attended my first candlelight vigil, then organized antiwar activities at my high school and later at Stanford. This paved the way for the questions I've been asking ever since—all revolving around how citizens might fulfill the promise of democracy.

Was I wrong when I spoke out in support of the Vietnam War? Should I have kept my views to myself until I learned all the facts? I don't believe so. Had I not acquired the habit of voicing my beliefs, I might never have taken a stand for *or* against the war. The lesson I learned—and it helped to discover this early on—was the importance of remaining open to other points of view and letting new arguments, information, and perspectives change my mind. I'm not saying that we should abdicate judgment and switch positions at the first sign of inconsistency or error. We should remain faithful to causes that make sense, and stir our hearts. But a mind that admits no new light eventually withers. A heart that remains closed inevitably grows rigid. Sometimes those who oppose us have the most to teach us.

LIVING WITH AMBIGUITY

Advocates for the perfect standard would have us believe that uncertainty ought to be an insurmountable obstacle to social action. Occasionally it should. More often it's a distraction. And uncertainty can also be a blessing. "Sometimes we are most open to conversion and transformation when we don't get it," writes Sister Mary Smith, of Portland's Franciscan Renewal Center, "when we cannot figure it out. We have to give it over. It is beyond our control, beyond our fixing, beyond our repair. The fact that we don't get it could be the best news of all. Because in not getting it we are opened up to a new way of seeing, a new way of hearing, and possibly a new way of living."

Smith isn't endorsing passivity, just reminding us that social involvement means little if it doesn't lead us into new spiritual terrain. The theologian George Johnson amplifies this point in *Beyond Guilt and Powerlessness.* "Most of us," he says, "are more comfortable with answers than with questions. We prefer closures rather than paradox. There is security with certainty. When faced with a problem we generally approach it with the assumption that information, insights, and proper action will bring satisfactory solutions. We want to fix things right now. . . .

"However, the reality of a broken world," Johnson explains, often leads to ambiguity rather than certainty. "What we thought, believed, assumed, or followed is suddenly brought into question. . . . long-held assumptions are discovered to be inadequate if not false! Receiving more information unsettles us rather than making things clear and easy. . . . It should not surprise us that our journey into the lives of those who cry for help will be discomforting."

It's also important to realize that those of us who work for social justice often have no choice but to pursue our fundamental goals by means that are sometimes unclear, ad hoc, and even contradictory. I remember one Vietnam-era demonstration that focused on the role of major oil companies in promoting the war. The demonstration was held in San Francisco. My friends and I drove to the city from Palo Alto, because there was no other cheap and efficient way to travel. As we stopped to fill up at a gas station along the way, it dawned on us that we were financially supporting one of the same companies we would soon be vocally opposing. We felt more than a little absurd. But it was the best choice available in the situation.

We learn to live with such contradictions in our personal lives. We love family and friends despite their flaws and missteps. A lonely few wait indefinitely for partners who match their romantic ideal in every possible way, but most of us take the leap of falling in love with people who, like ourselves, fall well short of faultlessness; then we do our best to love them for who they are. Anyone who has children knows that they are the very embodiment of unpredictability. We can influence but surely not control them. To all those who are dear to us we can only respond, moment by moment, as lovingly and mindfully as possible, improvising as we go. We embrace these necessarily uncertain human bonds, because the alternative is a life of isolation.

Public involvement demands a similar tolerance for mixed feelings, doubts, and contradictory motives. When we do act, others may view us as heroic knights riding in to save the day, but we're more like knights on rickety tricycles, clutching our fears and hesitations as we go. Gandhi called his efforts "experiments in truth," because successful results could only be discovered through trial and error. We take action despite our fears and less-than-perfect preparation.

How, then, shall we characterize those who participate in our society as active citizens? They are people of imperfect character, acting on the basis of imperfect knowledge, for causes that may be imperfect as well. I could be mistaken, but I think that's a profile any of us could match, given a willingness to live with ambiguity and all it implies, including occasional failure and frustration. That kind of imperfection may not be saintly, but living with it in the service of justice is a virtue.

WOUNDED HEALERS

I once took a workshop that psychologist Joanna Macy called "Despair and Empowerment." We used a variety of exercises and rituals to voice our bleakest feelings about the state of the earth and humanity, and then to work through them and find hope. Participants spoke about everything from the destruction of topsoil to the nuclear threat to one man's outrage about the rape of his sister. At one point Macy herself broke down, saying, "I do these damn workshops. People vent and cry. But nothing changes." Then she returned to being a steadfast guide.

Mock vulnerability can be used to manipulate others. Think of the politicians and televangelists who tell us they "feel our pain," then assure us that if we just give them our votes or our money all will be well. But Macy's genuine moment of doubt gave me infinitely more respect for her than I'd have felt if she had remained impeccably in command, untouched by the emotional vulnerabilities she'd called forth. She reminded me that when the people we look to as leaders acknowledge their own uncertainties, their visions become all the more human and accessible.

Taking a stand neither requires nor confers moral perfection. At best, in the Catholic theologian Henri Nouwen's words, we're "wounded healers," and in acknowledging this we can actually gain strength. I'm not suggesting we dwell on how our lives were ruined by every minor disappointment in our past. But I do believe there's value in reflecting on moments when we've felt genuinely beaten down or defeated. The process can help us put our lives in perspective and recognize our debt to those around us. It can nurture compassion and make us more patient with human frailty, confusion, and anguish. As the farmer and essayist Wendell Berry writes, "We can make ourselves whole only by accepting our partiality, by living within our limits, by being human—not by trying to be gods."

Virginia Ramirez, whom we met in chapter one, saw this as a key lesson from her strong Catholic faith. "To me," she said, "everywhere I go, and whatever I do, I truly believe that God is with me. I can ask Him to forgive my mistakes, and He'll give me the strength that I need. Sometimes this work is very hard, and I get tired. But I can talk with God if I have a bad day and think about what to do. I can look at other people and not judge them so harshly, because they have good qualities and weak qualities, just like me. If I make a mistake—like not listening to somebody, or talking to them rudely and hurting them—I can remember that human beings make mistakes and it's okay to make a wrong step. When I know God forgives me, I'm less afraid to fail."

Just as we can't determine all that will happen in our personal lives, we also can't dictate everything that will happen in the world, and we might as well admit it. What Thomas Moore says about the soul and psychology applies equally to the citizen and social action: "To care for the soul we will need to give up our limited ideas of what psychology is, our attempts to gain rational control over our moods and emotions, our illusion that our consciousness is the only sign of soul in the universe, and our desire for dominance over nature and fabricated things. We will have to expose ourselves to beauty, risking the irrationality it stirs up and the interference it can place in the way of our march toward technological progress."

Healing the world, in this view, doesn't lessen the need to build coalitions and apply political, cultural, and economic pressure to force giant institutions to act more humanely. But pragmatic approaches work best when we're honest about the limitations of our perspectives, and when we're willing to learn from changing contexts. As Madeleine L'Engle once wrote, "Only machines have glib answers for everything."

Vulnerability isn't always a strength. Some people are so personally besieged, it's all they can do to get by. They may have been raised, in the words of the anthropologist Mary Catherine Bateson, "to believe messages of disdain and derogation," to feel that their words and thoughts don't matter, and that even their cries and laughter are foolish. They may have so little confidence they can barely find their private voices, much less take difficult public stands. Even those of us who feel reasonably strong face periods when personal cataclysms overwhelm us. If we, our parents, or our children are ill, if we're going through a divorce, if we're struggling to find work, or if a loved one dies, we may be able to deal with little else.

If at times some people feel so individually overwhelmed that they must temporarily withdraw from the world, who can blame them? But meanwhile the rest of us can use their vulnerability, and our own, to appreciate more fully why compassion is needed, and to understand how seemingly personal troubles often have social and economic roots.

Marian Wright Edelman, founder of the Children's Defense

Fund, is yet another person who found more to admire in Martin Luther King, Jr. than rousing speeches and stalwart action. King was, she says, "someone able to admit how often he was afraid and unsure about his next step. . . . It was his human vulnerability and his ability to rise above it that I most remember. He didn't pretend to be a great powerful know-it-all. I remember him discussing openly his gloom, depression, his fears, admitting that he didn't know what the next step was. He would then say: 'Take the first step in faith. You don't have to see the whole staircase, just take the first step.' "

Chapter Three

One Step at a Time

People say, what is the sense of our small effort. They cannot see that we must lay one brick at a time.

— *DOROTHY DAY*

The journey of a thousand miles begins with one step.

— *LAO TZU*

When we think about the problems of the world, it's easy to feel overwhelmed and to become paralyzed. The way to avoid this, as Martin Luther King, Jr. suggested, is to proceed at our own pace, step by step, breaking down our goals into manageable tasks and not worrying too much about the precise political impact of every choice we make. Nothing gets accomplished when we try to do everything at once. Given how easily our hopes for a better world can be extinguished, this approach lets us fight for what we believe with reasonable expectations, patience, and a sense of balance. To borrow the classic Alcoholics Anonymous maxim, the best way to get involved in social change is "one day at a time."

This incremental process doesn't have to lead to dramatic public controversy. And it doesn't always produce immediately visible results. But invariably it alters those involved, in ways that can't be foreseen. As Gloria Steinem writes, "As for who we will be, the answer is: We don't know. . . . But we do know that growth comes from saying yes to the unknown."

The French theologian Phillipe Vernier offers a similar perspective on conducting a life of spiritual purpose: "Do not wait for great strength before setting out," he cautions, "for immobility will weaken you further. Do not wait to see very clearly before starting:

one has to walk toward the light. Have you strength enough to take this first step? . . . You will be astonished to feel that the effort accomplished, instead of having exhausted your strength, has doubled it—and that you already see more clearly what you have to do next."

As Steinem and Vernier suggest, such journeys yield rich and complex personal experiences, but you probably won't learn that by watching the nightly news, reading the morning paper, or going to the movies. Increasingly our knowledge of the world comes from stories scripted by others, stories whose characters and plot lines are stripped of the most important questions we can ask. Social involvement, in contrast, forces us to create our own narratives as we join with others to build a community garden, close down a toxic waste dump, organize our workplace, or encourage our neighbors to support a political candidate. There is no preordained plot, no characters free of contradiction and confusion, no tidy ending. As Alice Walker says, "It's a practice, like any other. You never get it completely." But since it's a story of your own making, you can start anywhere you wish.

The African American activist Julius Davis began under circumstances many would consider discouraging. As a teenager he'd spent most of his time doing drugs and committing petty crimes. Scorning everything about high school except sports, he was forced to repeat tenth grade, and barely graduated. Afterward he worked as an unskilled construction laborer and telemarketer. Mostly, he spent his time smoking pot, hanging out, and partying.

One day Julius was getting stoned at his cousin's apartment in the Bronx, dejected because he'd just broken up with a woman he'd hoped to marry. Idly leafing through a stack of records, he came upon the seminal Malcolm X speech "The Ballot or the Bullet," and put it on the turntable. He'd never read or heard anything like it. Ten minutes into the speech, he no longer felt high. Instead, he was transfixed by Malcolm's words, "like how he talked about all the wars we fight, when we won't fight racism and poverty, and

how if you fight for justice here, you'll know what you're fighting
for."

Julius thought about how he'd gotten where he was and what
he wanted to do. He started reading intensely—everything on Malcolm; Carter Woodson's *Miseducation of the Negro*; Saul Alinsky's
Rules for Radicals; and a self-help book that was a gift from his
uncle, David Schwartz's *The Magic of Thinking Big*. Feeling for
the first time that learning had meaning, he enrolled in Buffalo's
Erie Community College. There he began participating first in
black nationalist politics, then in multiracial coalitions with New
York's state Student Association, around issues like access to education. Julius eventually became the second African American
president of the national federation of student governments, the
U.S. Student Association. Later he worked for the Children's Defense Fund and an organization called Public Allies, which places
young, socially concerned men and women in community service
and advocacy programs. Each step led to another. Each opened up
new possibilities. Julius's picture of himself and his vision of what
the world could be emerged as he acted.

BEYOND THE COMFORT ZONE

When I ran cross-country years ago, my coach always urged me
to get beyond my comfort zone—that pace at which I could run
forever but would never win a race. That's what Julius did; he left
his comfort zone, an often painful and difficult process that Cornel
West describes as "stepping out on nothing, hoping to land on
something."

The psychologist James Prochaska has studied how people do
and don't manage to quit smoking, lose weight, or overcome alcoholism. If we're contemplating such changes, he says, we first
need to acknowledge what we gain from the self-destructive behavior—for instance, the ease of familiar patterns and the safety
of having a shield against the world. The same is true of social

involvement. Before we take the first step, it helps to consider elements of our lives that have previously held us back—our particular roots of inaction. It's difficult to overcome barriers of which we're unaware. But by bringing them to light, we can better gauge the effort that we'll need to overcome them, and that effort can in turn strengthen our resolve.

I'm not suggesting that social movements can prevail solely by sheer determination. But success is unlikely if we fail to develop the will to change, and if we do not acquire, however slowly and incrementally, confidence that change is possible. At the peak of the Reagan-era arms buildup, a West Los Angeles housewife named Suzy Marks and her husband, a real estate agent, were invited by their rabbi to come to a meeting on the nuclear arms race. Apart from voting, the couple had never participated in political activities. They'd paid little attention to the Vietnam War, for instance, concentrating instead on raising their kids. Now, however, the children were grown. Since the rabbi had specifically asked them, Suzy went to the meeting and then attended an interfaith conference, during which a nun invited her to participate in a Wilshire Boulevard peace vigil. Suzy was hesitant but went anyway, she says, because the arms race seemed "an ultimate issue that threatened all of us and all of our children." Standing on the street corner, she covered her face with her placard, showed herself briefly, then hid again, terrified that a friend might pass by and recognize her. Over and over she peeked out around the sign, then darted back again, like a rabbit in a carnival shooting gallery. After a dozen rounds of this, the nun laughed and asked, "Having problems?" Suzy admitted, yes, she guessed she was. And she ducked out a little more from behind her sign.

Since that initial vigil, Suzy has gone on to help spearhead a statewide initiative aimed at converting military facilities to other uses, to be arrested in a demonstration at the Nevada nuclear test site, to organize against California's anti-immigrant Proposition 187, and to join a women's trip of witness to Guatemala. More recently, she's worked on fund-raising and educational out-

reach for Liberty Hill, a community-based foundation that supports grassroots organizing among the poor and disenfranchised in
L.A.'s ghettos and barrios.

"Looking back," Suzy remembers, "my standing out on Wilshire Boulevard holding the sign was a turning point. It was okay
that I was scared. I think understanding my own ambivalence and
hesitation made it easier to reach out to people who are also reluctant to make themselves vulnerable by taking a stand. But it's
better to hold a sign in front of your face, put a scarf over your
head so your friends don't recognize you, or do whatever you have
to, than never get involved at all."

DAY-TO-DAY DEMOCRACY

The writer Frances Moore Lappé says the arts of democratic participation comprise skills and confidences that can be learned in
only one way—by practice. Think of kids learning to walk. They
pull themselves up with the help of a chair, take a step, stumble,
fall flat, then get up and try again. They're not deterred by failure,
even as we hover over them. They keep trying until they succeed.
To be sure, social activism is a more complex process than figuring
out how to walk. It can take us onto what can seem like new and
treacherous ground, where we know neither the language nor the
rules. But the principle is the same. Each step, no matter how awkward or hesitant, prepares us for the next. "Once you get involved," says fisherman Pete Knutson, "you start paying attention
to things in a different way. You see different social patterns and
political opportunities."

The political psychologist Ervin Staub has explored the ways
human destructiveness builds on itself. Torturers, concentration
camp guards, and death squad members, he says, generally undertake a series of increasingly brutalizing acts, each of which further
dehumanizes their victims and strengthens a sense that these victims have earned their suffering by their actions or character. Each

step confirms the sense, on the part of the perpetrators, that their actions are justified.

Conversely, Staub finds, those who take powerful humanitarian actions also learn incrementally. And when bystanders take relatively small actions to challenge injustice, this can trigger more significant responses on the part of others. Rescuers of Jews in Nazi-occupied Europe often responded first to the need of a friend or acquaintance, then went on to help strangers. Children who teach a younger child, write letters to people in the hospital, or make toys for poor kids develop more receptiveness to helping people in need than those who don't share such experiences. Humane morality, Staub concludes, "is learned through moral action."

I saw this process of sequential engagement in a Connecticut housewife named Alison Smith. While she was living in a small rural town, raising her kids, a developer arrived one Thanksgiving weekend, when no one was around, and cut a canal to drain the water from a large marsh that adjoined her backyard. "He was slimy and greedy," she says, "doing things on the sly. He filled in the land and built new houses. Gradually it dawned on me that we had wetland regulations, that he'd broken the rules, and that no one was doing anything about it. So I went to a town meeting of a couple hundred people, and waited for someone to say something. Nobody did. So even though I didn't know that much about the issues, I voiced my opinions as best I could, red-faced, hesitant, and embarrassed. And I found that all these other people were thinking the same thing. They'd say it to each other, but not in public. It was really hard for me to speak out, but it was also really neat."

Shortly afterward, a neighbor suggested that she join the League of Women Voters. "I told her I wasn't much of a joiner, but she kept asking me to different meetings and said I could bring my three-year-old daughter." Gradually Alison got involved, working mostly on inland wetland problems and recycling programs. "I was hesitant at first. I don't have a college degree. I'm more of a behind-the-scenes person. But I've always felt like someone who cares, even if I didn't always know what to do about it."

When Alison moved to Maine, her local League chapter in Connecticut bought her a membership in the League's Portland affiliate. Again, she focused on the environment, dealing with clean-air issues and campaigning for transportation alternatives. She helped organize a broad coalition of players—environmentalists, municipalities, the petroleum industry, marine-wharf owners—to pass a new state law on waste-oil recycling. "The more I did, the more confident I became. The more I felt I had something to contribute." By the fall of 1995, when the Maine chapter of the League called her to collect signatures to get a new campaign reform measure on the ballot, Alison, now full of conviction and passion, jumped at the chance.

"We've become so used to being disgusted with elections and politicians," she says. "We assume that almost anyone who gets in will be corrupt. But the decisions they make in our name matter hugely, often leaving us with even less power. I didn't know whether the initiative would pass, but I didn't want cynicism to rule my life. I'd like to see politics bring out the best in us, not the worst. I get tired when people complain all the time but never do anything to change things."

Maine's Clean Elections Act offered candidates for state office an alternative to the degrading and often corrupting process of financing their campaigns. Under its provisions, they could choose a Clean Election Option, whereby they'd pledge not to take private funding and to spend no money of their own, apart from some modest initial seed funds. They'd be required to demonstrate their grassroots support by raising a specified number of five-dollar contributions within their legislative or statewide district, and that money would go into Maine's Clean Election Fund. In return, candidates who ran under the Clean Election rules would receive enough public money to mount a full-scale campaign. The amount they got would be based on spending in recent comparable races. If privately funded opponents or outside political committees outspent them, they'd get enough additional money to stay competitive. The initiative also tightened limits on individual and corporate spending, strengthened the power of the state's ethics commission, and computerized campaign financing records to make them more accessible. It paid for the changes in part by doubling lobbyists' registration fees and adding a voluntary check-off to the state income tax.

By the time Alison joined the Clean Elections coalition, it included an array of organizations—from state affiliates of the League, Common Cause, Citizen Action, the American Association of Retired Persons (AARP), and Peace Action, to the state AFL-CIO and major environmental, women's, and gay groups. In a single day, eleven hundred volunteers qualified the measure by staffing tables outside polling stations. "I just sat at a table with a sign saying 'Do you want to take big money out of politics?' " recalls Alison. "Almost everyone who came over responded and signed."

The campaign worked closely with members of an allied research project that publicized in-state contributions from such sources as the tobacco and trucking industries. It was especially effective to invite the press to film a hundred-dollar-a-plate pancake breakfast that industry lobbyists held for the chair of the banking and insurance committee in the state legislature. These stories, says Alison, "helped us talk about the issue not only in speculative terms, but in terms of how wealthy interests were buying and selling our government. People felt they didn't have to accept this as the way things always had to be."

As she got more deeply involved, Alison met with newspaper editorial boards and spoke at local meetings, forums, and house parties—indeed, she talked wherever anyone would have her. "I felt nervous when the League asked me to do new things like speak at press conferences. 'Why on earth would they want me to do it,' I asked, 'instead of some expert?' They were shoving me into places that weren't familiar or comfortable. But I also found that as an ordinary person I had more credibility than the political professionals. The more I talked with people, the more I began to understand the issues. When people asked why I was involved, I'd tell them about the cynicism that seems to be destroying the very core of our democracy. I'd repeat over and over how if we could just break the links between money and politics, we'd begin to have a solution."

The Clean Elections Act passed with 56 percent of the vote. It carried Democrats, Republicans, and Independents, men and women, and every county in the state but one. Although the new legislation couldn't legally affect federal races, its popularity among voters helped persuade Maine's two Republican U.S. senators to buck party leadership and back serious campaign finance reform efforts in Congress. The initiative's passage also changed Alison personally. "It gave me a sense that I really can do something just by showing up to further a cause—this fundamental cause of democracy that affects everything I care about. I'm in it, as I said, to challenge the cynicism and despair, both my own and that of our society. Now I see other states taking our campaign as a national model and beginning similar initiatives. It's a wonderful message of hope."

Alison's story didn't have to unfold this way. Years earlier, when she noticed the developer's bulldozer, she could have said to herself, "I'm not the kind of person who gets involved." But by taking an initial step she said, in effect, without realizing where that step would take her, "I'm going to find out what kind of person I can be."

THE PATCHWORK CITIZEN

It's important to recognize that Alison's transformation did not represent a departure from her core values, the notions of responsibility and fair play that she learned when she was a child. Instead, she simply was applying them in new arenas. When Alison nervously attended that first town meeting, she already possessed everything she needed to take her first step into the unknown. The same is true of almost all social activists. Even those from apolitical backgrounds often credit their parents with providing a basic ethical framework. Families with strong ties to friends and neighbors may instill in their children an appreciation of community. Religiously conservative families in which biblical study is stressed can transmit a strong sense of the importance of caring and compassion, as was true for massage therapist Corrine Kelly. Whatever our backgrounds, they can provide us with ethics that are as relevant to the actions of society as they are to our personal lives.

Family experience, of course, is only one of many influences on character development. "We know," the psychologist Lillian Rubin writes, "that there are shifts and changes in identity as we take on new roles and adapt to different life stages. Each passage—from single to married to parenthood, for example, or from youth to midlife to old age—calls upon a heretofore unrealized part of the self. [Each part], when consolidated and internalized, leaves us with a new and different sense of who we are. But each new definition of self doesn't wipe out the last one. Rather, it is layered over all that came before, each successive self-image becoming part of the complex and often conflicting patchwork that defines the self."

Similarly, social involvement builds on who we already are, even as it changes us in unexpected and lasting ways. I saw this in Virginia Ramirez. For all the newness of her public commitments, she also built on long-standing beliefs, like her strong Christian faith. "When people ask me to do something I've never done before," she said, "I tell myself, I'm going to do the very best that I can, and God is going to give me the strength that I need. Fear can cripple you if you let it, but I always feel God's presence, so I say, okay, let's take that step, let's see what happens."

In fact, Virginia and other grassroots COPS leaders often used biblical passages in their training sessions, to make connections with participants' core moral frameworks. "We'll work from our personal stories, and from the Scriptures, all those sections that talk about justice. We'll look at our city, how divided it is between

rich and poor. The Bible talks about that too, and how it's wrong.
It gives us strength, and puts things in perspective. I've read it all
my life, but I'm reading it differently now."

Like medieval ragpickers, most of us tend to patch together our
models of activism from the social or cultural traditions at hand.
We choose what inspires us, what we can stitch to our previous
experience, what those we admire recommend by their example.
The process reflects a more general need to sort through our fa-
milial and cultural legacies, as we craft an evolving sense of self.
We "compose" lives of commitment, to use the term of Mary Catherine Bateson, by continually asking what we believe in, then de-
vising ways to participate in public life that mesh our convictions
with our circumstances.

The physician Deborah Prothrow-Stith was a third-year medical
student in the early 1980s when a teenage boy was admitted to
Boston's Brigham and Women's Hospital with a stab wound. As
she stitched him up, he described the argument that prompted the
attack, and said he'd take his own revenge as soon as he got out.
"Don't go to sleep," he warned her, "because the guy who did this
to me is going to be in here in about an hour, and you'll get all
the practice stitching you need!"

His words stayed with Prothrow-Stith and raised questions
about the scope of her responsibility. "Had he been a potential
suicide who had taken an overdose of barbiturates," she says, "my
job would have extended well beyond the lavage of his stomach."
She wondered why physicians educated the public about cigarette
smoking, excess weight, and safe sex but did nothing to address
the street violence that led to more than twenty thousand homi-
cides a year. "We were just stitching them back up and sending
them back out on the streets," back to the domestic equivalent of
a war zone, where in some neighborhoods a quarter of all children
had witnessed a murder. Prothrow-Stith realized that this violence
had reached epidemic proportions; it was a public health problem
that called for a public health solution.

Drawing on the experience that had moved her so, Prothrow-

Stith began working with city hospitals to develop follow-up strategies for patients admitted with gunshot or stab wounds, so that the factors that led to the incidents were addressed as well. She spent fifteen years developing violence-prevention curriculums for schools, and programs that taught conflict-resolution skills to teachers, students, police officers, health workers, businesspeople, church members, and public housing residents. By 1997, more than two years had passed since a person aged sixteen or under had died from a shooting in Boston.

Apart from the powerful results, what's most instructive about Prothrow-Stith's experience is that everything she did was an extension of her role as a physician, meshed with the broader sense of responsibility she learned from the African American church that helped anchor her soul. She merely expanded her mission as a healer one step beyond its traditional bounds.

I've observed many instances of normally apolitical interests, occupations, and obligations that have been converted into public causes. At the University of Michigan, for example, a group called Greeks for Peace persuaded a decent fraction of their politically detached fraternity brothers and sorority sisters that working for social justice was a logical extension of the ethic of community service to which most at least gave lip service. Two art majors in one of the sororities had said on more than one occasion that they liked the group's ideals but didn't have the time to come to meetings or events. Then someone asked them to make a banner for a march opposing Ronald Reagan's Central America policies. That, they said, they could do. They threw themselves into the task with all their energy and creativity. When banners and posters were needed for subsequent events, the two young women volunteered their services again. They had found their niche in the group by drawing on their passions.

I've mentioned psychologist James Hillman's concept of the *daimon*, the "acorn" of character that pulls us toward a specific vocation or a calling. In *The Soul's Code,* Hillman explores ways we can use this concept to look beyond our routine daily concerns,

and ask why we were put here on earth to begin with. It's a common belief that social activism is itself such a distinct calling—okay
for some, unsuitable for most. Hillman himself, however, rejects
this idea, as do others in his psychological tradition, such as
Thomas Moore. When I asked Hillman directly, he said it was
"simply nonsense" to consider public engagement a separate path,
appropriate only for the select few. Rather, he stressed, any true
calling impels us toward service to the community, even as the
shape that our service assumes will always be determined by the
particular passions, strengths, and gifts we have to offer.

Think again of Pete Knutson, and the unlikely coalitions he organized to restore the salmon runs. His social activism wasn't a
substitute for fishing, but an outgrowth of it. It was an extension
of feeling called to a vocation he considered challenging, worthwhile, and intimately connected with the health of the natural
world.

Some people have computer skills. Others play music, perform
theater, cook great food. Others are effective networkers who like
nothing better than to pull people together for common projects
they believe in, or persuasive speakers who can charm opponent
and friend alike. Not every private passion can be joined to the
common good, of course. But social activism that is in some measure an outgrowth of our deepest beliefs and values, of that patchwork creation we call the self, is most likely to endure.

THE JOURNEY OF A THOUSAND MILES

The Taoist philosopher Lao Tzu once said, "The journey of a thousand miles begins with one step." I can think of no one who better
exemplifies that precept than the one-hundred-year-old godmother
of Seattle's environmental movement, Hazel Wolf, who got her
political start in the eighth grade, in 1911. Hazel was always athletic, but her playground, like her classroom in Victoria, British
Columbia, was sexually segregated. Basketball was played by boys

and watched by girls. After Hazel talked with some of her friends, she approached the principal and said, "We want to play basketball too." "Girls don't play basketball," he said, dismissing her. "Of course we don't," Hazel responded. "We *can't* if we don't have balls or hoops." Taken aback, the principal agreed to furnish them if Hazel could raise two teams, which she did by that afternoon. Since that day, Hazel has led or participated in dozens of different causes, from labor issues to civil rights to the environment.

Whether we are eight, eighteen, or sixty-eight when we first venture into the public arena, our inaugural steps will almost certainly seem modest, even inconsequential. In the lesson of the familiar adage: We can't run without first learning how to walk, and we can't walk without first learning how to crawl. Derrick Bell offers a more eloquent formulation of the same idea: "It is the willingness to take on the small challenges of daily life that prepares one to take a stand when people's basic rights are threatened."

Even the most exceptional stories often begin with seemingly insignificant efforts. In 1996, when he was twenty-three, Adam Werbach became the Sierra Club's youngest-ever national president. His student health insurance had expired, he later joked, so he needed a job. Why not lead this 600,000-member organization?

Like Hazel Wolf, Adam also entered political life at an early age; he was eight. His parents were therapists in Tarzana, a town in the San Fernando Valley of Los Angeles. They liked camping, hiking, and other outdoor activities. They wrote checks to groups like the Sierra Club, Amnesty International, and the ACLU. When Adam first saw timber clear-cuts from an airplane, he "wondered what kind of monster created them. They were great slashes and gaps, like Martian footprints in the forest." Shortly afterward a Sierra Club petition came in the mail demanding that James Watt, Reagan's Secretary of the Interior, resign. Adam took it to his third-grade class and to his neighbors, to whom he'd already sold candy to raise money for school projects. People laughed, but at week's end young Adam had five hundred signatures.

As a child, Adam spent many hours in a nature preserve in the

Santa Monica Mountains, close to his house. In seventh grade, at
his all-male private school, he started an animal rights club that
focused on needless cosmetic testing. Adam's science teacher opposed the organization, calling its meetings an inappropriate use
of school time. He was mocked by many of his fellow students.
But the headmaster offered encouragement, as did other teachers.
Adam was elated when companies such as Clairol and Gillette gave
in to a national boycott and reduced their animal testing.

At the same time, Adam's Jewish faith reinforced his sense that
it was right to get involved. "I learned about the importance of
service," he says, "of giving back, and of doing the right thing even
if people disagreed, laughed at you, or otherwise gave you grief.
There's a whole Jewish tradition of *tikkun olam,* of working to
heal the world, which got imbedded in me as a cultural fiber. My
religion also helped me develop a sense that I wasn't just fighting
to protect my earth. I was fighting to protect the earth that God
created, which means it's a larger question than whether I want to
save a particular piece of wilderness."

Adam's rabbi was particularly encouraging, as was his highly
religious grandfather, who ran a clothing store and had helped
found a major local temple. Adam gave his bar mitzvah speech,
"my first pulpit," on the need to save the environment, then donated the money people gave him to Greenpeace, the Sierra Club,
and planting trees in Israel.

After Adam wrote up the animal rights group's difficulties and
successes for a national newsletter, teenagers concerned with environmental issues started calling him from around the country.
With his parents subsidizing his phone bill, he pulled together a
large informal network. Adam was now in high school, where he
started an environmental class, then attended a Vermont environmental camp called the Mountain School. "We hiked, camped, and
studied writers like Aldo Leopold, John McPhee, Bill McKibben,
and Henry David Thoreau," he says. "People were always saying
that we were too young to understand the issues. So I felt I had to
know them better than anyone else."

A few months later, in the fall of 1990, Adam returned to L.A. and stopped by the local campaign office of Big Green, a statewide environmental initiative.

"Who's organizing high school students?" he asked.

"Well, *you* are," responded the staffer in the office.

Within days, Adam had enlisted five hundred student volunteers by calling every active student he knew, then approaching high school environmental clubs, student government associations, YMCAs, Scout troops, and every other group he could find. The students canvassed, answered phones, and "did everything imaginable," Adam says. "Almost universally, they'd say 'I wish someone had called me before.' If I hadn't happened along, if I'd gone to a Dodgers game instead, none of them would have ever gotten involved."

The initiative was narrowly defeated by its lavishly funded opposition. But Adam was struck by the enthusiasm of his young volunteers, and wondered how many more students he could involve if only he had the resources to reach them. Of all the national environmental groups, the Sierra Club seemed to have the broadest grassroots base, so he started the Sierra Student Coalition (SSC).

Given the degree to which his peers were stereotyped as apathetic and passive, Adam figured the Sierra Club's national board would be wary of investing time or money, "even though," he says, "we were the generation that would be sustaining them." So he first approached the Southern California Angeles chapter, some of whose active members he already knew. The chapter donated seed money that Adam used to conduct a weeklong training camp, modeled on the Mountain School, where a racially diverse group of high school and college activists got the chance to hike, talk, roast marshmallows, take workshops, and plan strategies. Participants then launched SSC through their friendship networks and the newsletters and phone banks of local Sierra Club chapters. The group sponsored cleanups at local rivers, lakes, and ocean beaches, wrote letters and circulated petitions on NAFTA and the California Desert Protection Act, did educational outreach on childhood lead poisoning, and distributed black snow cones to dramatize opposition to oil drilling in the Alaska National Wildlife Refuge. When Adam went off to Brown University, he set up a national office at the school, staffed by the volunteer efforts of fellow students.

By September 1992, when Adam presented the SSC project to the national Sierra Club board, it had 25,000 members. Hesitant at first, the board finally gave the group official status. After one of the lengthy discussions, the eighty-three-year-old environmental legend David Brower encouraged Adam to run for the board himself. Adam prepared a statement for the ballot that went out to every member, and in 1994 was elected. He was twenty-one years old, the youngest national board member ever.

Adam had begun with his third-grade petition. Now he was helping set policy for one of the largest grassroots environmental groups in America. At the beginning, he could never have foreseen this outcome, yet each step he took opened up new possibilities. Each one led to the next.

"I still got some condescension," Adam says about his initial reception by his fellow board members. "Two of them walked up to the chair and said, 'Make sure Adam doesn't work on our project. We don't want a children's crusade.' I wouldn't call it a geriatric crusade if they were running it. I loved the club, but I also felt they had too much nostalgia. They still had a committee to dismantle the dam in California's Hetch Hetchy Valley, which was a noble cause we lost fifty years ago. I saw a tension between people like Brower, who's now back on the board, and who keeps pushing us forward, and some of the old guard who fired him as executive director in the sixties, and want us to be just a hiking club with lobbyists."

Again Brower encouraged Adam to run, this time for national president. "I think he saw me as the club's future. I obviously had some trepidation as to whether I had the skills to do it. Here I was barely balancing my checkbook, having gotten through college by working as a handyman and doing office temp work. I'd been accepted to Columbia film school, was singing in a rock band and trying to write a novel. Suddenly I'm thinking about applying to run a fifty-million-dollar-a-year national organization with a staff of three hundred. College doesn't exactly prepare you for that. But I also felt I had something to offer. I'd probably done my best organizing when I was eighteen. I had five years' experience since. I decided, 'Why not run?' "

To Adam's surprise, the board elected him. Under his leadership, the club has grown in members and donations, reversed a long-standing trend by lowering its membership's average age by ten years, and shifted $4 million a year from Washington, D.C., lobbying to local grassroots organizing. They've spearheaded boycotts of Shell Oil (for their support of a dictatorial regime in Nigeria) and Maxxam Corporation (for destroying old-growth timber in northern California), defeated fourteen of eighteen antienvironmental congressmen targeted in a recent election, and used such media as MTV and Adam's syndicated college newspaper column to reach out to a new generation. He's also led the Sierra Club into new alliances with hunters, farmers, fishermen, religious groups, and low-income and minority communities.

"I've learned that going ahead and doing the best you can is better than waiting until you have all the answers," Adam told me just after being reelected for a second term. "I learned that at the very beginning when I was foolish enough to think anyone would even listen to a third-grader gathering signatures. If I hadn't started back then, I wouldn't be here now."

Chapter Four

The Cynical Smirk

Irony has only emergency use. Carried over time, it's the voice of the trapped who have come to enjoy their cage.

—*LEWIS HYDE*

In a recent issue of *Harper's* magazine, I came upon an ad for Microsoft's on-line magazine, *Slate,* edited by former *Crossfire* host and *New Republic* lead columnist Michael Kinsley. "It's what everyone is talking about," the ad proclaimed: "media, politics, technology, high and low culture . . . all with a certain insouciant smirk that thinking people find compelling."

Which insouciant smirk, and which thinking people? My dictionary describes insouciant as "carefree" or "blithely indifferent." "Carefree" seems fine, even if it conjures up endless parades of Laura Ashley maidens in flowered summer dresses. But is indifference a virtue? Does the ad mean to suggest that *Slate*'s editors and writers stand above it all, and nothing they say really matters?

Praising any smirk, especially a "certain" one, seems worse yet. People smirk when they're full of themselves, smiling arrogantly, "in a self-conscious, knowing, or simpering manner." They know the score, you don't, and they're about to put you in your place. Multinational oil companies smirk. So do grade-school bullies and corporate raiders. William F. Buckley and Donald Trump smirk. Marie Antoinette's famed phrase "Let them eat cake" was an ill-timed smirk that cost her her head.

Yet *Slate,* or their ad agency, has decided that an ethic of contempt boosts sales. They present it as something to be proud of. All of us, the ad suggests, should approach life with such hip detachment. Merely knowing the right people and being able to drop the right insouciantly clever names and phrases exempts us from any broader responsibility to our fellow human beings. We simply need to acknowledge that the world is inherently corrupt, bought and paid for, and that all talk of changing it is naive.

This cynicism pervades our culture. "Everybody lies," says a veteran newspaperman quoted in the *Utne Reader,* "but it doesn't matter, because nobody listens." Imagine a man who tells his young son to jump from the stairs into his arms. The father catches the boy twice, but the third time steps back and lets him fall. "That's to teach you never to trust anyone," he explains, "even your own father." More and more we expect such betrayal. "That's just how things are," we say, then shrug and move on. We now take our cynicism as much for granted as the air we breathe, making it as great a barrier to hope and meaningful public action as all the other barriers combined.

I'm not trashing dark humor. I recently saw the performance artist Eric Bogosian do a scathing one-man show, *Wake Up and Smell the Coffee.* He mocked real estate agents selling homes in a gated community complete with ex-LAPD cops as guards and in-house microphones that monitored the coddled residents' every move. He also mocked liberals with shelves full of premium mugs from worthy causes. Bogosian's humor was bleak and unsparing. But the accuracy and intensity of his descriptions kept the audience rattled and thinking. He definitely explored the shadowy side of fine words and good intentions, but you can't write characters that powerful without caring, which is the opposite of cynicism.

To be sure, it's hard to act during a time when every sphere of life seems dominated by the desire for private gain, and when every value, ideal, and public symbol has a profit-seeking sponsor. A few years ago, Taco Bell took out ads in *USA Today* and other major newspapers. The fast-food company had bought the Liberty Bell, the ad explained, and would now call it the Taco Liberty Bell. The bell would stay at its same location, still accessible to the public, but under new ownership.

The ads turned out to be an April Fools' Day parody, but it felt too real for comfort. Congressional leaders already talk seriously of turning national parks over to Disney. Channel One broadcasts commercial-laden "infotainment" into public schools, along with suggested class projects in which students write commercials for Snapple and design art for Pepsi vending machines. Two London ad executives have recently begun consulting with NASA scientists on ways to project advertising logos onto the moon, using reflective mirrors. Why not auction off America's historic monuments to the highest bidder?

Cynicism takes the notion that every institution and every person is for sale, and enshrines it as an eternal truth. It insists that human motives are debased and always will be. Cynicism implies that no institutions, truths, or community bonds are worth fighting for.

A POOR SUBSTITUTE FOR HOPE

Cynicism wasn't always so disempowering. The first Cynics were a group of ancient Greek philosophers, most notably Diogenes, who caustically denounced the established culture of their time. Monklike ascetics who preached simplicity, self-discipline, and self-sufficiency, they offered a moral alternative to the empty materialism, legalism, and religious hypocrisy that had come to dominate Greek society. Back then, to be a Cynic meant to stand up for one's convictions.

To fully appreciate the corrosive effect of contemporary cynicism, imagine adopting the same approach toward our children, spouses, lovers, and friends that we often do toward public life. Pretend for a moment that instead of placing our trust in them, and forgiving their lapses and flaws, we greeted them with derision, suspicion, and indifference. How long would hope, love, or joy survive under those conditions? That's precisely the reason we resist cynicism in our personal relationships. We take chances on people, risking disappointment and heartbreak, so as to encourage their best qualities. Otherwise, decent relationships become impossible.

Cynicism in the public sphere is no less destructive. Take electoral politics, toward which our pessimism and contempt are more thoroughgoing than in any other aspect of American life. As National Education Association president Bob Chase worries, "We're coming dangerously close to believing that nothing is possible, except for a nation of corruption and greed. People in media and politics should be promoting integrity. But they give us a sense that everyone's on the take, that everyone's out for themselves, and that working for a larger common good is impossible."

Attitudes in the workplace aren't much better. We've come to expect an occupational culture in which meanness and insecurity prevail. "That's the way it is in the real world," we say, which means a world stripped of moral considerations. Even if we'd once hoped to tie our values to our jobs, too many of us now work just to survive, or to buy a few pleasures during our free time. Asked to account for the discrepancies between our private convictions and our economic roles, we respond, "I just work here." Or: "I'm only running a business." Or: "If I don't do it, someone else will." As *Doonesbury*'s creator, Garry Trudeau, points out, this attitude paints a categorically bleak portrait of human existence, with no possibility of redemption: We end up believing that all businessmen and politicians are dishonest, all religious leaders charlatans, all reporters cheap-shot hacks, all social activists fools.

More and more, cynicism occupies the mental and psychological space we once reserved for hope—at least for the kind of hope that might inspire us to take public stands. Better to expect nothing, in this view, than to set ourselves up for certain disappointment. Yet this very detachment renders us impotent, and thus eternally cynical.

THE EROSION OF TRUST

What's the alternative? It certainly isn't blind trust, which though less self-defeating and socially irresponsible than cynicism, is dangerous in its own right. I saw both during my three-year study of Washington State's Hanford nuclear complex, the largest in the world. Hanford's founding generation came in during World War II, producing the plutonium for the first atomic bomb (exploded in the New Mexico desert), as well as for the one that fell on Nagasaki, and later the raw materials for a quarter of all the atomic warheads in the world. They were proud of their work. The high school football team, the Richland Bombers, displayed a miniature mushroom cloud on its helmets, pep club banners, and school commencement programs. When a new test breeder reactor called the FFTF went on line, the town's largest church added "God bless the FFTF" to its list of daily prayers.

To me, nuclear work raised troubling moral questions: Hanford's repeated releases of radioactive gases, some deliberate, have left a trail of cancers and related health problems in communities as far as two hundred miles downwind; Hanford waste tanks, intended to be temporary, have leached hundreds of thousands of gallons of radioactive liquids into the ground; bombs made with Hanford plutonium have risked the potential annihilation of our species.

First-generation workers avoided these questions, choosing instead to immerse themselves in their jobs, building a team spirit and taking pride in the ethic of invention. "I could just as easily have been working in a coal plant," said one. "Or making lightbulbs." "My job," explained another, "was to make the machines work." Ultimately, Hanford's founding generation passed moral responsibility to those they referred to as "the men who know best." In Washington, D.C., explained the Hanford engineers, were congressional leaders and Pentagon officials who'd studied whether the building of nuclear weapons was right or wrong. They trusted them, they said, to make that decision.

The notion that a small group of specialists has a better grasp of key national choices than ordinary people exemplifies the moral distancing mechanisms common among the generations of the 1940s and 1950s. When men and women who came of age during that period later stayed silent in the face of obvious social ills, they did so largely because of their faith in our government leaders, and their belief in technical progress. Both of these impulses were strengthened by the Second World War, when the United States pulled together to defeat a common enemy. Could the Allied forces have taken Omaha Beach on D-Day without a very large number of young men who were willing to place their fate in the hands of the generals, their representatives in Washington, and ultimately their president? I'm not sure. But I do know that this same trust also made it easier to excuse dangerous governmental and corporate actions in all sorts of contexts, from Hanford to Vietnam.

Our institutional faith today has eroded, in part because of repeated betrayals by individuals and institutions we once trusted. We no longer believe the men who say they know best. However, we also don't believe we can challenge their judgments. In a disturbing twist, a large number of Americans, convinced that the country is simply doomed to be run by greedy crooks, have responded by retreating into private life. How did we arrive at this grim juncture?

This familiar blend of inflated skepticism and pervasive resignation was evident in a new generation of workers that arrived at Hanford in the late 1970s and early 1980s to build three new commercial reactors. (Only one of the plants limped to completion, saddling Pacific Northwest ratepayers with a multibillion-dollar debt load, greater than the national debt of Poland.) Unlike their older counterparts, most of these young men and women mistrusted the nuclear enterprise, but still showed up to build the plants every day. They cultivated an attitude of detachment, treating their work as an elaborate con game with an excellent paycheck.

"When these reactors go on line," several told me, "I'll be long gone—as far away as possible." One computer scientist whose world-weariness seemed particularly terminal joked, "Maybe the human species is like a company past its time—simply due for extinction."

Other young atomic workers rationalized their jobs by saying that since everyone else in the community accepted the reactors, they might as well accept them too, despite their personal qualms. "If this was somewhere else, where they didn't want these plants," said one, "I'd be the first to start protesting. But this is a nuclear town and it always will be."

"If I was back East and they were building reactors," said another, "I'd be throwing rocks, climbing fences, and getting arrested. Here, where else are you going to work? I tell you, I don't like that breeder, though, and when they start that sucker up I'm moving."

The young Hanford workers often voiced misgivings about the results of their labor and the process of their work. But they quickly brushed aside higher ideals like so much smoke from the high-priced dope they smoked. They joked about neophytes who bought their way into skilled jobs, underground pipes that led nowhere, improper welds, and other shoddy practices with potentially catastrophic consequences. Then they laughed, shrugged, and said they might as well get the money, since someone was going to.

You might call them realists, if by realism you mean the ability to accept almost any situation without moral qualms. But no matter how much Hanford's workers mistrusted their product, and regardless of any worries they had about the escalating stakes in the nuclear gamble, their occupational culture possessed no internal check that would stop them from going in day after day to help build reactors of questionable safety or weapons of mass destruction. As in industries with much less dramatic potential impact, the possibility of an alternative response wasn't part of their world.

"Won't Get Fooled Again"

Since I first wrote about Hanford in the early 1980s, America's cynicism has grown more insidious. We've come to equate moral conviction with delusion, and mock those who dare act on their beliefs. "It's nice that you're idealistic," we respond. "But what makes you think it matters?"

In the judgment of the Princeton philosopher Robert Wuthnow, this dismissal has deep cultural roots. "In an individualistic society," he writes, "caring is sometimes seen as an abnormality. . . . We do not even believe in sharing too deeply in the suffering of others. Our individual autonomy is too important. If caring for others becomes too demanding . . . we call it an obsession."

Even if we believe in some core notions of right and wrong, we often portray the unjust structures of our time as immutable, and that produces a sense that they can never be changed. A "radical" political scientist once explained to me loftily, "We're fooling ourselves if we think government doesn't serve powerful economic interests." True enough, for the moment. But he framed this as an inevitable state, as if history were out of our hands. He gave his students no vision to fight for, no foundation for action, only the prospect of joining him in the ranks of the all-knowing witnesses to human folly.

Cultivated or crude, cynicism is treacherous. It converts the sense of not wanting to be lied to—conveyed in the classic Who song "Won't Get Fooled Again"—into bitter protection against dashed hopes: If we never begin to fight for our dreams, there's no risk that we will fail. We can challenge the notion of "the men who know best" with new information—examples of how the powers that be routinely mislead us. But what can possibly challenge an all-encompassing worldview that, in the guise of sophistication, promotes the bleakest possible perspective on the human condition—the notion that everyone lies? The answer requires giving citizens something to believe in, a vision of connection powerful enough to help us begin once again to trust our fellow human beings.

DISTANT LIVES

I once shared a train seat with a young man, just out of the army, who was heading back to the small northern Washington town where he grew up. Friendly, wholesome, and innocent, he described the tedious routine of being a soldier, and how much he looked forward to living in his hometown and seeing his family again. Then he stopped speaking for a moment, as if trying to puzzle something out, and told me about the sex bars he used to visit in Korea. The dancers there, he said shyly, squatted on the tables and picked up coins with their genitals. "You know"—he bent down and gestured to his own—"like this." Once, a young woman about his own age was working, and he grew curious about what would happen if he heated the coins with his cigarette lighter. "I didn't mean any harm," he said. "I never thought it would hurt her." But she howled in pain, then ran out of the bar hunched over and screaming.

I believed the soldier harbored no conscious ill will toward that woman—or anyone else. But this only made his story more disturbing. It reminded me of our more general capacity for what theologians and ethicists call evil—the "militant ignorance," in the phrase of M. Scott Peck, that helps us deny the most destructive results of what we say and do. Did the military environment teach the young soldier to view the barroom dancer as something less than a full human being? Did he learn this lesson instead from his school, family, or friends? Or from his religion or the TV news? He had to acquire it somewhere. He wasn't any more intrinsically malicious than the rest of us.

Human destructiveness rarely comes in the shape of bloodthirsty madmen or sadistic monsters. In fact, those who cause the greatest harm these days are often so far removed from the consequences of their actions that they don't even perceive the connection. When I was in high school I had a friend named Tim. About the only thing we shared was a desire to go to Harvard. But we shot baskets in his backyard and speculated about sex. He taught me to play bridge, which he said would help me "get ahead in the world." I even slept over at his house while my parents took a vacation. In time, I realized that we had too little in common to sustain a friendship, however, and we grew apart.

Tim's father, whom I'll call Robert, worked for the Rand Corporation think tank in Santa Monica. He'd earlier been offered the job, Tim had told me with pride, of Nixon's national security advisor, before Henry Kissinger took it. Although Robert had turned down the position, he made regular trips to Washington, D.C., to meet with important people. What he actually did back there remained unclear until a couple years later, when I came across some of Robert's essays on foreign policy and military strategy. In works like *Insurgency and Counterinsurgency: New Myths and Old Realities,* he argued that any effort to win popular support in South Vietnam had little chance of success. Instead, he wrote, government forces should act as harshly as possible to prevent peasants from supporting our enemy, the Vietcong. We shouldn't be hamstrung by sentimental moralizing.

The "grunts," the ordinary soldiers, summarized this strategy crudely: "If you've got them by the balls, their hearts and minds will follow." The language Robert used was more erudite and technocratic, far removed from the stench of death in the Southeast Asian jungles. But U.S. forces seemed to follow his maxims—from the designation of so-called free-fire zones where saturation bombing raids were conducted, to an assassination campaign, the Phoenix Program, that may have killed as many as forty thousand civilians. Given Robert's role as an advisor at the highest levels of government, it seemed likely that he'd helped inspire these strategies. If so, he was responsible for infinitely more suffering than the young soldier with his cigarette lighter could ever have imagined.

I still have a photo of a party Robert and his wife gave for the young men in Tim's circle and for our parents. We sit in their high-ceilinged living room, with a tiled fireplace, trees filling a picture window, a piano in one corner, and drawings and paintings on the walls. Robert wears a suit and holds a drink. His wife sits next to him, listening attentively. The scene looks civilized, peaceful. Nothing links it to the massive death Robert helped bring about through his work.

Cynicism thrives in large, complex societies where cause is so easily divorced from effect. Under these circumstances, people such as Robert, the Hanford workers, or tobacco company CEOs can participate in immensely destructive enterprises, yet feel no guilt, no ambivalence, no direct responsibility. By contrast, the young soldier was forced to witness the pain he caused. It disturbed him, profoundly enough to confess and ask forgiveness from a stranger on a train. This action didn't erase the consequences of his action, the scars on the young woman's body and soul, but I believed he would never act similarly again. Robert experienced no such connection. On the contrary, like Henry Kissinger, he viewed his readiness to help destroy ordinary lives as a badge of intellectual rigor and toughness. Remote and untouchable, he was too distant from the suffering he helped create to even begin to grasp its human impact.

THE SOFT APOCALYPSE

It's more than bureaucratic detachment or cultural denial that produces our national mood of cynicism. Increasing economic uncertainty also plays a role. And to a large extent, concern about it is justified. Despite appearances, in recent decades conditions have changed in ways that leave most American citizens more insecure and more mistrusting.

Sociologist Todd Gitlin calls the resultant shifts the "soft apocalypse." The gap between rich and poor is greater today than at any point since the eve of the Great Depression. Even while the stock market has skyrocketed, companies have downsized, and real wages have stagnated—as they had since 1973—so that the average American manufacturing worker now makes less than those in eleven other countries, including Germany, Austria, Sweden, France, and Japan. The wealthiest one percent of Americans now control more of the nation's wealth than the bottom 95 percent. The United States has the industrialized world's highest rates of infant mortality, homelessness, and child poverty. We also lead in the rates of murder, rape, and other violent crimes, and in no country in the world is a higher percentage of the population in prison. We have the most billionaires, the highest executive salaries, the greatest inequality of wealth, the biggest military budget, including the most military aid to developing countries, and a commanding lead as the world's largest private arms trader. Even where things look good, as with the seemingly low unemployment rates of the late 1990s, the percentage of those unemployed would nearly double if corrected for involuntary part-timers and people who've simply given up on finding jobs. It would increase still further if we included our prison population and the array of criminal justice and security workers we pay to protect us from the hopeless and desperate.

While everyone is affected by the soft apocalypse, those with the fewest resources are especially vulnerable. High school students in New York City attend classes in cafeterias, locker rooms, and gymnasiums because their schools can't afford to build new classrooms. California and Florida now spend more on their prison systems than on higher education. Men's movement leader Michael Meade recently gave a workshop in the Southeast Ohio Correctional Institution. The facility started out as a school. Later it was converted into a minimum security prison. Then it became medium security. Meade calls it "a metaphor for our times."

It's a frightening metaphor. Increasingly, formal education is essential for any decent job, yet access to colleges and universities has actually been shrinking for those at the bottom. If you're in the top economic quarter of the population, your children have a 76 percent chance of getting through college and graduating by

age twenty-four, after which age such achievement becomes sub-
stantially less likely. If you're in the bottom quarter, however, the
figure is 4 percent. That's shocking enough. But consider this: In
1979, it was 27 percent—not great, but vastly better than it is now.
The decline is a result of repeated cuts and shifts in federal financial
aid, the eroding value of the minimum wage (which makes it far
harder for students to work their way through school), and the
reduction of public and private investment in America's most impoverished communities. No matter how smart, ambitious, and
hardworking you are, if you're poor, the odds are four in one
hundred that you'll acquire the education you need to escape poverty without an immense and protracted struggle.

This information may surprise you. It certainly contradicts the
dominant image of an American economy in unprecedented health.
How could we not be aware that the plight of our poorest neighbors is actually getting worse? We're unaware in part because our
society is so profoundly divided, and the lives of the poor are so
invisible. Jim Wallis, the editor of the wonderful radical evangelical
magazine, Sojourners, recalls how a friend, the civil rights historian
Vincent Harding, began to weep after yet another young African
American man whom they knew was lost to senseless street violence. "A whole generation of us is being destroyed," said Harding.
"At that moment," recalls Wallis, "I understood more clearly
than ever before why our society was allowing the deadly carnage
to continue. I realized that for most Americans who are white and
middle class, it isn't a whole generation of 'us' that is being lost.
Rather, it is 'them.' And we tell them what we think of them in
clear messages every day: they aren't important, they don't count,
they don't exist."

True words, and discomforting ones. Yet economic uncertainty
affects even the relatively comfortable. Whatever the state of the
stock market, few of us feel financially secure. Even if things seem
flush for the moment, our jobs are increasingly precarious. We
might be "outsourced," "downsized," or forced to work as "permanent temps." The emerging global economy constantly threatens

to move our jobs to Mexico, Malaysia, or budding high-tech com-
plexes in India and Ireland. Because our economic context is so
unstable, most of us feel we must hustle constantly, rarely pausing
to wonder why. What Barbara Ehrenreich has called "fear of falling" leaves us worrying about our children's future, how we'll get
by in our old age, and the skyrocketing costs of human basics like
health care. In a world that seems to be getting leaner and meaner,
we become preoccupied with our own private lives.

RADICAL FUTURELESSNESS

Any problem whose magnitude seems overwhelming can produce
this same mix of resignation and self-absorption. The global environmental dilemma is an example. As the Catholic monk
Thomas Berry writes in *The Dream of the Earth*, "We can break
the mountains apart. We can drain the rivers and flood the valleys.
We can turn the most luxuriant forests into throwaway paper
products. We can tear apart the great grass cover of the western
plains and pour toxic chemicals into the soil and pesticides onto
the fields until this soil is dead and blows away in the wind. We
can pollute the air with acids, the rivers with sewage, the seas with
oil—all this in a kind of intoxication with our power for devastation at an order of magnitude beyond all reckoning."

Think of population growth. In 1700, there were fewer than
700 million people in the world. By 1900, the number had slightly
more than doubled, to 1.6 billion. It grew to two billion in 1945,
despite two world wars and a global influenza epidemic. Since
then, global population has nearly tripled, and may reach nine billion in our lifetimes.

Think of agriculture. In the words of Timothy Weiskel of the
Harvard Divinity School, "Never before in the history of humanity
have so many people come to depend on so few plant species
grown in such restricted regions and subsidized by the net destruction of such quantities of non-renewables. In just fifty years hu-

manity has transformed global agriculture from a net source of captured solar energy into a net energy sink."

The bad news keeps coming. Antarctic penguins now have PCBs in their body fat. The rate at which we extinguish species—several thousand per year—is comparable to the great "extinction spasms" that doomed creatures like the dinosaurs. For decades the advanced industrial nations have been consuming a vastly disproportionate amount of the planet's resources. Now the poorest and most desperate countries are asking, reasonably enough, why they should be denied an equivalent share—which is to say, a similarly wasteful way of life.

Just reading these descriptions may make you feel more overwhelmed. It's understandable. Yet make no mistake: Solutions exist to address these problems, as well as others, from global warming to the depletion of the ozone layer to deforestation. They've inspired countless people—like Pete Knutson, Adam Werbach, Alison Smith, and Hazel Wolf—to get involved in environmental issues. But it's easier to adopt a kind of technological fundamentalism, like that of the initial Hanford workers, and assume that we can follow our current course indefinitely. Even if we have reservations about our present direction, it's tempting to succumb to what Robert Jay Lifton has called a "radical sense of futurelessness," and cease trying to imagine a better world, much less working to bring it about.

The prevalence of radical futurelessness is easier to understand when we realize that the problems we face today, environmental or otherwise, didn't reach their present scale overnight. They developed incrementally, which, in the case of a distracted and self-focused citizenry, means almost invisibly. I've heard it said that when frogs are thrown in boiling water, they jump out. But when they're placed in a pot in which the water is slowly brought to a boil, they let themselves be cooked to death. Similarly, we tolerate slow-burn crises so long as they don't touch us too directly and we have time to adjust to their effects. The sudden eruption of a large and intense military conflict, another Vietnam, would certainly inspire dramatic responses. By contrast, low-key yet devastating wars of survival occur daily on the streets of U.S. cities. Jobs disappear. Neighborhoods crumble. Lives are blighted. Young men and women die. Yet except for brief flickering moments, such as the Rodney King riots, the toll is invisible unless you're close at hand. Our steady assault on the environment also doesn't register, except for those paying close attention. The casualties of corporate raiding are equally hidden from sight. We rarely get a clear, unequivocal signal to tell us when things have gotten so bad that we must confront them.

As a result, by the time crises grow so big they can no longer be ignored, their sheer size can completely intimidate us, even if we're inclined to help. The vast number of issues adds to this feeling. Commentators use the phrase "compassion fatigue" to describe the resulting sense of saturation and hopelessness. We already feel overwhelmed. We're told that all options for productive change have already been tried and failed. So what's the sense of joining causes that seem doomed from the start? Why not restrict our efforts to domains in which we can reasonably hope to have some influence? Why not retreat into private life?

GHOSTS OF THE SIXTIES

Here's why not: Our personal lives are to a great extent shaped by decidedly impersonal forces. And we have far more power to influence those forces than we know. By retreating, we don't escape from the world so much as submit to it. We conspire in our own defeat. I'll return often to these themes, as well as to their corollary—that the surest way to improve our private lives is to act together with others in the public arena. But for now I'd like to explore another element in the general downsizing of hope, or at least of the kind of hope that makes us feel we can have a say in our shared common future: our culture's neglect and demeaning of efforts at change.

I've described how our cultural gatekeepers have buried or distorted the stories of America's most successful citizen movements: the abolitionist and women's suffrage campaigns, the union movement, the early civil rights efforts. By downplaying times when seemingly powerless people have nevertheless changed history, they've denied us many of our most inspirational models. But they can't erase the memory of an activist period that many of us lived through—the 1960s. So they've twisted its examples of citizen action into aversive images, making it far easier to dismiss current efforts for change.

Let's start with the caricatures. Again and again, activists of that time are portrayed solely as acid crazies wild in the streets, burned-out space cases, or militants waving copies of Mao's *Little Red Book* and chanting mindless slogans. The worst misrepresentations are the now pervasive stories of peace activists spitting on soldiers, which imply that most protestors were utterly contemptuous toward the young Americans sent to fight and die in Vietnam. To be sure, such images reinforce the belief of many soldiers that their country betrayed and disdained them. But when researchers who've worked with veterans have tried to track down actual cases, they've found next to none. U.C.–Santa Barbara sociologist Richard Flacks and University of West Virginia sociologist Jerry Starr both concluded that if such incidents happened at all, they were marginal. Yet the media present them as the centerpiece of that time.

Related images of activist callousness form a patchwork with those of apolitical "flower children," dominating current portrayals of the period. They crowd out far more complex and heartening lessons about what drove a broad spectrum of citizens to challenge their government and eventually help end the war.

The flip side of caricature is sentimentality, an unwarranted nostalgia that equally undermines our ability to act in the present. The more we romanticize the period as a Shangri-La when everyone seemed to care, the easier it is to treat current efforts toward change as naive and trivial by comparison. Thirty years later, reporters still describe all manner of dissident efforts as "sixties-style protests." It's as if present actions can at most be pale imitations.

If we spend our time mourning the eclipse of a more compassionate time, we forget how hard and lonely it often was to act then as well, and how much perseverance it took. It required far more than the snap of a finger to get 100,000 people to march against the Vietnam War. As late as 1966, no national antiwar demonstration had drawn more than 25,000 people, and more than 70 percent of students at the University of Wisconsin, a future radical hotbed, still approved of America's Vietnam involvement. In the spring of 1968, not one of thirty-nine major newspapers in a *Boston Globe* survey favored pulling out our troops, and Robert Kennedy continued to oppose unilateral military withdrawal in his early presidential campaign. I've mentioned how Martin Luther King, Jr. got savaged when he finally mustered the strength to speak out.

THE GREAT BETRAYAL

The most cynical media myth regarding the 1960s is that of the great betrayal—the notion that those who most fervently campaigned for change back then abandoned their various causes the moment they had the chance, compromised their principles, and headed straight to Wall Street and lives of greed. We've all heard "Big Chill" stories of Yippies converting into Yuppies and one-time protestors becoming corporate raiders. Until he died in 1994, the former Chicago Seven defendant turned promoter of selfishness, Jerry Rubin, seemed to get as much press in any given year as all the other former activists from the period combined. His omnipresent story made social involvement in general look transient and foolish, opportunistic and arrogant—hardly something to which we'd want to devote our time.

The notion of the great sellout has resonated particularly strongly among those who've grown up since the 1960s. "How can they tell us to act," young men and women say to me repeat-edly, "when they gave up all their values and left us the mess we're now facing?" This image makes those now coming of age feel they're alone in confronting America's problems. Even when their peers speak out for change, they decide that they're "merely in it for a fad," since they, too, will eventually betray their beliefs. They assume it's impossible to craft socially committed lives.

Conversely, media pundits have branded twentysomethings as universally self-indulgent and apathetic, as if they were missing a key chromosome for compassion or moral conviction. "You're writing a book on student values?" people asked when I was work-ing on *Generation at the Crossroads,* my study of their commit-ments and choices. "Do they *have* any values?" They delivered the question again and again, in almost identical words. Even many social activists embraced the same dismissive conclusion and con-descending tone.

The notion that all the 1960s activists sold out stems, first, from a conflation of the period's social movements with the far broader but often apolitical counterculture. Viewing the two streams as one was common from the start. The Nixon administration built its political support on the image of unwashed barbarians at the gates. Although social activists mistrusted the hippie focus on "dropping out," many often smoked the same dope, wore the same clothes, and were harassed by the same cops. At times both activists and their opponents found it convenient to magnify the movement's strength by claiming that every longhair was a potential comrade, a card-carrying member of "Woodstock Nation."

The conflation persists: Rush Limbaugh described a Bill Clinton White House decorated with flowers, paisley, and peace signs. Stu-dents I interviewed talked of those who "were hippies back then, and now all they care about are their Beemers." But smoking dope at a rock concert or growing out your hair wasn't the same as working for civil rights in Mississippi or even handing out antiwar leaflets at school. Some may have been inspired to dress and act the hippie part by aspirations like the activists' for a more compassionate world, and by a similar revulsion against the carnage in Vietnam. But the hippie style required no additional moral commitment, posed a comparatively minimal legal or psychological risk, and offered none of the discomfort or frustration that resulted from asking larger questions about America's direction. All the same, the image of hippies turned greedheads remains an easy one with which to tar the idea of sustained social commitment.

To show that the myth of the great sellout is false, we need only call to mind the variety of people still active today. Think of Marian Wright Edelman, Gloria Steinem, Alice Walker, Earth Day founder Denis Hayes, the populist U.S. senator Paul Wellstone and congressman John Lewis. Think of organizations that grew out of that period, such as Greenpeace, the National Organization for Women (NOW), and the National Abortion Rights Action League (NARAL). Think of major union reform efforts, the environmental movement, efforts to achieve greater parity for women and respect for the human dignity of gays. Studies of those who spoke out at campuses as diverse as Berkeley, Michigan, Florida, and U.C.– Santa Barbara have discovered that their involvement in social causes hardly ended with graduation. The sociologist Doug McAdam found, for example, that half of the students who joined Mississippi's Freedom Summer civil rights project in 1964 remain involved in at least one citizen movement. Compared to peers who never marched, or were only peripherally involved, this group remains far more engaged.

I don't want to make the picture sound too rosy. Dashed hopes are part of our current problem—for many of us, the people, institutions, ideas, and movements we once believed in turned out to be all too human and fallible. I'll talk later about activists—both from the Vietnam-era movements and from important efforts since—who've burned out from day-to-day pressures, the fragility of their political community, the difficulty of challenging entrenched institutional power, and doubts about just what to fight for in a highly confusing time. Many have shifted their focus from trying to change the world to filling in gaps left by shrinking social programs, or to leading ethical private lives. But that's very different from saying that they now stand for all that they once opposed.

Why have the media portrayed the legacy of the 1960s in ways that obscure its most heartening lessons? One reason is our sound-bite society. Far too often, reporters recycle each others' assumptions, repeating the same images, perspectives, voices, and quotes year after year. I also worry that a more insidious process is at play, part of the culture of the smirk. Even the mildest forms of social commitment imply that our actions make a difference, and that if we want a more humane future we're all going to have to help create it. That perspective can be threatening to those in a position to influence opinion, such as editors and reporters. It suggests that they have a moral responsibility to listen to voices that don't necessarily originate in Washington, D.C., or the corporate suites, and to question the actions of the powerful. Insouciant cynicism's more comfortable.

Democratic societies progress by democratic means—that is, when citizens participate fully and fairly in public life, working for the common good. The myth of generational betrayal disrupts this process by instilling the belief that speaking out for justice and standing up for freedom are transient youthful pursuits, and misguided ones at that. It implies that they'll be inevitably replaced by grown-up, realistic priorities, like making sure we come out on top in a world that's getting meaner. It forecloses even the prospect of our leading lives of conviction.

Cynicism salves the pain of unrealized hope. If we convince ourselves that nothing can change, we don't have to risk acting on our dreams. But the more we accept this, the more we deny core parts of ourselves. We deny even the possibility that our choices can matter.

RECLAIMING OUR HISTORY

As an alternative to this impotent realism, I'd like to propose a clear-eyed idealism, which recognizes that these are bad times for many people, but refuses to accept that the bad times are inevitable. This bears repeating, so as to avoid misunderstanding. I'm not promoting a culture of happy talk. It's important to dissect institutional arrogance and greed, to assess how it damages lives, neighborhoods, communities, and the most basic life systems of the earth. But too many social activists almost delight in rolling around in the bad news, like dogs in rancid fish. If that's all we do, we'll reinforce the belief that efforts to change things are doomed. We'll foster resignation and despair. So along with the bad news, we need to convey that which is capable of inspiring hope.

I'll explore how we can find this hope in the unexpected heroism of ordinary people, and in the movements for change that they've created. We can find it in our religious traditions—in the sense, as Virginia Ramirez said, that God provides strength for even the most difficult challenges. We can find it in the awe we feel at the complex majesty of the natural world, when watching an eagle or feeling the power of a river. And we can find it by reclaiming the historical legacies that can most inspire us.

It may always feel more than a little absurd to think that we might be able to change history. Recognizing that fact, and appreciating the irony in our situation, can be useful, especially when our efforts don't go as planned. But that same sense of irony becomes dangerous when it's used to justify passivity. As the poet and essayist Lewis Hyde points out, it becomes "the voice of the trapped who have come to enjoy their cage." Accordingly, we might think of a modern cynic as someone who's given up all hope of finding a door, much less a key. And we might remember that there are better ways to live.

Chapter Five

Unforeseen Fruits

*Most of the things worth doing in the world had been declared impossible
before they were done.*

—*JUSTICE LOUIS BRANDEIS*

I once went for a run in Fort Worth, Texas, in a grassy park along
a riverbank. I came upon a man shaking a tree. I hesitated, then
stopped and asked, "What are you doing?"

"It's a pecan tree," he said. "If I shake it enough, the nuts will
come down. I can't know exactly when they'll fall or how many.
But the more I shake it, the more I'll get."

This seems an apt metaphor for social involvement. Often our
efforts may yield few clear or immediate results. Our victories will
almost always be partial. But we need to draw enough strength
from our initial steps to help us persevere. "You have to begin
with small groups," said Modjesca Simkins, an eighty-four-year-
old African American activist from South Carolina. "But you reach
the people who matter. They reach others. Like the Bible says,
'leaven in the lump, like yeast in the dough' . . . it rises somewhere
else."

We liberate ourselves from cynicism by replacing the all-
knowing but soul-destroying smirk with compassionate curiosity
about our fellow human beings. When we do so, we find that there
is ample reason for hope. Even during the past decades of supposed
activist quiescence, and despite a mean-spirited national politics,
we have witnessed the emergence of important new visions. We've
witnessed the resurgence of an international environmental ethic:
More and more citizens refuse to accept the casual spoliation of
the earth. We've seen the development of a global women's movement that asks fundamental questions about age-old power rela-

tionships. America's new and far more engaged union leadership offers at the least the possibility of labor organizations willing to challenge the unchecked rule of global capital. It's easy to highlight the most discouraging aspects of our time. Yet every effort for change has its uncertainties, and every era its barriers and possibilities.

As I said earlier, this is all the more important to bear in mind when considering the major changes of the past. It's a mistake to presume that earlier movements were destined to succeed, that opportunities were greater then, or circumstances more favorable. America's major victories for democracy have never been easy or inevitable. Activists—the African American students and sharecroppers who spearheaded the civil rights movement, the labor organizers of the 1930s, the abolitionists who helped end slavery—have often braved physical violence far greater than anything most of us face today. Unless we're ready to concede that history has effectively ended, and that the current time is therefore inherently bleaker than any in human experience, we'd do well to keep faith in the possibility of change.

RIPPLES OF HOPE

We never know how acts of generosity and faith will resound in the world. In 1978, the Seattle therapist Ginny Nicarthy, who organized some of the country's early battered women's groups, decided to write a book for her participants. The public was still largely unaware of domestic violence. Ginny ran her groups without pay, through the downtown YWCA and a women's shelter called New Beginnings. She scraped together a meager living doing outside counseling on a $5- to $10-an-hour sliding scale. Wanting to give the battered women a glimpse of the road they'd have to travel to get out of their abusive relationships, Ginny assembled some makeshift handouts. The few existing books on the subject, she says, were academic tomes "hardly appropriate for women in the middle of the soup." So she began writing her own book, draw-ing on the stories she'd heard.

Twenty-four publishers saw her sample—and rejected it. The editors liked the writing, but they said that there weren't enough battered women in America to make up an audience—and even women who were abused wouldn't take on the stigma of walking up to a bookstore clerk to buy a copy. The editors didn't see any marketing potential.

The rejections left Ginny frustrated. "I knew the women needed the book. Every week more came into the group with black eyes and broken spirits. But I didn't know just how it would get out. Maybe I'd even have to publish it myself. But I was already so stretched working umpteen hours a day on different projects, with things so scraggly in terms of money. The whole situation felt over-whelming."

Ginny mentioned her circumstances to a group of friends who met weekly to talk, decompress, and reflect on their work. And one was moved enough to help. Jane Klassen, a therapist who co-led the New Beginnings group, admired Ginny's vision and spirit and knew how much the book would mean to women who, Jane felt, "had absolutely nothing to help guide them through." Though she had no resources beyond a modest income from her own ther-apy practice, Jane decided to give Ginny $500 to help her finish the book. "I was trying to live simply," Jane said. "I got a partic-ular satisfaction in helping a friend do something that mattered, rather than writing an anonymous check to a faceless agency. Ginny was doing important work. She'd always inspired me. I thought it might help."

Ginny was astonished. "It was such a testament of faith. It doesn't sound like much money now, but back then it was a month's living expenses. I could pay all these bills that were weigh-ing me down. I didn't have to worry so much. Jane's gift gave me breathing room. With all her trust in the project, I had to complete it."

Buoyed by Jane's faith and generosity, Ginny finished the book and showed it to a friend at a four-year-old Seattle publisher, Seal Press, that was printing feminist poetry and fiction. Seal hadn't done anything similar, but her friend felt the subject was important, and decided to go ahead. *Getting Free* sold modestly at first, primarily through battered women's shelters and support groups, but has now sold 150,000 copies, and has become the bible for women concerned about domestic violence. It paved the way for a slew of related books. It helped move the battered women's movement from the margins to the mainstream. "Back then," Ginny said, "no one wanted to touch the subject. The problem hasn't gone away, but at least people recognize the right of women not to be beaten. Now concern about domestic violence is respectable. It's social work. Some people even understand that it's a political issue, having to do with abuse of power."

Jane could not have predicted the results of her gift. She acted on an impulse, to help a friend do crucial work. Her gift of money translated into inspiration and energy that helped Ginny keep plowing ahead to complete the book despite all the rejections and frustrations. She helped it get out to make its impact.

The risks we take make a difference. As Robert Kennedy once said, "Each time a person stands for an ideal, or acts to improve the lot of others, or strikes out against injustice, he or she sends forth a tiny ripple of hope. And crossing each other from a million different centers of energy and daring, those ripples build a current that can sweep down the mightiest walls of oppression and resistance."

CHAINS OF CONCERN

Our actions don't always transform institutions directly. Change comes, to be sure, when we shift corporate or governmental policies, elect more accountable leaders, or create effective institutional alternatives. But it also comes when we stir the hearts of previously uninvolved citizens and help them take their own moral stands. It comes when we set in motion chains of concern that eventually help alter history.

Growing up, I attended the same Los Angeles temple as Suzy Marks, whose story I've already told. A few months after the 1967 Six-Day War in the Middle East, our rabbi, Leonard Beerman, gave a High Holy Days talk. We should be glad for Israel's survival, he said, and celebrate its creation of a vibrant Jewish society, but we ought to be wary of blindly celebrating military force. The message surprised even this liberal West Los Angeles congregation. Many bristled at it. However, it struck a chord inside me. It taught me the importance of raising hard questions, even if people won't always like what you say. That lesson has stayed with me to this day, and given me strength.

As a rabbi, Beerman was entrusted with offering a moral vision. He had a ready-made venue, a podium. But too many rabbis, ministers, and priests are silent on difficult issues, or slide over them by reciting platitudes. Beerman grappled with his own doubts and apprehensions while writing this talk and others, but that didn't prevent him from risking controversy with words that helped change people's lives.

Another wide-ranging chain of inspiration began with the teenage daughter of Lockheed engineer Robert Aldridge. In the early 1970s, she asked her father how he could work on "these terrible weapons," the Polaris and Poseidon missiles he'd helped design. At first Aldridge rationalized. Then, after painful reflection, he resigned his job and began to speak out against the arms race. A talk he gave inspired a Catholic theologian, Jim Douglass, to establish a peace community next to Washington State's Trident submarine base.

While Douglass was in jail for climbing the base fence (he prayed in protest near the area where the warheads were stored), Seattle archbishop Raymond Hunthausen visited him and celebrated mass. The two shared a religious language. Hunthausen had been relatively silent during the Vietnam War. But he was so appalled by the Trident's immense deadly potential—it carries warheads with a total destructive power two thousand times greater than the Hiroshima bomb—that he called the base the Auschwitz of Puget Sound and withheld half his federal income taxes in protest. This unprecedented step, together with the equally passionate voices of a handful of other bishops, moved the U.S. Catholic Congress finally to make a statement condemning the nuclear arms race. That, in turn, sparked study and debate in parishes throughout the nation, and began to set the tone for the end of the Cold War. Had Aldridge's daughter—and hundreds of others—not spoken out, the process would never have begun.

Some issues touch us directly, impelling us to immediate action. More often, though, our responses are delayed. We hear about common concerns on the TV news or read about them in the newspaper. We may even learn that citizens in our communities have made this or that issue their cause. But we still may pay little heed until a friend, or maybe two or three friends, take a stand. When we do finally get involved, we realize that all the other voices we've heard and seemingly ignored have led the way.

Historian Howard Zinn witnessed this phenomenon in the late 1950s and early 1960s as a young teacher at Atlanta's esteemed black women's college, Spelman. In the classroom, he spoke out for justice and encouraged his students to involve themselves in the nascent civil rights movement. At first, they held back. But as the movement grew, a few decided to take part, at first in modest ways. As that initial group became more confident, taking increasingly greater risks, others joined. In time, Zinn's students helped play key roles. And some, like Alice Walker and Marian Wright Edelman, went on to inspire thousands of others.

"Even the smallest, most unheroic of acts," Zinn writes, "adds to the store of kindling that may be ignited by some surprising circumstance into tumultuous change. . . . What the [civil rights] movement proved is that even if people lack the customary attributes of power—money, political authority, physical force—as did the black people of the Deep South, there is a power that can be created out of pent-up indignation, courage, and the inspiration of a common cause, and that if enough people put their minds and bodies into that cause, they can win. It is a phenomenon recorded again and again in the history of popular movements against injustice all over the world."

Courage can be contagious, spreading from those who are active to those on the sidelines, helping them overcome their isolation and fear and renewing their spirit. And the "spectators" are not the only beneficiaries of such leaps of faith. As Dave Hall, the president of Physicians for Social Responsibility, says, "I draw strength and energy from anybody who is doing something constructive about issues that matter."

BEFORE WATER TURNS TO ICE

Virtually all of America's most effective historical movements met with repeated frustration and failure before making significant progress toward their goals. At few points prior to victory could participants have proved that their individual efforts mattered. On the contrary, the reverse often seemed true. As the U.S. Supreme Court justice Louis Brandeis once wrote, "Most of the things worth doing in the world had been declared impossible before they were done." Only in retrospect does the link between small beginnings and profound social change become fully evident. Only then is the true value of persistence in the face of difficulty revealed.

Think of the apartheid-era campaign for South African divestment. American economic interests supported the apartheid government almost from its foundation. After the 1960 Sharpeville massacre, for instance, a consortium of U.S. banks (led by Chase Manhattan) invested heavily to shore up the Pretoria regime, which seemed on the verge of collapse. In response, one of the first Students for a Democratic Society (SDS) protests was held on Wall Street. Challenges to American economic support of apartheid surged and receded for the next twenty-five years. Then, after the U.S. Senate failed to pass a sanctions bill in 1984, a stream of people staged acts of civil disobedience at the main South African embassy in Washington, D.C., and at local consulates nationwide.

These protests in turn rekindled large-scale social activism on America's campuses. Even as their generation was being maligned as apathetic and uncaring, students organized rallies, petition drives, and marches, built protest shantytowns, staged sit-ins, and set up blockades—all aimed at persuading colleges and universities to divest themselves of stock in companies doing business in South Africa. Their movement caught fire as global television showed the South African government beating, gassing, and shooting peaceful demonstrators who challenged worsening economic conditions, substandard education, and a new constitution that would permanently disenfranchise black South African citizens.

At Columbia University, the divestment campaign was led by the Black Student Association (BSA). Participants used speakers, public forums, referendums, and door-to-door canvassing of the dorms to win support for their cause. They even secured an endorsement from the faculty senate. When university trustees refused to meet with the campaigners, a dozen students launched a hunger strike, and then a sit-in that they expected would last a few hours. Instead, several hundred people joined in, and the sit-in lasted three weeks. Not only did Columbia divest the following fall (while administrators insisted their action had "nothing to do with the protests") but its students inspired similar efforts across the country, prompting some 150 institutions to withdraw more than $4 billion in investment funds. The student movement proved to be the key factor in the U.S. congressional vote that finally approved sanctions against South Africa over Ronald Reagan's veto. By ending U.S. moral and economic support, this historic decision placed enormous pressure on the South African government and its white population to finally move toward democracy.

Movement participants acted mostly because they felt they had to do something, even if it had little impact on university policy. "Going into it, I wasn't at all sure the university would respond," said Winston Willis, who later headed Columbia's BSA. "I doubted the trustees would give in. Columbia's an immensely powerful institution. But a number of us felt so strongly about the issues that we were willing to risk arrest, suspension, or expulsion, and to sleep outside night after night in the sleet and the rain—in case maybe, just maybe, they would."

The sit-in was particularly hard for African American students on scholarships, many of whom were the first in their families to go to college and had no safety net of money and personal contacts. But letters and phone calls of support came from across the country. The students persisted, and their efforts bore fruit they had scarcely imagined. When Nelson Mandela was freed and came to speak in Harlem, Winston attended. He went, he says, "with a sense that I'd played a part, no matter how infinitesimal, in helping to get him out. Friends gave me a copy of that first ballot where blacks got to vote, which I still keep in our study. Recently another friend from those days, whose wife's father is now an official in the new South African government, went to visit. Desmond Tutu shook his hand and said, 'You don't know how important it was what you American students did.' We had no idea our actions would have such an impact."

None of us can predict when the causes we support will capture the public imagination, and our once-lonely quests become popular crusades. "Before water turns to ice," writes the psychologist Joanna Macy, "it looks just the same as before. Then a few crystals form, and suddenly the whole system undergoes cataclysmic change." The paleontologist Stephen Jay Gould has developed a theory he calls "punctuated equilibrium." Rather than occurring at a steady pace, evolution proceeds in fits and starts, Gould argues. Long stretches of relative stasis are followed by brief periods of intense transformation, when many new species appear and others die out. Although attempts to improve social and economic conditions usually proceed incrementally, it is impossible to foretell precisely when any of our endeavors will reach critical mass, suddenly creating change.

Nor can we predict when a single seemingly insignificant effort will produce powerful results. Shortly before the 1994 Congressional elections, a Wesleyan University student named Tess Rondeau was inspired by an environmental conference. With a few friends, Tess registered nearly three hundred fellow students concerned about environmental threats and cuts in government financial aid programs. Nearly all ended up supporting Congressman Sam Gejdenson, a Democrat of more-than-usual courage and vision. Gejdenson squeaked in to win re-election by just twenty-one votes, then recaptured his seat in 1996, and won by a landslide in 1998. Before they began, Tess and her friends feared that their modest registration campaign would be irrelevant, and worried that they'd come off "like politicians spouting a line." But they decided to go ahead anyway and do the best they could. Which to their surprise turned out to be very good indeed. Had they done nothing, Gejdenson would have lost.

SHORT-TERM ENCOUNTERS

Like our more personal journeys of learning and growth, wholesale social change rarely happens all at once. Most successes are partial. "A final victory," Martin Luther King, Jr. said, "is an accumulation of many short-term encounters. To lightly dismiss a success because it does not usher in a complete order of justice is to fail to comprehend the process of achieving full victory."

An excellent example of the cumulative impact of such short-term encounters is the dramatic shift in American attitudes toward nuclear power. Today we tend to take for granted the principles of environmental accountability that stopped the burgeoning construction of America's nuclear power plants. Many of us have forgotten that through the 1960s, the industry faced scant opposition, even from progressive activists. The radical folksinger Pete Seeger sang of a bright nuclear future, with energy too cheap to meter. The technology drew praise from the radical students of SDS. I grew up reading a Little Golden Book called *Our Friend the Atom*.

In the 1970s, a handful of citizen groups and dissident experts began to raise questions about the risks commercial reactors and their radioactive products posed to human health. The activists' alarm affected others, including a former navy ROTC cadet named Michael Lowe, who spent the mid-1970s helping build a nuclear power plant sixty miles north of Columbia, South Carolina. Over time, however, Michael became appalled at slipshod work practices and rampant cronyism. Eventually he resigned. Then he started reading about the risks of nuclear power, discovering among other things that the nearby reactor's cooling water would enter the Broad River, the source of Columbia's drinking water. He grew concerned about the safety of himself, his wife, and especially their two-year-old son, Malachi. "The managers didn't even care about the risks," he says; "they were distant enough that they could just abstract them."

"Even after quitting my job, I couldn't just leave the reactor," Michael explains. So with a small group of friends he formed the Palmetto Alliance to challenge the atomic enterprise in one of the most heavily nuclearized states in the nation. The group held community meetings, interviewed nuclear workers about the effects of radiation, and engaged state media and elected officials in discussions. Michael had recently finished a fifteen-day jail sentence for a civil disobedience protest at a local plant when a reactor at Three Mile Island, in Pennsylvania, had a partial meltdown and leaked radioactive material into the atmosphere. It was 1979. Nuclear power plants were under consideration nationwide. The warnings of the Palmetto Alliance and similar groups throughout the country suddenly took on new urgency. In South Carolina, local TV stations broadcast reports on the state's atomic risks. When trucks brought waste from the damaged Pennsylvania reactor, Governor Richard Riley cited their questionable paperwork and turned them back at the state line. The message? South Carolina should no longer be considered a nuclear haven.

It wasn't just Three Mile Island that changed things. Accidents with nearly the same potential for catastrophe had already occurred at the Detroit Fermi plant, at the Rocky Flats atomic weapons facility outside Denver, and at the Brown's Ferry plant in Decatur, Alabama. But the atomic enterprise had continued to grow. In the early 1970s, President Nixon projected a thousand nuclear power plants to be built by the year 2000. The Three Mile Island meltdown had the impact it did because a growing popular movement had been steadily exposing the downside of the nuclear enterprise, both environmental and economic. People held massive civil disobedience protests at New Hampshire's proposed Seabrook reactor, California's Diablo Canyon, and South Carolina's own Savannah River Plant. They spoke out and educated their communities. Eventually, public attitudes changed so much that building new nuclear facilities or dump sites in even the most politically quiescent areas of the country became virtually impossible. Twenty-five years have passed since anyone has put forward a plan to build a new nuclear reactor on American soil.

Looking back on his role in this transformation, Michael Lowe says he felt he had to take a stand "whether or not I had a chance to succeed. I did it as much as anything just to preserve some dignity." And he felt responsible "for Malachi, for his future." Such ordinary feelings as pride in workmanship and love of family can produce an extraordinary outcome when they fuel our involvement in public concerns.

GLOBAL RIPPLES

Sometimes we don't notice profound changes when they occur. Cultures shift, bit by bit. Ideas once branded as heresy become common currency. Under enough pressure, political and economic institutions follow suit. Think of the global shift toward sexual equality. It goes beyond the tremendous progress women like Ginny Nicarthy have made here in the United States on issues from domestic abuse to workplace opportunities to the admittedly beleaguered right to abortion choice. Despite serious backlash, women throughout the world now expect vastly more from their men, work, and communities than they did as recently as the early 1970s.

Jean Houston describes watching residents of a small village in India gather before their single TV set to watch a gorgeous dramatization of the Ramayana, a three-thousand-year-old epic central to Hindu culture. In the story, Princess Sita is abducted by a demon and carried away, then rescued by Prince Rama and an army of monkeys. Jean, like the villagers, was enjoying the production when an old woman turned to her and said "Oh, I don't like Sita."

The princess was too weak, the woman explained, too passive. "We women in India are much stronger than that. She should have something to do with her own rescue, not just sit there moaning and hoping that Rama will come. We need to change the story." She said her husband was also named Rama and her name was Sita, and that he was "a lazy bum. If any demon got him, I would have to go and make the rescue." The woman's fellow villagers laughed in agreement.

Houston realized she was witnessing an ancient myth undergoing change, and with it fundamental relationships of power. No one can chart the precise route feminist currents followed to reach this particular remote village, whether through Indian political leaders, outspoken local women, the international medium of television, or some combination of the three. But in Houston's estimation, the mere fact that the villagers were questioning traditional roles was an astounding benchmark of the global women's movement's progress and reach.

THE ONLY FAILURE IS QUITTING

We never know how the impact of our actions may ripple out. We never know who may be touched. That's one more reason why, although the fruits of our labors can't always be seen, they matter immensely.

I've mentioned Derrick Bell's April 1990 decision to take an unpaid leave to protest Harvard Law School's refusal to hire a single female Latino, Asian, or Native American professor. There were a few white women, a few African American men, and that was it. Although administrators made vague promises of change, they kept hiring more white men. Bell took a second year of unpaid leave, then requested a third, for which he had to obtain a routinely granted waiver of the standard rules. In his case, though, the university refused, saying that Bell must either return to his teaching duties or lose his tenured position. Bell chose to forfeit his lifetime position on the most prestigious law faculty in the nation.

This was a courageous moral stand, which drew national attention. It brought major pressure to bear on Harvard Law School, and called attention to the hiring practices of other law schools nationwide. Seven years later, Harvard Law finally relented, hiring an African American woman, Lani Guinier, away from the University of Pennsylvania. African American colleagues throughout the country have told Bell that they owed their tenure-track hirings in part to his protest. "The fact is," Bell writes, "that most of us in law teaching—whatever our qualifications and potential—are the beneficiaries of pressures, past or present, on campus or beyond." Note that the victories sparked by Bell's action came without out his foreknowledge and after he'd already paid a personal price.

Bell himself says he would not have been able to make such a sacrifice if not for another difficult moral decision earlier in his career; a decision that, in turn, had been sparked by another example of commitment. In 1957, Bell was a young lawyer for the U.S. Justice Department. He'd joined the NAACP a while before, and his bosses called his two-dollar annual membership a conflict of interest. Most of Bell's friends urged him to quit the NAACP and to work from within the system to change this policy and others. But Judge William Hastie, the first black federal judge in the country, urged Bell to follow his conscience. During World War II, Hastie had resigned as a top civilian aide to the secretary of war when the military refused to integrate its forces; his departure helped bring the issue to public attention, and Truman abolished military segregation a few years later. Bell decided not to give up his membership. When his superiors at the Justice Department transferred him to a meaningless backbench assignment, he resigned to head the Pittsburgh branch of the NAACP. There he started working with people like Thurgood Marshall on some of the most critical civil rights fights of the time.

As Bell said, what separates individuals who act to challenge injustice from those who stand aside is the sense of personal urgency they develop, "and the recognition that, in the real world, we cannot expect—and certainly should not wait for—the perfect solution." Had he not taken that first stand, Bell recalls, "I might have toiled on, unhappily, at the Justice Department for years at work less risky but certainly no less frustrating than my job with the Pittsburgh NAACP. More important, had I remained at the Justice Department, I would have missed the chance to work with the NAACP Legal Defense Fund during some of the most exciting years of the civil rights movement." And that was precisely the experience that prepared him for the stand he took at Harvard.

As Bell's experience suggests, a key ingredient of effective social action is faith that our efforts count for something. Sometimes we don't even recognize powerful victories when they occur, because their impact is hidden. In 1969, Henry Kissinger told the North Vietnamese that Nixon was threatening a massive escalation of the war, including potential nuclear strikes, unless they capitulated and forced the National Liberation Front in the South to do the same. Nixon was serious. He'd had military advisers prepare detailed plans, including mission folders with photographs of possible nuclear targets. But two weeks before the president's November 1 deadline for surrender, there was a nationwide daylong "moratorium," during which millions of people took part in local demonstrations, vigils, church services, petition drives, and other forms of protest. A month later came a major march in Washington, D.C. Nixon's public response was to watch the Washington Redskins football game during the D.C. march, and to declare that the marchers weren't affecting his policies in the slightest. His contempt fed the frustration and demoralization of far too many in the peace movement. But privately, Nixon decided the movement had, in his words, so "polarized" American opinion that he couldn't carry out his threat. Participants in the moratorium had no idea that their efforts may have helped stop a nuclear attack.

Nowhere is the need for a long view of social change more evident than in the case of campaigns that span generations. Think of the women's suffrage movement. When Susan B. Anthony began fighting for women's right to vote, her cause seemed a long shot. She worked for it her entire adult life, then died at the age of eighty-six, fourteen years before suffrage was ratified. In retrospect, Anthony played as pivotal a role as any single individual. Yet during her lifetime, success seemed far from assured. Only by trusting that sooner or later their actions would matter could she and others keep on until they prevailed.

LETTING GO OF THE OUTCOME

Few of us, I hasten to add, can pursue a goal day in and day out, year in and year out, without experiencing success or satisfaction of some kind. So it's important to act as wisely as we can, in the hope of winning tangible victories. But no amount of thoughtful strategizing and prudent allocation of effort can guarantee a specific outcome. As a local leader in the successful 1997 United Parcel Service strike put it, "We couldn't promise anything at the beginning. We didn't know how it would turn out. We could only say that our cause was important and that the more we stuck together, the more solid we would be."

"If you get involved in trying to heal the world," says Marianne Williamson, "you're not guaranteed specific results as you define them. You're not promised that because you're doing this, a particular organization will work or a particular cause prevail. But you gain the satisfaction of living your life for a higher purpose."

It's best to attend to the journey, in other words, and fret less about the destination.

While pregnant with her first child, my friend Stephanie Ericsson lost her husband to a sudden heart attack. In *Companion Through the Darkness,* her meditation on grieving, she explained, "Many books would prefer that we are neater about our pain. So they attempt to organize a process that is intentionally chaotic. . . . To acknowledge that there are mysteries we will never unravel is humbling and freeing at the same time. It is not a passive stance— resigning to darkness. It is an open stance, palms to the sky, as a receiving vessel. For vessels are meant to be emptied and filled, emptied and filled, emptied and filled."

Social change work seems to involve a similar process. The forces that impel any of us to act and take risks will always, at their core, remain a mystery, one that "the talkers talking their talk," to use a phrase of Walt Whitman's, will never be able to explain. We can only glimpse the reasons by means of what Whitman called "faint clues and indirections." Fighting for our deepest convictions requires relinquishing control and accepting messy uncertainties. It demands working as well as we can at efforts that feel morally right, and then having faith that our labors will bear fruit, perhaps in our time, or perhaps down the line, for somebody else. "If you expect to see the final results of your work," wrote the journalist I. F. Stone, "you simply have not asked a big enough question."

The principle of keeping on regardless of apparent results recalls the religious view that true strength comes, paradoxically, from vulnerability, from knowing our limitations, and from a suffering that opens the door to compassion. As Jim Wallis of *Sojourners* writes, "Never achievement or success . . . but rather the giving of ourselves in faith leads to life." Our challenge, from this perspective, is not to predict what God has in store, or master some nebulous dialectic of history, but to live rightly, love our fellow human beings, and cherish God's creation. We can do this on a personal level, one to one. We can also do it politically, by working to create a society that nurtures human dignity.

America's dominant culture insists that our lives have no such broader significance, so we dare not vest them with purpose. Yet we can see how political silence feeds on itself, breeding isolation and despair. And how acts of faith and courage, conversely, can build on one another, opening up new possibilities. We owe much to those who acted with vision and conviction in previous times. The risks and commitments we undertake today may leave a better world for those yet to come. We can view our lives as a bridge between past and future.

"It helps to remember," says Atlanta's Sonya Vetra Tinsley, "how many changes there've been that were someone else's radical struggle for social justice. Whether the minimum wage, child labor laws, public schools, even jails instead of chopping people's heads off. When you first learn about injustice, you get all fired up. You want to fix it that day. You figure that if you only join this or that organization you'll solve it all in a couple years. After a while, you get humbled by the process. You realize that you're working for things you might not even see, and that you need to have faith that the effort is worthwhile.

"So much needs to be done to educate people," adds Sonya, "on how the freedoms and rights we take for granted didn't come about through chance, coincidence, or benevolence, but through struggle and intention. There's very little of worth in our society that someone didn't fight for."

We need to remember this even when our efforts appear utterly futile, when we seem to be rolling Sisyphus's rock up a hill only to watch it roll back again and again. In the early 1960s, my friend Lisa Peattie, now a retired MIT professor, was a young widow with four small kids. She took two of them to a Washington, D.C., vigil in front of the White House, to protest nuclear testing. The vigil was small, a hundred women at most. Rain poured down. Lisa's children were restless. Frustrated and soaked, the women joked about how President Kennedy was no doubt sitting inside drinking hot chocolate, warm, comfortable, and not even looking at their signs.

A few years later, the movement against nuclear testing had grown, and Lisa attended another march in Washington, considerably larger. Benjamin Spock, the famous baby doctor, spoke. He described how he'd come to take a stand. Because of his stature, his decision had influenced thousands, and would pave the way for his outspoken opposition to the Vietnam War. Spock cited his growing worries about radioactive contamination. Then he mentioned being in D.C. a few years earlier, and seeing a small group of women marching, with their kids, in the pouring rain. "I thought that if those women were out there," he said, "their cause must be really important." As he described the scene and setting, and how much he was moved, Lisa realized that Spock was referring to her group.

Chapter Six

The Call of Stories

What is most important to me must be spoken, made verbal and shared,
even at the risk of having it bruised or misunderstood.

—AUDRE LORDE

We work for justice, I've come to believe, when our hearts are stirred by specific lives and situations. Virginia Ramirez challenged the ills of her community only after watching her elderly neighbor die needlessly. She wasn't motivated by an abstract statistical analysis, however scandalous, of local poverty, deteriorating housing stock, or unequal investment in different neighborhoods. She learned those numbers later. Instead, she responded to a particular human story, which spurred her to rethink her own life. Virginia displayed a quality that's critical to social engagement: the capacity to feel empathy, to imagine ourselves as someone else. "Nearly all acts of altruism and self-sacrifice at any level are tied to this particular ability of the human imagination," says Carol Bly.

Businessman Chris Kim was inspired to act by listening to the story of a fourteen-year-old African American boy. The boy stole a pair of pants from the clothing store Chris ran in his minimall in a poor south Seattle neighborhood. Chris and another Korean store owner grabbed him, called the police, and were ready to press charges. Then Chris thought about Christ's message of responding with forgiveness, not retribution. He decided to talk with the boy and his parents. "We always say we love our neighbors, but we never do it and risk something that belongs to us. He was a teenager, a young kid. It could have been anyone in a desperate situation, even one of my kids. I thought I should try and understand, not just turn him over to the police."

After Chris and the boy talked, the boy apologized, and said what he really wanted was a job. Chris hesitated briefly, then hired him as a clerk. The boy's mother sent Chris a note saying his compassion had changed her view both of Koreans and her son's life. Moved by the experience, Chris started working with local organizations that educate black youth. "Through my lifetime," Chris admitted, "I didn't have a good feeling about black people. It wasn't from direct experiences, but you hear so much in the media, about all the violence. So I tried to treat this kid as another human being, like myself, my family, my friends. I wanted to be part of solving the problems."

Chris's involvement was supported by an existing foundation of belief, in this case his Christian faith. But it took a direct connection with the boy and his world to induce Chris to put those beliefs into practice. It took a willingness to exercise his moral imagination, to expand his sphere of concern to include someone from a completely different background.

As a result of wrestling with his responsibility to the boy, Chris began questioning himself, especially his business practices. He consulted local neighborhood leaders, brought in new African American shops to his minimall, and sponsored an annual neighborhood festival. He tried to make the mall a place where people of all races and ages would feel welcome. It still felt strange staking his money and time to try to help people who, as he says, "aren't even my own race of Koreans. But I'd wanted to set an example for my children. Once you start to share with others, it gets easier. What I did wasn't anything fancy. But I felt such a priceless taste of love coming back. I got closer to some other human beings who I'd never have gotten to know. Once I've done something like that, I can't go back to what I was before."

SPECIFIC LIVES

New information—the number of America's children in poverty, the record percentage of wealth controlled by the rich, the thousands of acres of old-growth forests and fertile topsoil that have been destroyed—can give us a sense of the magnitude of our problems and help us develop appropriate responses. But it can't provide the organic connection that binds one person to another. By contrast, powerful individual stories create community, writes Scott Russell Sanders in *Utne Reader*. "They link teller to listeners, and listeners to one another." They let us glimpse the lives of those older or younger, richer or poorer, of different races, from places we'll never even see. Showing us the links between choices and consequences, they train our sight, "give us images for what is truly worth seeking, worth having, worth doing."

In a time when we're taught that our actions don't matter, stories carry greater weight than ever. They teach us, Sanders suggests, how "every gesture, every act, every choice we make sends ripples of influence into the future." Indeed, it's no exaggeration to say that the stories that gain prominence in public dialogue will significantly shape public policy.

This means that we are more likely to challenge homelessness if we hear the testimonies of people living on the street. We will work to overcome illiteracy after gaining a sense of what it's like to be unable to read. COPS derived its political agenda from stories like the one Virginia told about her neighbor. Ginny Nicarthy's battered women first shared their anguish and rage, then, with the support of the group, began to change their situation. Psychological studies of those who rescued Jews during the Holocaust found they differed from their peers in their ability to be moved by pain, sadness, and helplessness. "If one woman ever told the whole honest truth about her life," writes poet Muriel Rukeyser, "the world would split open." I'd say the same would be true for any man.

As you may recall, there are dangers inherent in trying to grasp too much at one time, in wallowing in the bad news. As Joanna Macy reminds us, "Information *by itself* can increase resistance [to engagement], deepening the sense of apathy and powerlessness." Stories about particular individuals and specific situations usually have the opposite effect. By giving unwieldy problems a human face, they also bring them down to a human—and thus manageable—scale. That's why learning what it's like for a single child to grow up with inadequate food, education, and medical care, with hopes damped and broken, can help us understand the moral ramifications of allowing this to happen to millions of children every day. Similarly, feeling the loss of a specific place that's been environmentally desecrated, or adopting and reclaiming it, can give us the strength to face the larger truth—that destroying the living forms that Thomas Berry calls "modes of divine presence" has become our culture's routine way of doing business.

Concrete, particularized stories help us feel the emotional weight of the world's troubles without so burdening us that we despair of ever being able to change things. As the philosopher Richard Rorty reminds us, the best way to promote compassion and solidarity is not by appealing to some general notion of goodness, but by encouraging people to respond to specific human lives. Responsibility in this view is not an abstract principle but a way of being. It exists only in the doing.

THE STORY OF THE EARTH

Recently an entirely new group of stories has emerged, which taken together might be called the narrative of the natural world. They can help us to "hear within us the sounds of the earth crying," in the words of Buddhist monk Thich Nhat Hanh. Adam Werbach's concern about the environment was first aroused when he saw massive forest clear-cuts. Michael Schut, of the faith-based environmental group Earth Ministry, describes the profound sorrow he felt hearing about Alaskan wolves being hunted from helicopters. "How am I possibly diminished by a wolf's death? What difference could the shooting of a few Alaskan wolves possibly make in my life? . . . Yet I tell the story anyway. . . . It speaks to me of the potential extent of the circle of human compassion, a sign of connection with all of creation. I felt and shared in another's loss, even when the 'other' is one with whom I didn't realize I shared an intimate connection. For the moment, the perceived walls of my separation came down."

Few of us will go as far as some of the deep ecologists in calling for a "biological egalitarianism" whereby we extend coequal standing to all living creatures. But I'm heartened by the worldwide passion for Gary Larson's "Far Side" cartoons, which give a voice to those the Sioux Indians call the creeping people, the standing people, and the swimming people. A group of bears stumble across campers in their sleeping bags and exclaim, delightedly, "Sandwiches!" Two chipmunks comment on a woman squatting down to feed them nuts, "I can't stand it. . . . They're so *cute* when they sit like that." A duck in a bar complains, "I tell you she's drivin' me nuts! . . . I come home at night and it's 'quack quack quack' . . . I get up in the morning and it's 'quack quack quack.' " "I've heard all kinds of sounds from these things," explains a saber-toothed tiger after eating a caveman, "but 'yabba dabba doo' was a new one to me." Such images remind us that we aren't the sole creatures in the world that live, breathe, procreate, play, and suffer. We need not sentimentalize nature to recognize, as Scott Russell Sanders says, "that we belong to the earth, blood and brain and bone, and that we are kin to other creatures."

Five hundred years ago, Martin Luther spoke to this kinship when he likened the world to a divine text: "God writes the Gospel, not in the Bible alone, but also on trees, and in the flowers and clouds and stars." Today, ecotheologians like the Catholic monk Thomas Berry and ecopsychologists like Theodore Roszak offer a complementary image, based on recent developments in modern science. They write of the need to understand our lives and ground our choices in the context of the largest possible story, what Berry calls "the grand liturgy of the universe."

In the last century, the convergence of physics, biology, and astronomy has led to the creation of a new master narrative for the cosmos, which writers like Roszak and Berry, and physicists like Fritjof Capra, believe supports far more respect for the earth.

Through theories like that of the big bang and the discovery of quarks and quasars, the universe has been revealed, they explain, not as a dead and static entity—as scientists ever since Isaac Newton had viewed it—but as a changing and unfolding *process* that has steadily produced greater and greater complexity, including, on our particular planet, a vast biological flowering. The Gaia hypothesis of chemist James Lovelock and biologist Lynn Margulis explores complementary territory, creating a metaphor of the earth as a living entity, continually adapting to help nurture life.

The vast grandeur of these systems doesn't provide us specific prescriptions for our lives. But to recognize that we are connected to the forces that power the stars can remind us that when we work to heal the world, we do so in resonance with an immensely complex natural order that's been evolving for billions of years. As Roszak puts it, "The same atomic rudiments, the same chemical constituents, the same laws and principles extend from the cellular substance of our blood and bone to the farthest galaxies."

THE BROWN-EYED GIRL

The sense of being part of and responsible to a larger world inspires us to act for human dignity as well. A Long Island teacher named Carol McNulty felt inspired to take a stand after watching a video of a brown-eyed Salvadoran girl. Though only fifteen, the girl had worked for two years making fifty-six cents an hour sewing clothes for the Gap and Eddie Bauer in a Salvadoran *maquiladora*, a factory inside a free-trade zone. Her eighteen-hour days left little time for eating, sleeping, or even going to the bathroom. She had to buy her food from the company store. Attending high school was out of the question, though she said shyly that she'd like to someday. The factory bosses prohibited workers from talking with each other, and when some of the bolder ones tried to organize, they were fired.

"I'm very intuitive about people's eyes," Carol explains. "The girl was in a documentary called *Zoned for Slavery*. I saw such a look of helplessness in her eyes. My own children's eyes are so bright and cheerful. Hers were equally beautiful, but so beaten down and clouded by despair. It's wrong for children to live like that—undernourished, without hope, literally chained to machines. She was just one young woman whose life was so blocked. If you multiply that by all the others, it's horrendous."

It angered Carol that this child—in Carol's words, "made in the image and likeness of God"—could be so abused for greed. After watching the film with the peace and justice group of her local Catholic parish, she joined a weekly vigil at a nearby Gap store. Each Saturday morning, like citizens at other stores across the country, she and a dozen others handed out literature and talked with customers. They demanded that the corporation's contractors treat workers decently.

The group that started the Gap campaign, the National Labor Committee, was originally founded to support threatened trade unionists and human rights activists during the Reagan-Bush Central American wars. Now it challenges companies like Wal-Mart, Guess, Disney, Victoria's Secret, and the Gap for shifting production from U.S. factories to the cheapest possible sites overseas, then letting their contractors mistreat workers. Shirts made for 30 cents at the young woman's Salvadoran *maquiladora* sold in the United States for $20 or $30. She and her fellow workers could barely afford to eat. The situation outraged Carol to her core.

For years she'd thought little about such matters. She considered Vietnam "a horror," as did her husband, Bill, a teacher turned carpenter. But they were too busy raising their six kids and paying their bills to do anything about it. When Reagan insisted that his Central American policies were working, they believed him. Then the Gulf War erupted, and Carol and Bill joined a nascent peace group in their church. They couldn't understand why so many people "treated the war like a carnival, while we found it so wrong and tragic, and so hypocritical, given how much our country had supported Saddam Hussein in the first place."

The war got Carol thinking about "all the poverty, hopelessness, and drug use" in the low-income school where she taught. Shortly afterward, she saw *Zoned for Slavery* at her church, and decided to take a stand. Like Suzy Marks ducking behind her sign in West Los Angeles, Carol found it hard to be visible in her home community. Yet every Saturday for two months she and Bill stood in front of the Gap store, braving biting winter rain and freezing snow. They were joined by a nun, some students, young mothers, a longshoreman, a union organizer, and a handful of others. Village trustees considered using antisoliciting laws to force them to leave. One claimed the group had cursed people, physically accosted them, and harassed them in their cars. When Bill challenged this falsehood, the trustees refused to let him address their meeting. They said they didn't want to give him another platform for his protests.

The attacks frightened and disturbed Carol. "People lied so blatantly, it shook me up. It was so much easier to put a dollar in the collection plate each Sunday and think that this would buy eternal salvation. But I kept focusing on that young girl in the film and all the others she worked with. Their images kept me going."

Meanwhile, pressure continued to build against the Gap and its policies. The National Labor Committee coordinated a nationwide effort whereby citizens picketed stores, young *maquiladora* workers traveled from city to city and talked to TV stations, churches, civic groups, and schools, and the national media ran exposés. "We felt these young women were incredibly courageous," said a National Labor Committee staffer. "If people just had a chance to hear them talk directly, we knew they'd be moved."

In the face of this rapidly growing public outcry, the Gap capitulated, pledging to ensure that contractors allow independent monitoring by churches and human rights groups and free access by unions, and treat their workers with greater respect. Amazingly, the campaign had won.

"We celebrated with signs thanking the Gap for doing the right thing," said Carol. "Standing out there every week was hard. But it helped me to remember that the mothers in Central America love their children the same way I love mine. They bleed and feel pain like we do. We're not better than they are just because we're more comfortable."

For years, Carol said, she and Bill "were always the good Catholics who attended mass every Sunday, ate fish every Friday, and did all the rituals. But that's not enough. It's hard to worship God or find peace with your soul if people are starving in poverty, or when the air and water are filthy. It's wrong when companies fire people and their stock goes up. Or when they make money on the suffering of children—like that girl whose eyes grabbed my heart. We don't know that what we do will change this. But we've got to have the faith to try."

THEY DIDN'T KNOW THE LANGUAGE

Like the organizers who arranged the speaking tour for the young Salvadoran women, the most successful activists know the power of stories to move people's hearts, so they weave the richness of personal example into their arguments. If particular institutions are exploitive, racist, sexist, ecologically destructive, or otherwise oppressive, effective activists don't rely on mind-numbing rhetorical labels to arouse concern. Instead, they describe precisely how the institutions damage people's lives or degrade the environment. They frame policy proposals in terms of particular consequences. They continually link their arguments and visions to specific situations.

"It's so easy to get wrapped up in legislative widgets instead of our core values," says Adam Werbach. "One of the first things I changed as Sierra Club president was the way we always talked in terms of bill numbers. Now we name them and describe them, which gives people a sense of what they're actually about."

In the late 1980s, Oregon state employees, who were predominantly female and universally underpaid, began fighting for a living wage. Their unions started the campaign by hiring experts to draw up more equitable pay schedules. The resulting task force surveyed every category of job, then presented an elaborate report in the most neutral technical terms. At the request of top-level managers, they added more data. Eventually the study became so unwieldy and abstract that ordinary workers felt it had nothing to do with their lives, or their gut sense that their labor was undervalued. "Most of those affected couldn't even talk about the proposals," recalled the economist who chaired the task force, "because they didn't know the language, all the personnel-oriented, management-oriented terms. It left them completely out of the discussion." Lacking popular understanding or support, the effort collapsed of its own weight, dead on arrival at the legislature.

Then the unions shifted strategy, arranging for public-sector employees to speak for themselves to the media, community groups, and their elected officials. They posed simple but very telling questions. Why did women who took care of children at university day-care centers earn less than workers monitoring animals at local private research labs? Why did public-sector secretaries earn less than mail carriers? Why did nursing-home aides earn less than entry-level workers at insurance companies and banks? Testifying before the state legislature, they explained that their jobs mattered greatly to them, as well as to the community, then asked the senators how much they thought they earned. Holding up pay stubs as proof, they shamed the legislators with the reality of their economic plight: some made so little for full-time work, they needed food stamps to get by. The union won pay raises and other concessions that made working conditions more equitable. It triumphed by letting their members tell their own stories, in their own words.

STORIES AS TRAPS

But stories can mislead as well as reveal. How do we know which to heed? "Why, sometimes," says the White Queen to Alice in *Through the Looking Glass*, "I've believed as many as six impossible things before breakfast." Rush Limbaugh tells stories, and tells them well, which is part of his power. But time and again his stories betray the people and events they purport to depict, by twisting the truth.

The problem goes well beyond outright and preposterous lies, like Limbaugh's claims that "Styrofoam and plastic milk jugs are biodegradable." (Or that there are "more acres of forest land in America today" than when Columbus landed in 1492. Or that "Vince Foster was murdered in an apartment belonging to Hillary Clinton.") Far more damnable is the habit of Limbaugh and his cohorts of stripping stories of their actual contexts, and of highlighting the unrepresentative detail or exceptional incident, as when they give the impression that most welfare mothers drive new Cadillacs, live the high life, and eagerly squander our tax dollars. No doubt, in a handful of cases, something like this happens. But most people on public assistance struggle desperately to survive, and together families getting direct cash assistance consume just one percent of the federal budget. Even if the individual example happens to be true, it sheds no light on the overall situation.

Stories also mislead when ordinary citizens become poster children for the powerful. As the journalist William Greider points out in *Who Will Tell the People*, corporations routinely push through self-serving congressional bills by hiring public relations firms to organize "grassroots" lobbying efforts involving small business people. "Responsible Industry for a Safe Environment" is actually a front group formed by the National Agricultural Chemicals Association to thwart government regulation of pesticides. The "Alliance for a Responsible CFC Policy" is a creation of Dow, DuPont, and Amoco, opposed to banning the ozone-depleting chlorofluorocarbons these companies produce. When trying to eliminate or undermine the Endangered Species Act, the Clean Water Act, and other federal environmental legislation, extractive industries often will underwrite campaigns that appear to comprise small landowners and ordinary workers. After revealing internal documents were leaked to the *Los Angeles Times,* Microsoft recently backed away from a plan for its media handlers to commission "spontaneous" local newspaper articles, letters to the editor, and opinion pieces challenging antitrust efforts in key states.

Talk show hosts and corporate PR flacks aren't alone in ignoring, obscuring, and misrepresenting context. When, for example, reporters describe pending legislation or policy decisions, they rarely mention, much less analyze, the behind-the-scenes role of money and power in shaping them. In spring 1997, Bill Clinton signed what he and congressional leaders from both parties heralded as a "middle-class tax cut." They'd promoted the bill by evoking images of Joe and Jane Taxpayer—overworked, overburdened, and much in need of relief.

But you may be surprised to learn that almost half the "relief" went to the wealthiest 5 percent of Americans, and more to the top 1 percent than to the bottom 80 percent. The bottom 40 percent received virtually nothing. Our political leaders didn't say, overtly, "We're giving yet another tax break to the rich because they're nice and give us money." But with deep cuts in capital gains taxes as its centerpiece, the bill seemed the ultimate ratification of a dubious but increasingly dominant belief—that those who make their money from speculative investments are wiser and more worthy than those who live off wages as factory workers, clerks, and hospital orderlies.

The way most of the media covered the story, you'd never know that the bill benefited the rich. Instead, they uncritically regurgitated its supporters' misleading rhetoric, referring again and again to the hardworking Americans who were about to get a long-deserved break. Since most ordinary citizens actually gained little or nothing, they'll be ripe for embracing further regressive tax cuts down the line, especially if the media fail to unmask the populist images used to promote them.

SOLVING FOR PATTERN

So how do we separate true stories from false ones? How do we sort through the contending claims without reverting to the eternal detachment of the perfect standard? How, in short, do we restore context? One way is to evaluate conflicting narratives. Sometimes real stories clash, in their content and implications. Appropriate solutions to social problems often represent compromises between legitimate competing interests, requiring us to listen to those who disagree with us, acknowledge truths in their positions, and try our best to find common ground. People will always disagree over policy. But good policy can't be developed unless all relevant voices are taken into account, not only those of the well-connected and wealthy.

In her memoir, *Dead Man Walking,* Sister Helen Prejean describes feeling compelled to challenge capital punishment after she heard the story of convicted killer Pat Sonnier. Later, she came to know the parents of a girl whom another convict she was counseling had murdered. Through them, she also began to work with victims' rights groups. Acknowledging the pain the parents suffered at their daughter's brutal killing didn't negate Prejean's reasons for challenging capital punishment. But it did broaden her vision.

The moral complexity of Prejean's vision differs greatly from the clutter we experience in our media-saturated culture. This clutter leaves us so distracted, we have little attention left to address the core issues of our own lives—or the issues of our times. We know more about Arnold Schwarzenegger, Demi Moore, and the now-departed Princess Di than we do about our neighbors down the street. And far more, if we're financially comfortable, than we do about those who struggle economically. What kind of athletic shoes we wear, sport utility vehicle we drive, or which TV shows we watch has become more important than how we live.

We can help restore context by asking who profits from particular institutional choices, and who's lied or been honest in the past.

Sometimes we create this kind of accountability with hard numbers and facts. When Washington State's giant timber and aluminum interests tried to ban the family fishing operations that had started holding them accountable for their impact on declining salmon runs, they did so under the banner of ecological concern. But Pete Knutson, his fellow fishermen, and their environmental supporters countered by publicizing the actual track records of Initiative 640's major backers.

Pete's campaign publicized the dollars given by these backers and provided numbers, maps, and charts showing where salmon runs had declined and how degraded watersheds had caused these declines. He and others helped make it clear that the initiative's claims to environmental stewardship were false. They helped voters learn enough to defeat the measure.

Such information can contribute to a sense of larger context. It's useful, for example, to read the statistics on welfare mothers and discover that, contrary to public myth, most hardly squander the money they get from the government. Rather, they struggle to afford proper health care and child care, and to get support in finding jobs and access to alcohol and drug programs if needed. So I'm not suggesting we dismiss hard numbers.

More than anything, however, we come to understand the relationship between particular stories and their overall context by following an approach that Wendell Berry calls "solving for pattern." "A bad solution is bad," writes Berry, "because it acts destructively upon the larger patterns in which it is contained . . . because it is formed in ignorance or disregard of them. A bad solution solves for a single purpose or goal, such as increased production. And it is typical of such solutions that they achieve stupendous increases in production at exorbitant biological and social costs."

Good solutions, Berry suggests, recognize that they are part of a larger whole. They accept given limits and disciplines. They solve more than one problem and don't create new problems. They answer the question "How much is enough?" A good solution, he

says, "should not enrich one person by the distress or impoverish-
ment of another."

"In an organism," Berry concludes, "what is good for one part
is good for another. What is good for the mind is good for the
body; what is good for the arm is good for the heart. We know
that sometimes a part may be sacrificed for the whole; a life may
be saved by the amputation of an arm. But we also know that such
remedies are desperate, irreversible, and destructive; it is impossible
to improve the body by amputation." We can contribute to the
well-being of our society, the body politic, by applying a similarly
holistic ethic of interdependence, and by listening to those whose
voices are too often excluded from public discussion.

"LOVE YOUR HEART"

In her novel *Beloved*, Toni Morrison describes the farm where her
character Sethe grew up as a slave: "It never looked as terrible as
it was and it made her wonder if Hell was a pretty place too. Fire
and brimstone all right, but hidden in lacy groves. Boys hanging
from the most beautiful sycamores in the world." Social crises
don't always signal their presence. They become apparent only
when those who bear the scars of the crises speak out, insisting
that their stories become part of the public dialogue.

This is especially true if we come from communities whose
voices are habitually ignored, demeaned, or despised. Otherwise,
the powers that be are likely to dismiss the crises we face by explaining, in the words of the psychologist Edward Opton, "It
didn't happen, and besides they deserved it." We know that our
lives and those of our neighbors refute such characterizations, but
the only way others will know is if we tell them—if we take control
of defining who we are.

"No, they ain't in love with your mouth," says Sethe's mother,
Baby Suggs, as she holds prayer meetings in the woods. "Yonder,

out there, they will see it broken and break it again. What you say out of it they will not heed. What you scream from it they do not hear. What you put into it to nourish your body they will snatch away and give you leavins instead. No, they don't love your mouth. *You* got to love it." And more even than your mouth, she says, "More than your life-holding womb and your life-giving private parts, hear me now, love your heart."

We need to recover both our voice and our heart, even when the process is hard, and even in the face of people who will do their best to deny the very core of our being. "What is most important to me must be spoken," wrote the poet Audre Lorde, "made verbal and shared, even at the risk of having it bruised or misunderstood." As our religious traditions point out, our very pain, vulnerability, and suffering can actually bring us closer to God by opening us up to compassion. For only when we begin to voice the difficult truths of our experience can we begin to change them and build better lives for ourselves and our communities.

Effective social movements often begin when once-silenced people resolve to tell their own stories. In different ways, under widely varying circumstances, they state, in effect, "This is who I am. This is how my community's hopes and dreams have systematically been spurned and destroyed. And this is how things have to change." I'm heartened, in this context, by the wave of homeless people's newspapers that has spread across the country in recent years. In their pages those who live on the streets describe their experiences for readers who think of homelessness as a faceless social problem. The benefits to participants are both immediate and long-range. Money from the newspaper sales helps the vendors survive. At the same time, the very process of articulating their stories gives homeless men and women a new measure of control over their circumstances, and a sense of worth and purpose. It gives them a vehicle to talk about their lives.

As this example makes clear, problems tend to remain invisible, and thus unaddressed, until they're described in human terms. As in most cities, Seattle's construction trades were almost entirely white and male until protests in the late 1960s opened them up to minority and female membership. Recently, while workers were building Seattle's new baseball stadium, ugly graffiti attacking blacks, women, and gays began to appear in the construction site bathrooms. A hangman's noose was found. Objects fell from overhead without warning perilously close to people. Though no one could be absolutely certain, the likely culprits were members of a new outside crew of high-steel workers, whose foreman had already gotten into a fight with the on-site affirmative action officer.

In response, the project's black workers joined with a small number of women and sympathetic white men to distribute a leaflet calling for a meeting. Anxious about the outcome of a potential confrontation, the construction supervisor said that he wouldn't allow the gathering. Nor would he permit anyone to name the people involved in the attacks. The head of Seattle's Building Trades Council then intervened, arguing that the incidents dramatically affected the job climate. The meeting took place, as planned, on the construction site. A white carpenter said that the incidents insulted everyone on the job. A Native American cement finisher described the pride he took in his skills, and the times he'd repeatedly confronted prejudice. A black woman electrician talked about sexual harassment at work, citing specific incidents. A black man, himself straight, said he'd first viewed homophobia as a trivial concern, then realized it was no different from any other attack on a person simply for who they were. Four hundred and fifty largely white hardhats responded again and again with applause while a handful of high-steel workers watched silently from a nearby scaffolding. The harassment quickly stopped. "It wasn't a redneck site," said an African American electrical worker who'd helped open up the Seattle building trades twenty-five years before. "There were just six or seven bigoted people, who now felt totally marginalized. Once the workers began to speak for themselves and name the problem, everyone else came along in support."

"No matter who we are," writes Gloria Steinem, "the journey toward recovering the self-esteem that should have been our birthright follows similar steps: a first experience of seeing through our own eyes instead of through the eyes of others . . . telling what seemed to be shameful secrets, and discovering they are neither shameful nor secret . . . giving names to problems that have been treated as normal and thus have no names . . . bonding with others who share similar experiences . . . achieving empowerment."

The Gift of Being Human

What if we aren't victims of social injustice? What's our role in speaking out for change? Those of us who are relatively privileged are used to finding our interests and needs attended to. Contentedness, though, can induce insensitivity, even among people who are caring and generous. That's why we may consciously need to work to avoid becoming what Carol Bly calls "lucky predators," who by casually accepting the gifts bestowed by fortune, inadvertently circumscribe the lives and dampen the aspirations of countless others. No matter how well off we may be, we're spiritually impoverished whenever our society treats people with contempt, pillages the earth, or cannibalizes our common future.

"I keep thinking of the benefits of my own upbringing," writes Sister Helen Prejean, "which I once took for granted: I can read any book I choose and comprehend it. I can write a complete sentence and punctuate it correctly. If I need help, I can call on judges, attorneys, educators, ministers. I wonder what I would be like if I had grown up without such protections and supports. What cracks would have turned up in my character? What makes me think that I wouldn't have been pregnant at seventeen? How law-abiding would I be?"

It strengthens and deepens us, if our background is similarly comfortable, to read Toni Morrison, listen to a laid-off steelworker, or hear the testament of a welfare mother. If we truly heed such stories, they can liberate us from insulation and nurture our sense of broader connection. By "connection" I mean much more than an increased willingness to give money to hungry children or recycle our trash. I mean the recognition that our fates are fundamentally linked to other people, and to the earth, and that whether or not we're conscious about their impact, our choices do shape the world, making it more generous or more callous.

If we've led relatively insulated lives, then hearing the stories of those who have not can open us up to a greater understanding. When we truly see the face or hear the voice of a person fighting for dignity in a culture that denies it, we enlarge our horizons, as happened with Carol McNulty after seeing the Salvadoran girl. As the educator and social critic Jonathan Kozol suggests, too many of us purchase our comfort and security at the cost of building walls around our hearts. It doesn't help anyone to wallow in guilt. But we need to look at how we've erected our own internal gated cities, what it would take to dismantle them, and what we might gain by doing so. It's a miracle, says the African American theologian Howard Thurman, "when one man, standing in his place, is able, while remaining there, to put himself in another man's place. To send his imagination forth to establish a beachhead in another man's spirit, and from that vantage point so to blend with the other's landscape that what he sees and feels is authentic. . . . To experience this is to be rocked to one's foundations."

Once again, we are reminded of the personal rewards of social engagement. The psychologist Lane Gerber works with Cambodian refugees. Reflecting on their accounts of surviving violence and brutality—many had witnessed the murder of their families— Lane described an unexpected paradox. The refugees' stories were horrible. They gave him nightmares. Yet he also felt honored, even uplifted, to be able to listen in support. As a colleague of his recalled, "I felt such sadness and heaviness as I talked with a man about his suffering and loss. Yet I also felt more alive somehow. Those things shouldn't go together. But they did. I remember thinking that something sacred was happening, and thinking, 'This is why we were born. This is what it is to be human.' "

"There's something about what we hear from these survivors," said Lane, "that teaches us why we live. It's the opposite of a situation one woman described, where the Khmer Rouge prohibited her and the other concentration camp prisoners even from talking with each other—under threat of death. 'We all suffered,' the woman told me, 'but we suffered alone so the suffering was useless.' It shakes you to work with these stories. But you also feel privileged to hear another's cry and give recognition to their suffering. It touches your core vulnerability and lifts you beyond your individual self. It's a strangely hopeful experience."

SELF-HELP FOR SOCIETY

I've talked of how other people's stories can expand our view of the world. Social involvement also changes the way we think about our own personal stories, the narratives of our lives. As James Hillman writes, each of us needs "an adequate biography: How do I put together into a coherent image the pieces of my life? How do I find the basic plot of my story?" Everyone has such a larger explanatory story, which provides guidelines for the choices he or she makes, and provides a sense of meaning and purpose. But for most of us, these narratives ignore the possibility that civic involvement could play a significant role in our lives. We might even say that the most stunted area of human potential is the capacity to think through our convictions and act on them.

Our culture encourages us to view ourselves in isolation, to embrace Margaret Thatcher's pronouncement "There is no such thing as society—there are only individual families." But to me, this notion denies what makes us human. Those who take committed stands develop different explanatory stories—new definitions of self—which encourage their impulses to shape a better world. When the nun from COPS visited Virginia Ramirez, she asked what Virginia cared about. All of us care about something, so there's no better way to get our fellow citizens involved than to draw out their deepest concerns and ask them to think about public choices that affect their families, communities, and hopes for a better common future. When people like Virginia rethink their personal stories, they begin to build a sense of connection and responsibility. They recognize that their actions can matter. They nurture a faith that the work of healing the world is worth doing, whether or not they see immediate results. They learn to view their personal stories as intertwined with history.

Nowhere are stories of individual reinvention more prominent than in America's self-help tradition. Here are writers and lecturers who tell us how to find love, improve our careers, raise wonderful children, and generally make our way in the world. They tell us how to succeed financially, pull ourselves out of unhealthy relationships, and overcome neuroses and addictions. Self-help counselors convey their lessons in parables, affirmations, stories of how others have overcome their difficulties and fears. They encourage us to tell and retell our own stories, describing how we've been wounded or have wounded ourselves. They suggest that we imagine acting with wisdom and strength, and living more resolutely. They ask us to take control of our fate.

The self-help tradition offers many useful lessons for those of us wanting to change society. In the most basic terms, it teaches that we often can do more than we think possible. Like Alcoholics Anonymous members, we can break self-destructive habits and assist others trying to do the same. We have the power to transform our lives, provided we stop viewing ourselves as passive victims of our circumstances. We can grow, adapt, and escape old traps.

The future, this tradition reminds us, isn't fixed. Although we can't control how others will act, we can choose our own actions and responses. And, paradoxically, when we withhold our consent from injustice and actively challenge it, we often force people who've been acting oppressively to change their behavior as well.

Ultimately, self-respect and a sense of responsibility come from the same sense of connection. "Love your neighbor as yourself," says the Bible, which means that we need to do both. If, as Jean Houston suggests, "another word for sin is unskilled behavior," then moral and personal development go hand in hand.

As I've mentioned, many activists describe their motivation by saying they want to be able to feel self-respect when they look in the mirror. It's worth remembering that the mirror also reflects our internal demons. "If we attempt to act and do things for others or for the world without deepening our own self-understanding," writes Thomas Merton, "our own freedom, integrity, and capacity to love, we will not have anything to give to others. We will communicate nothing but our own obsessions, our aggressiveness, our ego-centered ambitions."

Too often, social activists neglect the universal need for psychological nurturance and individual growth. All of us can benefit from examples of perseverance and possibility, and from heeding the damage our emotional problems can do to others. At its best, the self-help tradition reminds us to listen closely to the inevitably personal reasons why people decide to act for change. This tradition also sheds light on the factors that make activists burn out. A scathing critique of present-day America is of little use in the absence of a hopeful vision of the future.

A THOUSAND POINTS OF DENIAL

Still, the self-help tradition has its limits. It too rarely challenges the extrapersonal forces that cause human suffering. And the insistence that we can do whatever we set our minds to can promote complacency among the privileged and help foster a way of thinking that blames those most wounded by our society for their own problems.

When Jonathan Kozol gave a talk to an affluent Dallas audience, he spoke of what he called the "savage inequalities" between rich and poor school districts across the country. At one point, he described how the desperately poor community of Camden, New Jersey, spent barely half as much per child as the affluent suburb of Cherry Hill, five miles away. Cherry Hill's children were growing up in homes filled with books, homes in which computers were as common as TVs, while Camden's children faced every imaginable obstacle. But New Jersey education funding was based on local property taxes, and Camden's tax base was minimal. Texas, Kozol pointed out, had a similarly imbalanced system; but when he suggested that statewide funding be equalized, the Dallas audience rebelled. Social problems can't be solved by throwing money at them, they said. Children can succeed if parents just teach them persistence and character.

Taking the audience at its word, Kozol then suggested that they send their own kids to Dallas's inner-city schools. Since their families possessed the necessary moral resources, they should have no problem flourishing, while the poor kids could commute to the suburbs. But the Dallas crowd didn't like that, either. Later, remembering all the sparkling diamond necklaces and jeweled bracelets, Kozol said, "I finally understood the meaning of 'a thousand points of light.'"

It's easy for those of us blessed with comfortable circumstances to assume that everyone has options equal to our own. But when we insist that we each have the power to shape the direction of our own lives, and that all problems are therefore individual problems, we ignore the social and economic context in which resources and opportunities are apportioned. Indeed, one reason for arguing that the poor choose poverty through their actions is that to think otherwise raises troubling questions about whether our own good fortune might in part be due to privilege or chance, and not merit.

The self-help maven Deepak Chopra teaches, "You are your own reality. You create it; you carry it around with you." Is it any wonder that a woman attending a Seattle New Age conference explains that welfare recipients "just need to wake up and realize their mythic selves"? Such willful insensitivity to context can easily reinforce the perfect standard. After reading Chopra's books, with their constant stress on self-improvement to the exclusion of other commitments, a young Website designer I know said, "I used to think it was important to help people, and that I could develop myself by serving others. Now I realize that I have to get myself together a hundred percent before I can help anyone else."

Imagine a spiritual leader like Jesus, Buddha, Isaiah, Gandhi, or King expressing that sentiment, or using phrases like "prosperity consciousness" or Chopra's talk of "saying no to negativity." The idea is absurd. "I was going to throw the money changers out of the temple," a Chopra-like Jesus might have explained, "but I didn't want to be a negative person."

The most troublesome consequence of this way of thinking is that it exempts even the most powerful economic, political, and social institutions from all responsibility for the state of society. Take the extreme case of slavery. Who created that reality? Was it the slaves or the slavemasters who needed to wake up and think about their actions? Such contemporary social problems as unemployment, discrimination, and inadequate health care may not be as dramatic as slavery, but no amount of positive thinking or self-actualization is going to solve them without common public action. True, a few scattered individuals will, through uncommon effort, outside support, or enormous good luck, surmount the institutional hurdles that stand in their way. But until the hurdles themselves are addressed, the dreams of most in their communities will continue to be crushed.

CHANGING THE THINGS WE CAN

Even more-compassionate perspectives in the tradition of individual uplift may inadvertently encourage passivity, by downplaying economic and political sources of human pain. I've found some valuable lessons in Stephen Covey's *Seven Habits of Highly Effective People.* But it disturbs me when Covey writes that "it is our willing permission, our consent to what happens to us, that hurts us far more than what happens to us in the first place." He tells the story of a woman in one of his audiences who was a full-time nurse to "the most miserable, ungrateful man you can possibly imagine," a man who constantly harped at her and found fault with everything she did. Initially, the nurse was outraged at Covey's suggestion that "no one can hurt me without my consent, and that I have chosen my own emotional life of being miserable." Then she thought further, and, according to Covey, realized that she did indeed possess the power to choose her response to her noxious patient.

I respect aspects of Covey's message: Sometimes we have to make the best of difficult situations; it's better to come up with creative responses than to bemoan our circumstances endlessly; and although we can't always control the actions of others, we needn't internalize their craziness. But such prescriptions, in isolation, fail to take into account the larger institutional context that so often constrains our choices. Maybe the nurse felt trapped, forced to keep her job, no matter how thankless or ill-paid, because no others were available. Rather than accept whatever tasks were handed to them, maybe she and her colleagues needed to organize a union to ensure that they could set limits to their commitments, receive a living wage, and get enough time off so they wouldn't burn out or take out their frustration on their families, themselves, or other patients. For all the importance of empathy, maybe this particular occupational setting wasn't the place for endless forbearance, or for automatically embracing the familiar women's role as long-suffering caretaker. Perhaps, instead, it was a place to challenge the unreasonable burdens that Covey's well-intentioned words ultimately rationalized.

Somewhere between the assumption that all can be changed if we merely wish it, and the impotent resignation of the cynics, lies a far more practical yet hopeful outlook. To a degree, it's expressed in the famous Alcoholics Anonymous prayer that has nourished millions of people: "God, grant me the serenity to accept the things I cannot change, the courage to change the things I can, and the wisdom to know the difference." We can view this as a justification for timidity. It's used that way at times. But we can also see it in its most powerful light—as a challenge to expand our definition of what we can change.

DIGGING UP THE LAND MINES

We can learn this expanded definition of possibility from people who, with courage and generosity, work to create a more just world. Though vastly underrepresented in our national dialogue, their stories can help us envision a future of reciprocity and fairness, wisdom and compassion, in which the human spirit can flourish. Their examples can help us balance public goals and personal pressures, give us perspective on our journeys, keep us going when times get tough. We need their stories to inspire us.

Many of the most effective and inspiring activists draw heavily on their own stories in charting their path. In 1992, East Palo Alto, California, had the highest murder rate in America. Five years later, serious crime in the 25,000-person community had dropped nearly 90 percent, thanks in large part to a long-time San Quentin inmate named David Lewis, who'd spent seventeen years in prison.

Even in his mid-forties, David looks intimidating: He's a six-foot-two, 220-pound African American man with a shaved head, a handlebar mustache, and eighteen-inch biceps, one of which is adorned with a fading tattoo and a scar. But his eyes and voice are no longer edgy and desperate. Patient, reflective, and forgiving, David is a very different man today than he once was.

David started his downhill slide when he was ten. Though he was undiagnosed at the time, he had dyslexia. His school responded to his resulting slow progress by placing him in a class with mentally retarded kids, where the teachers did little but baby-sit. Over the years, he heard civil rights activists, from the Black Panthers to his Baptist preacher uncles in the South, refer to education as the key to the black future. But David's teachers told him he had no educational future at all. There was nothing to be gained by trying.

Bored, angry, and powerless, David began drinking and skipping school, making, as he now says, "a conscious decision to take whatever substances would change the way I felt." His grandmother always kept liquor on hand as a medicine for sorrow. When President Kennedy was shot, she had stared bleakly at the TV until David, age eight, brought her a bottle. The only time his dad could talk with his white neighbor was when they were drunk. David soon supplemented his own liquor consumption with marijuana and barbiturates. When David was fifteen, Nixon cracked down on the marijuana trade, and heroin flooded the streets. "It felt really good to take a shot of dope," he says. "It took all my pain away."

David soon found other kids similarly scorned, discarded, and wanting to get back a sense of worth however they could. "We'd come up to a random person, the biggest grown man we could find, and knock him unconscious with a single punch. I could do it with either hand. People on the street started treating me with respect."

David grew bolder, entering drug dealers' apartments with a sawed-off shotgun. "I'd fire it at the ceiling, then clean them out. I never killed anyone to prove how crazy I was, but I was crazy enough to threaten people. I liked being the kid with no future—the kid people were afraid of." When David was eighteen, he and three friends were caught while robbing a gas station of $156. The judge sent him to San Quentin.

David was tough enough to master the prison environment quickly. He felt at home with his fellow inmates, who'd also learned to survive score to score and crime to crime. Many were also dyslexic, and had been similarly excluded from school. The clanging gates, at first terrifying, became familiar, almost reassuring. Although David joined a prison affiliate of the Panthers that talked revolution and claimed to strictly oppose drugs, he and the group's other key leaders spent most of their energy finding ways to get high. Their political efforts crumbled.

Two and a half years later, David was released, only to be

turned in a month later by a onetime friend, to whom he'd sold $20 worth of heroin. This time the sentence was ten years to life.

Prison became steadily more comfortable, despite its physical harshness. David found a pet mouse and "fed it, played with it, tried to teach it to play chess, did everything but make love to it."

He was released a few more times. But in each case, life outside prison seemed like a strange hiatus from real life, inside the walls. An uncertain spectator in an alien world, he'd eat food from the kitchen pot and sit on the toilet with the door open. "I had no social skills," David says. "I felt like God had left a component out of me, and that I didn't fit."

He also kept returning to heroin. "I always thought I could regulate it, not let it master me. Then I'd do something crazy to get back inside, where I had a place and a reputation. If I was hungry, I'd get a gun to take what I needed. Someone else could work and stand in line, but I wasn't going to."

David's turning point came while he was getting ready to watch the 1989 World Series on a small TV set in his San Quentin cell. The ground started shaking. It was a major San Francisco earthquake. "I felt helpless and hopeless, locked in a cage. I heard the Bay Bridge had collapsed. I thought of my twenty-seven-year-old son, who I'd had when I was seventeen. I'd spent half my life behind bars. Now he seemed headed for jail, too. I wondered if both of us might die here."

This sudden sense of vulnerability, David now believes, was the key to his transformation. In prison, people admired his toughness. It didn't matter that it led nowhere. More respectable people practiced a similar denial, David felt, in their endless striving to consume. "Only when I began to question and doubt could I change."

But wanting to change, David discovered, wasn't enough. He was full of resolve the next time he got out of prison, but still had no clear models for a different way to live. Aside from a few men who'd embraced more religion than he could handle, he knew of no long-term inmates who'd "broken free and gotten a regular life with the job, house, wife, dog, goldfish, and a car that you don't have to steal."

David's probation officer found him lying beneath a bridge with a needle in his arm, then got him into a rehab program. There he saw a video called *Breaking Barriers,* in which the veteran convict turned leadership trainer Gordon Graham described prison as a comfort zone, where people came to feel more at home than they did outside. Inmates needed to ask themselves what kinds of situations they'd gotten used to, said Graham, a former boxer, and whether these situations served their long-term needs. They needed to avoid continually going back to them.

"I'd never seen anyone really change who was like me," David said. "Gordy spoke in a language I knew, because he'd been in prison all those years. He showed me how I was stuck, like a broken record going rup, rup, rup in the groove, and how the survival skills I'd learned didn't work. He helped me get past just endlessly repeating."

David stayed in the rehab program nine months, got a job as a painter, and began attending Alcoholics Anonymous and Narcotics Anonymous meetings. They were his medicine, says David, "just like someone sick with diabetes needs insulin, or someone whose kidneys don't work needs dialysis. If you don't remember what you've been through, you're doomed to keep doing it, which means something dreadful will bite your ass like you never want to think about." After David appeared in a Bill Moyers TV program on an African American men's support group he was part of, he got a call from East Palo Alto's mayor. "She wanted me to help stop the community violence. I was one of the people who'd helped sow the land mines of violence to begin with. When you have a war like the war in our streets, it's the people who sow the land mines who know best how to dig them up."

A POLITICS BASED ON STORY

Using his own story to anchor his social vision and teach him what
to fight for, and with support from San Mateo County, David
started a drug and alcohol rehab center called Free at Last. Its
approach stemmed directly from the lessons of his life and the
culture of his fellow inmates. Instead of hiding the program, the
staff tied it to the community with a highly visible storefront center. They kept it open late, so people could drop in and get support
at almost any time. By day, a hundred people were enrolled in the
center's formal programs. At night, Free at Last outreach workers,
led by David, visited bars, crack houses, and shooting galleries to
test people for HIV and offer them treatment programs. "Most IV
addicts are out at night. So it doesn't work to have a clinic that
follows the standard medical model, open eight to five, and expect
people to come to you. You have to go to where people are. We
got trained in how to draw blood and give the tests, so we didn't
need a nurse. We'd pass out bleach and condoms as a way to draw
people into the rehab programs. They'd listen to us because we'd
been in gangs with them and shot dope with them. We'd been
there."

Monday night was a bad night for murders in East Palo Alto.
"On the weekends you're getting high," David explains. "You've
got your money, your drugs, maybe a girl. Then it's Monday, your
money's gone. You have to start all over, broke and hurting. That's
why all the blues songs talk about 'Stormy Monday' and 'Blue
Monday.' You have to steal to get what you need. That's when
you feel desperate and people kill each other.

"We developed one of the early Midnight Basketball programs
for Monday and for Thursday, which is another bad night. To
join you have to be a school dropout or on parole or probation.
Our players attend a workshop at eight in the evening, where
they talk about their lives and learn about alternatives. Then
they play in the basketball games, with community coaches. We
give them somewhere to go when they're likely to be the most

vulnerable and reckless. They don't have to go blow someone away."

David built the clinic through state and private grants and community health program contracts. He drew no salary, keeping his other job as an HIV outreach worker, but guided the organization on how to work best within the street culture. He even enlisted some Stanford students from their sanctuary just a few miles away across the freeway. The thirty-five-person staff developed residential services for women going through rehab, so they didn't have to be separated from their children. Free at Last challenged liquor store licenses, advocated for access to treatment programs, and ran domestic violence groups for women and for the men who abused them. Together with Gordon Graham, David also led prison workshops nationwide, developing prerelease programs that addressed the vast gap between prison culture and the outside.

"Lots of things I do today use the same energy and drive as when I was crazy. You don't go into a person's house and rob them with a shotgun without emotional faith. It's just as scary as asking for a hundred thousand dollars from the president of the Robert Wood Johnson Foundation. I just discovered a way into being a powerful person instead of being a fool." Within a few years, three-quarters of the people who graduated from Free at Last's programs remained clean, sober, and gainfully employed. East Palo Alto's serious crime rate dropped 87 percent.

David wanted to see a new politics coming out of the stories of the recovery movement, where "we start in a dark room, lift the shades so we're able to see, and begin fighting for a fair chance for our communities. If they'd had 'three strikes' laws when I was in prison, I'd never have been released. But I'm not an exception, just an example of what can happen when people get the support they need, in a language they can understand."

SHARED VULNERABILITY

If we want to create a more just and humane common future, we can begin by acknowledging our shared vulnerability. David Lewis started to change not when he felt in command, but when the Bay Area earthquake made him feel like a helpless beast, confined and powerless. For Virginia Ramirez, change came when she witnessed but couldn't prevent her old neighbor's needless death. And for Sister Helen Prejean, it came when she was unexpectedly touched by the humanity of the murderer Pat Sonnier. We rarely change when we're cruising along, insulated from the world—only when we drop the barriers that separate us from other human beings, admit that we don't know all the answers, and listen closely to others, to the world around us. Our lives shift when our heart becomes so open, in Alice Walker's words, that "the wind blows through it."

A parallel process occurs when we share our stories of engagement. Once we've been involved in social causes for a while, it's easy to forget our initial hesitancy. Reflecting on common journeys can remind us of the origins of our commitment and help us reach out to people who are paralyzed by the fears and debilitating self-definitions that once blocked our involvement, too. Theologian James Cone describes how the black church uses religious testimony "not only to strengthen an individual's faith, but also to build the faith of the community." The more we tell and retell stories about our commitments, the more we can strengthen our hope.

At its best, reflecting on the larger contexts of our lives can help us connect with the stories of others, and with a larger narrative of being. If we focus solely on our own experiences, we will hear nothing but the echoes of our obsessions. But if we look for ties to a broader common story, in which we all partake, we can develop the vision we need.

Chapter Seven

Values, Work, and Family

Finding the right work is like discovering your own soul in the world.
—THOMAS MOORE

*I have always believed that I could help change the world, because I have
been lucky to have adults around me who did.*
—MARIAN WRIGHT EDELMAN

We often hesitate to get involved in our communities: We're too
busy, we say. We've got all we can handle raising our children,
paying the bills, and holding on to our jobs. Given our day-to-day
responsibilities, we're lucky if we can find a few spare hours each
week for pursuits that revive us. It's hard to imagine how we might
make room for public commitments.

The pressures are real, especially at our workplaces, where we're
dominated more and more by a politics of the whip. Whatever our
jobs, most of us face the constant strain of working longer and
harder, doing more in less time and often with fewer resources,
worrying continually about being downsized. This is true whether
we're on a factory assembly line, writing code for a software company that's chronically late with its releases, or teaching the kids
of the poor in an underfunded school. If we're going to have a
decent future, and not become "losers" in an increasingly divided
economy, we're told that we need to become the salesmen of our
own lives, wheeling and dealing self-promoters who make career
advancement the center of our existence.

In *The Overworked American,* Harvard economist Juliet Schor
examines the emergence of this Alice-in-Wonderland world, where
we have to scramble faster and faster just to stay in the same place.

Americans' working hours, she points out, have been steadily increasing for the past thirty years. Between 1969 and 1987 alone, the average American worker's time on the job jumped by over 160 hours per year, or the equivalent of an entire extra month at work. The average workweek has continued to increase since, and threatens to expand even more as congressional Republicans push to end overtime pay (a deterrent to employers who'd otherwise insist on long hours) for sector after sector of the workforce.

That doesn't even take into account many workers' ever-lengthening commutes. My brother-in-law was recently downsized, for the second time in four years. A Los Angeles video producer, he's skilled, sharp, and creative, but his employers closed their video divisions. In another era, those jobs would probably have been more stable to begin with. Had he lost a job, he'd probably have moved to a neighborhood near his new place of work. Now, even if his next position is an hour or more away across the city, he can't risk selling his house and moving, because he doesn't know how long the new job will last. With no efficient mass transit and more companies treating their employees like disposable parts, he may be forced to commute an even longer distance. He'll squander hours of his life and clog the freeways along with all the other people crisscrossing the city to and from uncertain and increasingly stressful jobs of their own.

Not only do we spend more time working to get by, we receive fewer benefits, despite America's recent economic boom. We take fewer vacations, and they're usually shorter. Once we could rely on employer-funded pensions and Social Security, confident that if we worked long enough, our old age would be provided for. Now, for most of us, retirement has become a crapshoot. We save what money we can, then try to parlay it into the largest possible nest egg by spending hours studying investment-related articles, listening to financial talk shows, poring over mailings from a hundred different mutual funds, and hoping we'll make the right choices. Merely identifying and evaluating the various possibilities is exhausting. Recently, while trying to understand a "simple IRA," I spent fifteen minutes wending my way through voice-mail purgatory, then another hour on the phone with assorted staffers of a mutual fund. Afterward, I was more confused than when I began. Meanwhile, brokerage firms salivate over the idea of privatizing Social Security; they run costly self-serving PR campaigns to convince us that one of our most successful social programs is fundamentally flawed, and going bankrupt. Brokerages would benefit greatly from such a shift. They're eager to take their cut. But markets that go up can also go down. And do those of us without significant wealth really want to spend our lives poring over all the investment options?

Our circumstances in general feel more overloaded and uncertain. Cuts in federal financial aid combine with the declining real value of the minimum wage and with escalating tuition to make college an increasingly severe financial burden. This nation used to compensate for its lack of universal health care coverage with employer-paid insurance. Now, with the exception of congress-members and corporate executives, employees shoulder an increasingly large share of these steadily rising costs, and are left on their own to figure out the baroque mazes of HMOs and insurance plans. For a staggering 45 million Americans, medical coverage consists of nothing but a prayer: "I hope no one in my family gets sick anytime soon." Gradually, guarantees that once allowed most of us to take our basic survival for granted have eroded. Small wonder that the common good has become an uncommon concern.

Of course the very policies and practices that make it easier or harder to get by are themselves the fruit of political efforts. Without the legislation that established rent control, for instance, an award-winning high school science teacher I know would not be able to live, work, and raise a family in New York City. Nor would tens of thousands of other teachers, subway conductors, garbage collectors, and janitors, without whose labors the city would grind to a halt. Income-contingent loan-repayment programs—programs cut drastically by the Republican Congress—began to allow young women and men to pursue occupations that all of us would agree are vital to the well-being of our communities, but that traditionally don't pay well. These and other humane and far-sighted measures were brought about by elected representatives, advocacy groups, and the actions of ordinary citizens. The more we define common solutions to the pressures we face, the more chance we have that those pressures will ease.

OVEREXTENDED PARENTS

But that won't always erase our immediate burdens, particularly if we're trying to juggle work and family. We often feel we're giving our children barely enough time as it is, so understandably we're reluctant to take on additional public commitments. We race constantly to find baby-sitters, juggle money, keep track of the kids' schoolwork, and make sure they are fed and bathed and have clean clothes. If we have a bit of breathing room, we may try to pull them away from the TV or their computer games for a few scarce minutes. But middle-class parents often forgo even this opportunity by falling into the "soccer mom" trap, shuttling children from lesson to lesson, sports team to sports team, and play date to play date—in a gas-guzzling minivan or sport utility vehicle, of course. This frantic way of life often leaves everyone exhausted, kids and parents alike. What's the alternative, we ask, in these perilous and paranoid times? For their protection, we explain, children must always be supervised, even if it means scheduling every free minute of their lives.

Raising children can also make us more economically fearful. Because we're concerned about their futures, we shy away from public controversies that might risk our jobs. We buy life insurance, save for college, move to pricier neighborhoods with better schools, and provide every imaginable material convenience. No matter how economically successful we are, we can always justify the struggle to earn more by saying we're only trying to give our children the additional comfort and security they deserve.

Especially when our children are toddlers—and most in need of parental care—it may be all we can do just to go to work, come home, spend as much time as we can paying attention to their needs, and catch a few scarce hours of sleep. Group efforts like baby-sitting co-ops can help, as can childcare arrangements at political events. At our workplaces, we can continue to promote ideals we believe in. But sometimes we're simply not going to be able to do everything. Pete Knutson recalls feeling totally overwhelmed while trying to keep his domestic world afloat early in his marriage, although the desire to preserve a decent future for his kids eventually prompted him to take public stands. Virginia Ramirez's children were largely grown when she first got involved in COPS, but her husband and mother still pressured her to keep her focus on her family.

Veteran activists are no less affected by parenthood. "My kids are three and nine now," explains a therapist long involved in global peace issues. "They've brought a radical change in my life. I find myself doing things I can work into family life: tutoring at their inner-city public school; making phone calls; writing letters; staying involved through my Catholic church, which is a very engaged, multiracial congregation. But I'm not going to as many meetings. I'm not doing civil disobedience. I see time opening up as they get older, and look forward to all the things I'll be able to do, political and otherwise. I see myself as one of those women who will jump back in intensely when my kids are just a bit more grown."

As I've suggested earlier in this book, a personal crisis, like getting laid off or having to care for a sick child may leave us no choice but to pull back from social involvement and focus on more private concerns. But in general, we may have more choices than we think.

A Low Overhead

Later in this chapter I'll discuss how our children can inspire us to participate in the public arena. For even though the demands of raising them leave us with less time for social involvement, the actions we do take can give them much-needed models of integrity and commitment and help make their lives richer and more meaningful, to say nothing of leaving the world in better shape for them. I'd like to look first, however, at strategies to deal with the pressures of our work lives.

For most of us, time crunches are serious but not insurmountable. True, the amount of time we devote to work, commuting, and various family responsibilities has been steadily increasing. But those hours still aren't comparable to those faced by activists of a century ago, such as the labor activists who challenged the eighty-hour workweek even as they continued to put in their shifts. By and large, we have it far easier than the black sharecroppers and domestic workers who made up the unglamorous core of the civil rights movement. They struggled to take care of their families, faced pervasive racial discrimination, and still made time to challenge their situation. The day after Rosa Parks was arrested, she went in to work at her job as a department store seamstress. When he became head of the Montgomery chapter of the NAACP, E. D. Nixon continued working as a railroad porter. Neither had a choice. Both nonetheless benefited from their involvement, and in ways that weren't always obvious. "My feets is tired, but my soul is rested," said an aged participant in the Montgomery boycott.

So why does it *seem* that people like Parks and Nixon had more latitude to act than we do? It's important for us to realize that some of the pressure we feel is self-induced. "If you want to do anything creative," says the writer and peace activist Grace Paley, "keep a low overhead." Public commitment is an immensely creative activity, but it's hard to pursue if our lifestyle's so expensive we need a six-figure income simply to get by. In *Your Money or*

Your Life, Vicki Robin and Joe Dominguez explore this phenomenon, describing how the American addiction to consumption damages our souls. They then suggest systematic ways to examine how we spend our money, and make sure we really get enough satisfaction from each expenditure to justify the time and energy we invest in it. In the process, they encourage us to ask a radical question: How much is enough?

Simple lives can still be rich. As a young street artist once told George Orwell, "The stars are a free show; it doesn't cost anything to use your eyes." And Robin and Dominguez aren't arguing for sackcloth austerity. In their view, it's fine to enjoy particular discretionary items and experiences that offer real and sustained satisfaction. But they insist, rightly I think, that many (if not most) consumer purchases do no such thing, and they suggest we cut back, saving the money we'd otherwise spend to buy back our lives. If we do this enough we can work fewer hours, retire early, or shift to occupations more congruent with our values. True, Robin and Dominguez's approach works best if we earn enough to allow for discretionary spending in the first place. But just about everyone in America is affected by our culture's growing materialism; poor teenagers, for example, crave $150 Air Jordan basketball shoes just as much as their affluent suburban peers. And that means that just about everyone can benefit from spending money more wisely.

The results of stripping down our economic needs will vary from person to person, but often they're dramatic. For fourteen years, my friend Mary Hanson worked as a water treatment operator for Seattle's local municipal utility, involving herself in peace issues on the side. Along the way, she bought a house, which she shared comfortably but modestly with three roommates. By 1990, when she was forty-four, she was able to quit her full-time position. Since then, Mary's survived on the rent paid by her housemates, and her income from a twelve-hour-a-week job, assisting the business of a friend. Today she devotes most of her life to peace and environ-

mental causes. "I get so much satisfaction out of my involvements," she says. "I don't feel a need for all that other
consumption."

A young African American woman working to reduce commer-
cialism in public schools echoes these sentiments, looking back on
when she was employed by an accounting firm and wearing a new
string of pearls. "I didn't really fit that job," she says. "I made
good money and bought a fur coat. I still have it. But I don't need
lots of money. I don't need pearls. Poetry readings are cheap. I'd
rather go to a house party than a club. I don't feel I'm missing
things."

My favorite song from the Jewish Passover ceremony is "Dayenu," which means "It Would Have Been Enough":

> Had the Lord only brought us out of Egypt . . .
>   it would have been enough.
> Had the Lord only sustained us in the desert . . .
>   it would have been enough.
> Had the Lord only given us the Torah . . .
>   it would have been enough.

We have little of the "Dayenu" spirit in American culture. We
dream of making it big. We constantly pursue more wealth, status,
and material goods, whether or not they bestow true satisfaction.
When we joke that "he who dies with the most toys wins," we
underscore the extent to which we're possessed by our possessions.
As the historian William Appleman Williams wrote, "Once people
begin to acquire and enjoy and take for granted and waste surplus
resources and space as a routine part of their lives, and to view
them as a sign of God's favor, then it requires a genius to make a
career—let alone create a culture—on the basis of agreeing to limits."

Absent genius, there's always ingenuity. A lawyer I know
worked out a job-share arrangement whereby she and two others
split two full-time positions at the Seattle Public Defender's office.

This gave her four months on and two months off; she used the time off to join delegations investigating human rights crises in areas like Guatemala, El Salvador, and the Palestinian West Bank. She'd then come back to Seattle and report on what she'd witnessed.

TRUE REJUVENATION

Making the best use of our time and energy is more than a matter of reducing expenses. Often we spend time that we might use to get involved in our communities recovering from the stresses of our lives. We all have our favorite ways to do this: gardening, running, bicycling, or hiking, reading novels or self-help books, surfing the Net and learning new software programs, watching TV, solving crosswords, attending spiritual seminars, even following every twist and turn of political events as if they were a spectator sport. I'm not suggesting we necessarily give up these activities. The tangible and intangible satisfactions we get from them can help us remain sane, relaxed, and healthy. All citizens possess souls, and all souls require periodic rejuvenation. But in excess, even the most wonderful pastimes can swallow up our lives. And some are fundamentally distracting and numbing—indiscriminate TV-watching, for instance. If we cut back on some of our diversions, we can use the time we save for community involvement.

My own favorite time-waster is listening to Seattle Mariners baseball games on the radio. They give me a sense of drama and excitement, make me feel twelve years old and innocent, provide fresh hope each spring. And if I listen to one game a week, I still get a great deal else done. But baseball can easily consume untold hours—if I let it. If I listen to four, five, or six games, that's fifteen hours of my life. I insist I'm in control of my addiction, then find myself obsessing about how the bullpen blew another game, or why the team made another lousy trade. Before I know it, my surplus time has slipped away.

Whatever our private passions, they're subject to the law of diminishing returns, just like the cycles of endless consumption that Vicki Robin and Joe Dominguez question so perceptively. Beyond a certain point, the effort isn't worth the outcome. Think of Martha Stewart, and her insistence that we can and should express our most powerful creative desires entirely within the domestic world. It can be delightful to fix up a house, plant vegetables and flowers, make wonderful meals for our friends. But Stewart turns such modest domestic pursuits into an all-consuming enterprise. If we only have the right furniture and flower arrangements, she says, create flawless English gardens, and serve immaculately coordinated meals, then all will be well: salvation through interior decor.

Religious traditions call this idolatry—worshiping the unworthy and transient gods of distraction and decoration over our sacred connections to our fellow human beings, and to the living fabric of our planet. The alternative requires striking a balance between the havens that nurture us and the work that needs doing in the world. It means learning to draw pleasure from our modest domestic comforts, but refusing to let them dominate our lives.

WORKING TO GET BY

Even living simply, we need to work to survive. Often, we work at jobs that we hope are useful, but conduct our prime efforts to change the world in our off hours. I think of carpenters, accountants, bus drivers, and computer programmers who conduct their activism on the side. Alison Smith, of Maine's campaign reform initiative, had a low-level job at the university. The pioneering Seattle environmentalist Hazel Wolf spent years earning a modest living as a legal secretary, while juggling an array of political involvements and being a single mother to her daughter.

We may make a strong personal impact in demanding human service fields, such as teaching, nursing, or psychotherapy. But even these, as I've suggested, are subject to larger social forces. Dedicated community doctors and nurses see their ability to do their jobs well continually undermined by the efficiency measures and massive paperwork demanded by managed-care organizations; they're forced to make quicker and more mechanical diagnoses, with little time to engage their patients as people. Teachers, counselors, and social workers face similar speedups, particularly if they're serving less affluent populations. If we want to change social structures, much of our work will take place outside the confines of our jobs.

Corrine Dee Kelly, for instance, loved her vocation as a massage therapist, but also took on children's issues through her Unitarian church. At a time when no one would pay her to run her battered women's groups, Ginny Nicarthy supported herself by seeing individual paying clients. Using skills she'd developed with COPS, Virginia Ramirez worked as a health outreach trainer, while she continued her community organizing.

A longtime friend, Nick Licata, worked for fifteen years as an insurance agent. He used his flexible schedule to get involved in everything from creating low-income housing trusts and a public-interest video center to organizing environmental campaigns and challenging massive public giveaways for Seattle's football and baseball stadiums. A grassroots campaign elected him, at age fifty-one, to the Seattle City Council, although he was significantly outspent by his opponent. Now he addresses the same issues from that podium.

RIGHT LIVELIHOOD

It's a gift to be able to work directly on issues we care about, and earn our living in the process. We don't have to divide our lives. We can fully invest our passions. "Finding the right work," says Thomas Moore, "is like discovering your own soul in the world."

Usually the livings we make as community activists are modest. They require that we live frugally, and even so, financial pressures can force difficult choices in a culture based on always wanting more, and an economy where life at the bottom is hard. But when we do find such jobs, they let us focus our time and energy in ways consonant with our deepest personal urgencies. We may find such work by joining existing networks, whether local community projects or branches of national organizations like the Sierra Club. We also may start our own projects, like Michael Lowe with Palmetto Alliance, and Sonya Vetra Tinsley with the organization that produced her interracial music concerts.

Even when social engagement itself doesn't provide an income, it can lead to unexpected career opportunities. When a young woman named Barb Meister was "a fragile and self-conscious freshman" at the University of Nebraska, she rarely read a newspaper. She didn't vote in the first national election for which she was eligible. She rarely spoke up in class. Her most daring accomplishment had been entering her prizewinning cows in local fairs.

Then America's family farms began going belly-up. Barb's parents were forced to file for bankruptcy, but they also joined some activist farmers' organizations. Their involvement inspired Barb to start a student group, so she and others could educate their peers on the issues that affected Nebraska's farm communities. Later, she based a career, as she says, on "what I'd done, what I knew, the issues I was grounded in." By the time she was twenty-five, she was second in command of the entire Nebraska Department of Agriculture.

We never know where we'll find what in the Buddhist tradition is known as "right livelihood." I was recently stunned to see my friend John Weeks interviewed in *Best's Review*, the bible of the insurance industry. John talked about the future of alternative medicine, arguing that it should be integrated into HMO and insurance plans. He'd started in the field in 1983, doing fund-raising and public outreach for Seattle's John Bastyr College of Natural Medicine. John was no expert when he began, but, he says, he liked "the idea of finding ways to heal that relied more on supporting the body's own recovery system. Plus, I was so happy just to have work that fit my values."

Bastyr gave John "a chance to build something, and to fully engage myself for the first time in my professional life." He'd dropped out of Stanford, worked as a furniture mover and taxi driver, written for an alternative paper, assisted a maverick state legislator, and organized eastern Washington wheat farmers to fight a huge proposed coal plant. But he'd always felt rootless, drifting from cause to cause. Bastyr provided not only a paycheck, but also a home.

John used his organizer's skills to reach out to initially wary media. He helped secure research grants that enabled alternative medicine advocates to begin proving to critics that their treatments were legitimate. He worked with elected officials of both parties on issues like the relation of natural medicine to insurance programs. He also shepherded Bastyr through the lengthy process of becoming accredited, making it the first school of alternative medicine in the country to gain this legitimation. "We had to pass through that narrows," John says, "to have any significant influence on health practice in America." John then pulled together a team of naturopaths whose knowledge and credentials gave them a chance to be heard by Congress. They convinced political leaders as diverse as liberal Tom Harkin and conservative Orrin Hatch to support the federal government's first Office of Alternative Medicine, within the National Institutes of Health. John also helped the alternative health care movement reach people outside the middle class: He convinced Washington State authorities to develop the nation's first publicly funded community clinic where conventional physicians and naturopaths work side by side, learning from each other, while providing services to low-income patients. More recently, he's navigated the complex terrain of HMOs and giant insurance companies, showing them cost-effective ways to integrate alternative medicine into their plans.

Before his Bastyr job, John was intense, restless, constantly dif-

fusing his energy. A chronic underachiever, he always had entre-
preneurial skills but no context within which to use them. Now,
having staked out his own territory, he marshals resources, organizes unlikely coalitions, and converts the once-private impulses of
people already using alternative medicine into leverage for political
and institutional change.

"I never thought this work would become my career," John
says. "But I feel lucky. I've volunteered for a lot of causes, but I
always felt like I was fragmenting my time. Now I get paid to work
on specific issues I believe in, which lets me focus more clearly. I
get to do this work that I care about immensely as my livelihood.
I met my wife through this, and we have our two kids. I've built
wonderful friendships, because there's nothing like creating something together that takes all your heart, sweat, and tears."

Granted, John's work occupies an unusual niche that has
opened in recent years as Americans have expanded the ways they
maintain their health. He's been able to offer major medical institutions alternatives that promise both to save money and to improve their participants' wellness. Making a living in this field is
far easier than earning $20,000 a year trying to organize poor
communities, with half of your time taken up by fund-raising. But
if we're lucky enough to find paying work that helps change the
world, we can have a powerful impact.

WE ENERGIZED EACH OTHER

Even when our jobs have no direct link with social issues, we can
use them to address larger questions. Chris Kim transformed his
minimall into a center that helped tie together the surrounding
community. Fisherman Pete Knutson brought the lessons of an ancient way of life to bear on preserving the Endangered Species Act
and working for habitat restoration. Deborah Prothrow-Stith gal-
vanized public health workers to address youth violence.

What would happen if doctors and nurses began fighting to

guarantee health care for every American? If cops, firefighters, and social workers talked openly and compassionately about the homeless families they see on the street? If every teacher spoke out concerning the social inequities that make it impossible for many children to learn? If more scientists became advocates for the environment? Wherever we are employed, we can develop and support purchasing plans that make use of recycled goods, encourage our companies to hire the jobless and invest resources in neglected communities, and work to make our operations as ecologically sound as possible.

Whatever we do, we aren't likely to get far unless we join forces with others. Indeed, viewing our workplaces as mini-societies is the first step toward trying to make them socially and environmentally responsible. The former Dominican priest Matthew Fox suggests we take an active role in forming workplace communities, so we can "gather to tell our stories" and as a group create new and more generous visions of our vocations, "whether it's education or health work, religion or parenting." Without such support, Fox suggests, our most humane instincts will be frustrated, no matter how committed we may be.

No one is saying this is easy, or always successful, particularly in contexts we neither own nor control. But employees working in concert can produce astonishing transformations. At Chicago's Inland Steel, America's fifth-largest steel producer, four African American employees became concerned about how minority employees were treated. "The paper policies were fine," says saleswoman Scharlene Hurston, who'd been at Inland for fifteen years, and was thirty-nine years old at the time. "But they weren't carried out. When you were involved in meetings, you always felt like you weren't part of the group. You felt you were invisible. Although you'd speak up and have a reasonable opinion, your ideas would be ignored or discarded. Then someone else would bring up an almost identical proposal, and everyone would jump to embrace it. Forty percent of our plant workers are minorities. But it stops when you get to the upper levels. Out of two hundred managers in sales and marketing, we had three African Americans, and we were better than most departments. We felt totally isolated.

"We'd go to the colleges and recruit these great young African American graduates," she said. "Then they'd come to us asking about things that we'd encountered for years: being excluded from meetings; hearing things that were subtly or not so subtly racist; having managers or supervisors not communicate key information; being passed over for promotions."

Fed up with the lack of progress, Scharlene began meeting informally with three other African American colleagues. Each had approached management individually to discuss advancement practices, only to find their complaints dismissed. They echoed Scharlene's judgment "that the situation violated principles I hold very dearly, about doing what's right and truthful and honest." Over a period of months, they brainstormed together, finally deciding to approach Steven Bowsher, a white general manager they respected. Inviting him to dinner, they told him about the racist jokes, derogatory comments, and overt and covert obstacles that they and others had faced at Inland. Although Bowsher was sympathetic, he found the examples abstract and remote from his experience. But he was interested enough to take a two-day race relations seminar led by a longtime civil rights activist, and unexpectedly saw his company with new eyes.

"Suddenly, we weren't talking at each other," Scharlene Hurston recalls, "we started to talk *with* each other." Bowsher had his entire team of managers attend the seminar, then established an aggressive affirmative action plan. His department systematically promoted minorities on the basis of their total years of experience and the general strength of their skills, even if they'd been stuck for years at the lower levels of the corporate hierarchy. After some prodding from Bowsher, Inland's president attended the same seminar, convened a meeting of top officers to deal with racial issues, and seriously solicited the opinions of women and minority employees.

Scharlene's group met resistance, of course. "When you take on something controversial, you're going to get shot at," she says. "We all had colleagues who explained to us how our future looked so bright—if we just divorced ourselves from those other people who were causing trouble. Most of our opponents weren't bad people. They were simply ignorant, afraid of controversy and change."

But that didn't stop the reformers. "We energized each other," said Scharlene. "When one of us got tired, the others were there to pick them up." Besides, it was no longer just the four of them. Each major department and manufacturing plant now had a group to address issues of racial and sexual inclusion. When Bowsher became head of the Ryerson Coil division, one of the company's largest, he appointed Inland's first African American general manager and first Latino and female plant managers, conducted a major campaign against sexual harassment, and revoked a long-standing policy that made the office areas off-limits to ordinary workers. When the division finally turned a profit, after years of losing money, he attributed its success to unleashing the energy and creativity of workers who felt they had the respect and support of management.

"A corporate culture takes forever to create and forever to change," said Scharlene. "But the issues have been legitimized. We've learned the art of negotiation and the strength of solidarity. Before, there were little pockets of questioning, or people denying that these issues existed at all. Now people aren't nearly as afraid. They're much more ready to speak up."

PART OF A MOVEMENT

Scharlene and her co-workers were fortunate to find the sympathetic senior manager, Steven Bowsher. But what if our employers are wholly resistant to our ethical claims, and threaten us for

speaking our convictions? I've talked much in this book about finding our moral voice, but many of us risk losing our jobs if we
express this voice at work.

No matter what our situation, getting the companies we work
for to take a more socially responsible path is hard. That doesn't
mean change is impossible. In his terrific book, *Aiming Higher,* the
former Ralph Nader staffer David Bollier describes a number of
businesses that have combined ethical action with marketplace success. But such efforts require us to mesh causes we believe in with
the tasks that we're assigned, changing corporate culture while
serving as the subordinates of others, and questioning the assumption that businesses need not concern themselves with a larger social good.

This task becomes a lot less daunting if we have some protection
against being capriciously fired—if we can express our beliefs without fear of losing our jobs. And the only source of such protection
I know of—unless we're at the absolute top of the hierarchy—is
that much-maligned institution, the labor union.

Unions seem far from the domains of the soul. Hostile stereotypes associate them with corruption, ruthless power, and needless
confrontation. They seem to belong to an earlier period in this
country's history, one whose brute industrial forces and harsh
working conditions many of us would prefer to think we've left
behind. Yet since most of us are the employees of others, no other
institution can more effectively help us bring our values into our
workplaces.

In his compelling memoir *Which Side Are You On: Fighting for
Labor When It's Flat on Its Back,* the labor lawyer Thomas Geoghegan describes a dispatcher who'd worked at a trucking company
for years, then was abruptly fired following a heart attack. When
the dispatcher wanted to challenge his firing, Geoghegan asked if
anyone could testify about his work record. But everyone the man
knew was a fellow dispatcher or foreman, afraid to risk his job.
Finally, the man had an epiphany. "Hey, why didn't I think of it?

The guys in the *union*. They can testify for me, and they won't get whacked."

Like all other nonunion employees in America, Geoghegan writes, everyone else in the company could be fired "at will . . . for any reason, good or bad . . . or for no reason at all." But the union men, who happened to be truck drivers, could be fired only for cause. "They, unlike the supervisors, could stroll into court, testify, and just walk past the Boss and wave."

Although they've sometimes betrayed their promise, unions give those of us who are ordinary workers our best chance at a genuine say in our workplaces, with security grounded in more than employer benevolence. They protect us against capricious management decisions—for instance, against being fired for voicing discomforting truths. If we're in a union, employers find it harder to play us off one against another, as expendable pawns in the global marketplace. In a way all too rare in our cynical time, unions build solidarity, a sense of common purpose. They promote the profoundly spiritual recognition that "an injury to one is an injury to all" and that our fates are inextricably joined, as Martin Luther King, Jr. said, "in an inescapable network of mutuality, tied in a single garment of destiny." Years after she started the Boston baby-sitting coop, I met my wife, Rebecca Hughes, through the National Writers Union. So unions can tie us together in other ways as well. I felt drawn to Rebecca in part by the same spirit that moved her to take public stands.

Unions can also give us a say in shaping history. We forget, or are never taught, their role in helping to bring about the eight-hour day, Social Security, unemployment insurance, and Medicare. Nor is it widely known that unions like the United Auto Workers provided key support for the civil rights movement, or that longshoremen's locals worldwide helped end apartheid by refusing to load ships destined for South Africa.

U.S. unions have been in decline for the past twenty years, even as union membership has grown in Canada, where economic conditions are comparable, but where workers face far less hostile labor laws. Yet a wave of new leaders offers fresh hope. While in Seattle recently, AFL-CIO president John Sweeney visited strikers at a power-tool warehouse, met with a new group trying to organize software workers, then spent two hours talking with a parade of rank-and-file activists who wanted to voice their concerns. "I don't remember Lane Kirkland ever doing this during the sixteen years he was in charge," said one woman, amazed. "But Sweeney's taking time to listen to folks all over the country." His presence alone gave people a sense of being part of a nationwide movement.

Beside setting aside a third of the national AFL-CIO budget for organizing, labor's new leadership has also built new alliances by helping to create community-based networks like Jobs with Justice. Union activists are now coordinating their efforts with environmentalist and religious groups. They're registering voters, mobilizing retirees, and trying to enlist members to support local struggles. Each victory in this renewed effort leads to others. Inspired, in part, by the Teamsters' successful 1997 UPS strike, ten thousand US Airways workers signed up with the Communications Workers of America. In Las Vegas, citywide support helped over five hundred workers at the Frontier Hotel win a six-year battle to improve their working conditions. These and similar campaigns have succeeded largely on the basis of community ties like those that made possible the labor movement's classic organizing drives decades ago.

THEY LEARNED TO STAND UP

The starting point for many of the people involved in these efforts is a basic wish to preserve their dignity—a desire they share with other community activists. When Jorge Rivera was hired at ASI, a small Boston mattress factory with forty production employees, he was paid only $7.50 an hour, but promised quick raises to $10 or $11 an hour. Once on the job, Jorge learned how to coil inner springs, build frames, and sew padding and fabric. He assembled displays for trade shows and helped sell the company's high-end mattresses to customers. Some days he'd work sixteen hours straight. But his promised raises never came.

"I let it pass for six months," Jorge says, "then after another six months I asked what happened to the original offer. I was giving the best of myself, but they said I had to wait a little while." He finally got a 50-cent raise, but by that time well over a year had passed. "It was like they were using me, acting like I was stupid, so I said, 'I want the raise that you talked about when I got hired.' I was getting madder and madder, until one day I just stayed home and told them I was going to look for another job. They called and offered me nine-fifty because they didn't have anyone else to do the work I was doing."

At that point Jorge realized, as he says, that "all these other people in the company hadn't had a raise in three years. People wouldn't even get their overtime unless they went to the office and complained. I told them, 'You have to do what I did. Go and speak up.'" But most were afraid to. Jorge was born in New York City of Puerto Rican parents; most of his coworkers, though, came from Central America and knew only Spanish. "So I started speaking out for other people, because I spoke English."

The factory had other problems. The workers' bathrooms were filthy. "Like we were animals. Nobody cleaned them. The drinking water from our fountain came out green. They didn't give you safety belts for your back when you lifted heavy mattresses. We used a lot of hot metal glue from a pump gun, but they didn't give us gloves or masks."

When Jorge began talking openly about these and other issues, he says, "the manager told me to look out for myself and they'd take care of me. I felt bad because these were my partners. I was trying to make conditions better so people would be happy and increase production. They kept telling me to just worry about myself."

Around this time, another Boston firm, the Richmark Curtain Factory, fired ten employees for trying to organize a union, and several hundred workers walked off the job. After a six-month strike, and with the help of widespread community support, they won the right to be represented by the textile union, UNITE. When Jorge heard of the Richmark workers' success, he and a few other people from his job met with a UNITE representative. "I also started talking with people inside the plant and asking them how they felt about getting paid just five or six dollars an hour, when in that same hour they made three or four top-quality mattresses that sold for eight hundred dollars each. 'Management doesn't make five dollars an hour,' I said. 'You can't buy a house with that money. You can't raise a family.'"

Jorge knew his actions were risky. "But I had to do it for the people who were there, even if lost my job." The managers called a series of company-wide meetings. "They said that if the union came in, the owners in England would have to close the plant. That's the first thing they always say."

But momentum continued to build. Jorge addressed groups of people during his lunch breaks. "I'd go floor to floor telling them I'd be speaking, then we'd gather and talk about the need to stick together. The management could see us, but they didn't know what we were saying, because we spoke Spanish and they didn't."

When the mattress workers finally had a vote, the union won. But ASI offered to increase base wages by only 16 cents an hour. Jorge and the other workers felt they had no choice but to strike.

"It was one in the morning when we decided," Jorge recalls. "We hardly even slept. Instead, we woke up early and met people at the entrance, saying 'They didn't give us nothing, so we're not going in.' Only five workers crossed the picket line. Even some people who'd voted against the union and had been with the company for years and years were with us. One person had worked there for thirty-three years. These were old men and women who'd worked hard all their lives and gotten nothing. I was so happy to see them I almost cried."

The workers built outside support with the help of UNITE and organizations like Jobs with Justice. "We had a reporter from the paper," Jorge says, "mediators from the city, people from all different unions including the Richmark workers, old people from the neighborhood. We told our customers about the strike so they'd call and put pressure for delivery. The company ran out of inventory. Our boss saw these things and we told him, 'You don't do something, you're going to have people from all over the world coming in.' "

After five days, the company settled. Workers received an immediate dollar-an-hour raise and a guarantee of additional raises for each of the next two years, plus sick days, health insurance, and two weeks' paid vacation. The bathrooms were cleaned, and there was talk of a cafeteria. "Now people dare to talk with the boss and tell him what they feel," Jorge explains. "They go by themselves to the office, with the problems they have. They learned to stand up for themselves."

SHELTER FROM THE STORM

Gaining more dignity and security at our jobs is one example of how common public efforts can give us more personal breathing room. Public commitments can also influence other aspects of our private lives, including, most importantly, our children. The connection there is sometimes harder to see, and we often tend to shy away from social involvement precisely because we fear we'll make our kids' lives more difficult, or financially insecure. "You want to protect the institutions instead of challenging them," explained a woman who cut back her community organizing when the stresses grew too harsh. "Once I had a kid, I was no longer a single person. I had to balance everything against what it would mean for my son." Some parents even claim they're fighting for their kids when they work to keep their schools and neighborhoods white and privileged.

It's reasonable to want to shield our children from economic risk and the social ills of our time. We want to help them keep their innocence as long as possible. Yet that innocence is already under assault, from both the pervasive cynicism of our culture and the genuine crises that we face. We best serve our children not by hiding from the world, but by giving them models of ways to live with courage and integrity.

As the psychologist Mary Pipher writes in *The Shelter of Each Other*, the "junk values" taught by our media culture are toxic. They tend to make kids fearful, self-doubting, and alienated from their families and themselves. Pipher places the blame for this on the fact that multinational corporations have become the culture's storytellers, teaching children what life is all about, and conveying a worldview centered on the rituals of consumption.

Film critic David Denby makes a similar point in a recent *New Yorker* article. He describes wrestling with the impact on his kids of a media culture in which "people possessed solely by the desire to sell have become far more powerful than parents tortuously working out the contradictions of authority, freedom, education, and soul-making." The worse part about this culture, Denby says, is "not mere exposure to occasional violent or prurient images but the acceptance of a degraded environment that devalues everything—a shadow world in which our kids are breathing an awful lot of poison without knowing that there's clean air and sunshine elsewhere." A world, in other words, in which the insouciant smirk is constant and everything is disposable.

It's not enough, however, to insulate our children from this constant media barrage. We also need to make our own beliefs clear to our kids, and create alternatives compelling enough for them to respond. "Families need to both protect their members," Pipher says, "and connect with the world." Social engagement, she believes, is one way of helping both our children and ourselves find deeper meaning and purpose. She describes how she and her thirteen-year-old daughter, Sara, volunteered at a local soup kitchen for a year. Spending time with adults who were doing work they believed in, Sara found a respite from "a shallow and mean-spirited peer culture." She saw the value of her own efforts. In the process, mother and daughter renewed their own common bond.

If we shield our children from issues we care about, our silence can too easily connote indifference. When they worry about the environment, urban violence, or people sleeping on the streets, they do so because they feel the empathy and compassion that we want to nourish—or, at times, because they're legitimately afraid, for reasons we should hardly dismiss. Rather than wrapping them in a domestic cocoon, we can explain an adult society that might otherwise induce despair or callousness. The more they see us responding to the world's problems, the more they gain a sense of hope and purposefulness. Without our guidance, they may be moved and disturbed by such crises, yet remain silent to protect *us* from questions they sense we'd rather not face. This collaborative silence can become like the denial in alcoholic families, where people offer rationalizations like "Oh, your mother's just sleeping. She's taking a nap on the floor."

In poor communities, the need to shelter our children is more urgent. They live closer to violence. Social injustices affect them more personally and at an earlier age. As parents, we may have to explain fear, bigotry, greed—and why they can buy guns, liquor, and drugs at any hour of the day but have to take a bus miles to find school supplies, groceries, or library books. As Robert Coles writes, "A black child of eight, in rural Mississippi or in a northern ghetto, an Indian or Chicano or Appalachian child, can sound like a disillusioned old radical." But families in these situations can also teach rich lessons of struggle.

Even for more affluent families, public commitments can bring difficult choices. In their study of community involvement, *Common Fire*, Laurent Parks Daloz, Sharon Daloz Parks, and their colleagues profiled the director of a community credit union who raised her children in the same low-income neighborhood that the credit union served. Given that she and her husband had alternatives, she wondered whether it was fair to raise a child in this setting, where "instead of waking up in the morning and seeing lots of lovely flowers and beautiful homes," the child sees poverty and despair. "Is it good for your child to see children with no decent shoes or sweaters in winter? Is it good for your child to see people whose only home is a grocery cart?" But the woman also remembered looking out the window and seeing her husband and daughter helping a homeless man gather and crush cans for refunds. "Then again, they benefit from this too—maybe more than we know." She taught her daughter an ethic of connection, rather than one of retreat.

How directly we expose our children to social ills is an intensely personal question. Dedicated activists wrestle, if they have a choice, over whether to send their children to underfunded, low-income schools, to live in dangerous neighborhoods, or to risk time away from them in jail for causes they believe in. There are no easy answers. But as Marian Wright Edelman puts it in *The Measure of Our Success,* protecting our own children "does not end in our kitchen or at our front door or with narrow attention just to [their] personal needs."

Writing to her own sons, she says, "You must walk the streets with other people's children and attend schools with other people's children. You breathe polluted air and eat polluted food like millions of other children and are threatened by pesticides and chemicals and toxic waste and a depleted ozone layer like everybody's children. Drunken drivers and crack addicts on the streets are a menace to every American child. So are violent television shows and movies and incessant advertising and cultural signals that hawk profligate consumption and excessive violence and tell you slick is real. It is too easy and unrealistic to say these forces can be tuned out just by individual parental vigilance." If we want our children to live generous lives, we need to give them ideals to inspire them.

More than that, if we want truly to protect our children from the destructive forces of contemporary society, we have to meet those forces head-on. And that effort will work best if conducted in a spirit that affirms our human connections. Think of the possibilities: If we had strong public schools, we wouldn't have to fear that our daughters and sons will be unsafe, neglected, or poorly taught. Those of us who have the latitude wouldn't be spending hours navigating them through elusive magnet school programs, or opting out entirely and working extra hours to pay for private education. If we created a decent social safety net, we'd worry less about where to find the money to pay our kids' medical bills. If we had a less violent society, we'd more readily let our children roam the neighborhood with friends, instead of watching their every move or keeping them in the house in front of the TV. If we could worry less about their futures, maybe we'd be less obsessed with shuttling them to round after round of outside lessons and activities, all supposedly to prepare them to succeed. We may believe we can make our homes into castles, but whatever we do, the world will bleed in.

PASSING THE TORCH

A few years ago, I attended a national student environmental conference. A thousand young activists sat on a grassy field, talking about their projects and listening to speeches. Then a speaker asked them to "stand up if you love the Lorax." Everyone stood, except me. I was trying to remember who the Lorax was. It finally came to me—the Dr. Seuss creature who fought to save the trees. Just then, a young woman turned to me and said, with fond remembrance, "My mother read it to me when I was a little girl." I looked around and realized that everyone's mother or father must have read it to them when they were young. They'd learned, early on, a sense of connection with the human and natural world, and a respect for its power and enchantment. Their commitments stemmed from how they were raised.

Beyond shaping the world that we will pass on to our children, our actions offer models for their lives. As James Baldwin once wrote, "Children have never been very good at listening to their elders, but they have never failed to imitate them." Whether or not we choose social engagement, we influence our children simply by being who we are and living as we do.

Socially engaged parents don't automatically turn their kids into social crusaders. But when interviewing college students, I met countless individuals involved in important issues who referred to adult models: "My first demonstration, I was in a baby stroller"; "My mom's been going to marches and meetings ever since I can remember"; "Our church has always worked with the homeless."

Young women and men whose parents remain actively engaged are far more likely to view social involvement as a natural human activity. Early on, many learn to reflect on their personal choices and those of society, to challenge misleading authorities and institutions, and to think about the kind of America they want to help create. They also learn skills needed in public life, like the ability to articulate beliefs, engage differing perspectives, and enlist new allies. It's worth trying to make society live up to its highest ideals, they learn, even when doing so is difficult. Connecting with traditions of engagement, they gain a sense that human actions can make a difference.

By contrast, children who grow up in politically detached households learn to fear and mistrust civic involvement, to regard it as the task of "some other kind of person." These are tough times, they're taught. Personal survival is paramount, while social involvement is a luxury. The absence of family models of involvement also feeds their cynicism by encouraging the view that social change efforts are futile or actually make matters worse. If these children are ever to take on public issues, they'll first have to question the values they grew up with, resolve conflicting loyalties, and find new mentors outside their family. The barriers are that much greater.

Not all socially engaged citizens inherit commitment from their families, of course. But being part of such a lineage can give us confidence, direction, encouragement. AFL-CIO president John Sweeney's father, a rank-and-file participant in the bus drivers' union, took young Sweeney to union meetings and repeatedly told him that the union was responsible for every raise he got. Sweeney says that this experience, combined with Catholic social justice teachings, shaped his vision of a world where labor would be respected.

Marian Wright Edelman's father, a minister, built the first black home for the aged in their segregated South Carolina town. He also constructed a playground and canteen behind his church, so that black children would have a place to play. "I have always believed that I could help change the world," she recalls, "because I have been lucky to have adults around me who did."

Recently my wife, Rebecca, and I were showing her ten-year-old son, Will, the film *Newsies*, an unlikely Disney musical about a turn-of-the-century newsboys' strike. It was hokey and sentimental, but we loved it. "I was in a strike once," Rebecca mentioned to Will. "You were?" he said. "That's really cool. Tell me about it."

Of course, Will's vision of a strike involved Disney urchins singing, dancing, getting into punch-outs, and firing their slingshots at bad guys. Rebecca had left the University of Wisconsin after participating in a teaching assistants' strike that failed. But her union's efforts may have helped prepare the ground for similar graduate-student organizing efforts that later succeeded elsewhere—in the University of California system, for example, and at Yale. It also taught her new skills and gave memories of shared commitment that still inspire her.

Though the movie was romanticized, its links with Rebecca's history made its message that much more real. But Will's models of involvement aren't just historical. He hears Rebecca make phone calls for the National Writers Union and sees my letters on public issues in our local paper. He accompanied us when we delivered door hangers for our friend Nick Licata's City Council campaign—racing up and down apartment hallways, turning the task into a game. A few days later, when Licata won by a narrow margin, Will was delighted to have played a part in the victory.

The tenor of our behavior matters as much as the actual issues we take on. If we're part of a vital community and delight in the people we work with, we demonstrate that engaged lives can be vital and rich. If our involvement descends into factionalism, bitterness, or guilt, or if it starves our kids of attention, we teach the opposite lesson. The social activists profiled in *Common Fire* talk time and again of "listening from the stairway" as children, overhearing adult conversations about a larger public world. Many of them saw a steady and diverse flow of visitors in their homes. They encountered people from radically different social, racial, and religious backgrounds. Though their childhood environments varied widely, "common to most," the book's authors say, "was a core of love surrounded by a kind of porous boundary allowing interchange with the wider world, planting seeds for participation in an enlarged sphere."

YOU FORGOT MY BOOK

Children will always be children, of course, as well they should be. My stepson Will still prefers Mel Brooks movies and Terry Pratchett novels to political debates. A couple of years ago, we participated in a largely Jewish vigil challenging Israeli prime minister Benjamin Netanyahu's obstruction of the Middle East peace process. We took Will, but forgot to bring extra snacks and a book for him, and he was sullen and cranky the whole time. "But it's for peace in the Middle East," Rebecca explained plaintively. "I don't *care* if there's peace in the Middle East," he said. "You forgot my book." Finally, Rebecca took him to get some pizza.

In a similar vein, Marianne Williamson describes a terrible argument about Barbie with her six-year-old daughter. Marianne said the doll was impossibly skinny, cared only about shopping, and was a bad role model in general. Then she discovered this note from her daughter to Barbie: "Dear Barbie. I love you so much, but my mommy hates you." Marianne gave up, recognizing that her daughter was learning to stand up for her own choices. That for the moment she happened to choose Barbie probably wouldn't ruin her.

Jon Kabat-Zinn, of the University of Massachusetts Medical Center, has spent years integrating meditation with mainstream medicine. Someone once asked him about teaching meditation to kids. Children follow parents' examples, Jon replied. If you practice a spiritual discipline, your kids will observe what you do. They may express interest, at which time you can show them how to meditate, but otherwise you live the life you believe in, and they learn from that. To insist that they follow your example is likely to provoke them to do precisely the opposite.

Encouraging social engagement is a similar process. If we want our children to feel confident enough to take stands of their own, we need first to love and care for them. We can partake with them in what Jon and his wife, Myla Kabat-Zinn, call the everyday blessings of family life—sharing daily meals, watching them play, holding and consoling them when they're sad. Our house overflows with Will's toys. But none of them gives him (or me) more pleasure than our daily rituals: We chase each other around and around the wall between our kitchen and a hallway, while I make monster noises and he responds with glee; then each night, before he goes to sleep, we crowd onto his bed while Rebecca reads to him. As the psychologist Alice Miller has stressed, our children need to be loved not for how they perform or what they believe, but simply for who they are.

If we're involved in our community, speak openly about the causes and principles we believe in, and invite our children along when appropriate, they'll get the message on their own, even if they can't articulate it until they're older. When they're willing to listen, we can talk about our traditions of social commitment. We just can't compel their involvement.

Nor do we want to create clones who blindly follow us. Planned Parenthood's head, Faye Wattleton, differs strongly with her mother on abortion. Both draw from their lifelong experience in the church. Wattleton's mother has even prayed that her daughter will change her mind. But they maintain a bond of love and respect, and Wattleton credits her mother's integrity with helping to inspire her. Our kids need to think for themselves, learn from our limits and strengths, and find their own causes and commitments, in personal and public life alike.

AN ETHIC OF FAIRNESS

In *The Little Virtues,* the Italian essayist Natalia Ginzburg argues that we should teach our children "not the little virtues but the great ones. Not thrift but generosity and an indifference to money; not caution but courage and a contempt for danger; not shrewdness but frankness and a love of truth; not tact but love for one's neighbor and self-denial; not a desire for success but a desire to be and to know."

The little virtues have their place, Ginzburg says, "but their value is of a complementary and not of a substantial kind; they cannot stand by themselves without the others, and by themselves and without the others they provide but meagre fare for human nature." Only the great ones, which we hope our children will spontaneously develop someday but which in fact must be taught through example, can inspire a deeper sense of purpose.

The example we provide needn't be one of direct political involvement. Equally important is that parents pass on an ethic of fairness, encourage their children's own voices, and help them reason through complex issues. They can do this through nurturing a general sense of connection with the human and natural world. Each night, Margaret Mead's grandmother talked about the day's events while brushing Mead's hair. By age four, as Mead later wrote, "I was treated as a full person, whose opinions were solicited and treated seriously." She in turn extended the same respect to her daughter, Mary Catherine Bateson, who recalls both her parents "giving me real tasks and sitting down and having serious conversations."

Morris Dees, the founder of the Southern Poverty Law Center, grew up in Alabama, the son of poor tenant farmers, neither of whom was politically engaged. But Dees's father was highly egalitarian. He was the only white farmer in the area who invited blacks over to share meals, or who drank from the same bucket in the fields. The manner in which he lived conveyed in vivid terms a moral perspective that, Dees says, continues to motivate his lifework.

But in an era when our national motto has become "Invest in America: Buy a Congressman," our children need more than general encouragement of ethical behavior. They need practical models of commitment, which they won't get from the routine flux of our culture. It would be great if schools conveyed to students how much more democracy means than just voting. But they rarely do, and consequently students graduate with no sense of the movements and ideas that might most inspire their lives.

In fact, each institution in our society presumes that another institution will instruct young men and women in the principles and practices of active citizenship: Families assume civic involvement is taught in school; teachers think it's taught in houses of worship; religious leaders address private morality but defer difficult questions of social justice to those in the political arena; politicians, in turn, talk much about "family values," but do little to encourage real citizen participation.

If we want our children to lead lives of commitment and compassion, they're going to need tangible examples of people who act on their convictions with courage and integrity. They'll need a connection to history, so they'll have a sense of what it means to persist. They'll need to feel confident speaking out on controversial issues, negotiating conflicts, and cooperating with others. All adults, in all social roles, provide examples, whether we mean to or not. Everyone, therefore, is responsible. But by the same token, everyone is in a position to make a difference, by giving children the models that can inspire them.

OTHER PEOPLE'S CHILDREN

Ultimately, our children give us a reason to take a stand. Again and again, activists I meet describe their kids as living links to the future. David Lewis, trapped in his cell during the Bay Area earthquake, wondered whether he and his son would both die in jail. Suzy Marks first began to duck out from behind her sign and speak out against the arms race because she wanted to do what she could for what seemed the ultimate issue in her children's lives. COPS demanded that San Antonio build storm sewers because kids in the city's low-income neighborhoods drowned in yearly flash floods. South Carolina's Michael Lowe paid little heed to the nuclear reactors he was building, until he realized that the water his young son drank came from an aquifer they might contaminate. Later, when he was tried for civil disobedience at one of the reactors, an all-black jury listened attentively while Michael and his fellow protestors compared their action to "trying to prevent bullets from going to a gun that's going to kill our children." To Michael's amazement, they were acquitted.

I've mentioned how activists use the image of looking into a mirror, to take stock of their lives and choices. Our children serve as this mirror, reflecting who we are as well as who we might become—if only we make the effort. We want them to be proud of how we live, and what we stand for. "The young man who stole from my store," said Chris Kim, "could have been anyone in a desperate situation, even one of my kids. If I set myself a standard of how to love people, I believe my own children will follow."

In the most intimate way, children represent the future. Pete Knutson wants his two sons to be able to fish if they want to. He wants "everyone's kids to inherit a healthy planet." Alison Smith worked for campaign reform so her children would not have to grow up in a cynical world. A woman who now organizes Boston garment workers started her political life in Poland, hiding Solidarity leaflets in her young son's diapers in the hope that she could help create a country in which he'd have a say.

Many of the whites of Jackson, Mississippi, responded to de-segregation by sending their children to private schools. As a result, the political base for school taxes shrank and public funding declined precipitously. Without a strong educational system, those left behind seemed doomed to a future of despair. But in 1989, a group of white professional parents, convinced that their children needed to learn in real-world classrooms among children whose diversity reflected our society, decided to send their kids to public schools and to recruit other families to do the same.

The group they formed, Parents for Public Schools, enlisted 600 families like themselves who would normally have fled the system. Then they approached middle-class African American parents who'd similarly left. They helped pass a $35 million school bond issue—Jackson's first since desegregation—and created a model for parents in other cities from Cincinnati to Houston. Though they had fears about their decision, they felt that abandonment of the public schools would shortchange their children by passing on to them a meaner society. Also, as one parent said, "I want my children to know kids of different backgrounds, not just those who are white and middle-class. I want them to be educated in a world like the world that they're going to live in."

As these parents recognized, our most fundamental responsibility as citizens is to love not only our own children, but other people's as well—including children we will never meet, who grow up in situations we'd prefer to ignore. Marian Wright Edelman writes to her own sons about the need for this expanded vision of caring. She describes her "sometimes difficult, even frantic, efforts to balance my responsibilities to you, my own children, and to other people's children with whom you must share schools and streets, the nation and world. Paradoxically, the more I worried about and wanted for you, the more I worried about the children of parents who have so much less. When one of you got a high fever, painful earache, asthma attack, or sports injury, how reassuring it was to be able to pick up the phone and call our pediatrician and take you right in. How enraged I am to think that other parents cannot ease their children's suffering and their own fears because they happened to be born on the wrong side of the tracks, the wrong color, or to lack a job with health insurance or the means to get healthcare."

Too often, we're taught to ignore or excuse the pain inflicted on the distant and not-so-distant children of others. To be sure, we'll always listen most attentively to our own children's cries. But if we don't heed the cries of others' as well, America will be lost, and we'll risk losing our souls. As the Buddha said, we need to "love the whole world as a mother loves her only child." For only then do we honor the ties that bind us together—that make us human.

Chapter Eight

Village Politics

To carry the message of a cause in a community when you are a generally respected neighbor is far better than when you do it as virtually your sole activity in public.

—*KARL HESS*

In Florence, South Carolina, Baptist preacher Bill Cusak had never organized anything more controversial than a revival meeting. But in the mid-1980s he became concerned about whether the nuclear arms race would destroy his granddaughter's future. So he approached a biologist at a local community college, who'd written a letter on the issue to the morning paper. They began to meet with a few others. Together, they built a peace community from scratch, by speaking and showing a video on the arms race at every church, PTA association, and garden club that would have them. They enlisted a local African American pastor and evangelist to help bridge the community's racial divide. And they talked with younger members of some interested congregations, in the hope that they would then approach their friends.

One of the first groups Bill addressed was the local Rotary Club, of which he was a longtime member. "They kind of treated me like I had the plague," he recalled later. But he felt he had to do it anyway. "Basically it takes like to reach like: youth to reach youth; blacks to reach blacks; Catholics to reach Catholics. And," he said with a sly smile, "I even think it takes Baptists to reach Baptists."

Although the responses weren't always encouraging, even the Rotary Club members gradually began to ask Bill about war and peace issues that the local newspaper reported on, and generally stopped treating him like a pariah. Over a period of years, his and others' efforts slowly changed the town's culture, making it more hospitable to open discussions of difficult social problems.

FACE-TO-FACE OUTREACH

The process changed Bill. "It's been like a crowbar to my soul, cracking my personality, opening up depths to go beyond that superficial intellectual process of detachment. It laid a foundation for a style of life I'll be following as long as I breathe. I've had to think about the reality of my Christian faith instead of just the abstractions. I've started looking at different situations, like people in poverty, and asking how Jesus would respond."

More recently, Bill's been organizing a local shelter for homeless women and children, using many of the community networks he had when working against the arms race. He hopes to find one volunteer for each person in the shelter, both for the sake of the homeless families and "so the volunteers can get a sense of what it's like to live on the street."

We could call Bill's approach village politics, using face-to-face networks and existing communities to address larger issues and principles. This approach taps into the web of independent organizations that political theorists call civil society. These organizations include schools, churches, temples, bicycle clubs, softball leagues, PTAs, baby-sitting co-ops, the community groups that Chris Kim approached in transforming his minimall, and Pete Knutson's association of gillnet fishermen. At times, these networks insulate us from difficult social problems, segregating us by class, race, and belief system. Yet they can also provide a powerful structure for raising critical public issues with the people likely to take our perspectives most seriously: colleagues, coworkers, neighbors, and friends.

The more these groups are independent of governmental or corporate power, the more latitude their members have to think through ideas and act on them together. "In such *havens*," writes the sociologist Eric Hirsch, "people can easily express concerns, become aware of common problems, and begin to question the legitimacy of institutions that deny them the means for resolving those problems."

When dialogue begins to take place in these intimate venues, previously uninvolved people can find new ways to speak out and influence common choices. As the political scientist John Gaventa points out in *Power and Powerlessness,* his study of a resource-rich but economically devastated Appalachian valley, power isn't only a question of who prevails when issues are contested. It also hinges on the rules and institutional structures that allow access to debate, and the mechanisms that "prevent conflict from arising in the first place."

Village politics can give us a way to challenge these mechanisms. Granted, Bill Cusak's thirty-thousand-person town of Florence enjoys some advantages: It's small enough that people know each other across the divides of occupation, religion, and culture. But even cities such as Los Angeles, New York, and Chicago are vast patchworks of smaller communities. Each neighborhood, business, fraternal organization, or church group represents a potentially fertile field for public dialogue. We each have access to some of these communities, and the chance to use them to promote more humane social visions. Think of Adam Werbach, still in high school, enlisting five hundred volunteers for the California environmental initiative, by approaching every youth organization he could find. When we use such networks to reach out, we can build on existing bonds of human conviviality and connection, and we have the advantage of acting where people know us. As Karl Hess, a former Barry Goldwater speechwriter turned Vietnam War opponent, once wrote, "To carry the message of a cause in a community when you are a generally respected neighbor is far better than when you do it as virtually your sole activity in public."

Neighbor-to-neighbor outreach has long been crucial to the growth of successful citizen efforts. We saw this when COPS worked within churches and neighborhoods in the San Antonio barrios. We saw it in the church-based opposition to U.S. Central America interventions. We saw it when citizens in Maine worked through every conceivable community organization to pass their pioneering Clean Elections initiative. We see it when factory workers debate a union organizing drive, or when women in a beauty salon discuss the treatment they receive at their jobs.

In my description of the step-by-step journey toward activism, I mentioned an innovative University of Michigan student group, Greeks for Peace. As the group brought critical social issues into the habitually conservative domains of their university's fraternity and sorority system, people who otherwise would never have taken an interest began to respond. They might never have walked across the quad to hear exactly the same issues discussed by exactly the same speakers, but they'd go to events held in safe and familiar environments, when they were invited by their peers. "So much politics," said one of the founders, "is geared for those already involved. We wanted a vehicle for people to be with their friends and learn to take a stand together."

Following the Christian Coalition's strategy of working through local community networks, an organization called the New Party has begun to run progressive candidates for a variety of local offices nationwide. In the past few years, they've won 150 of the 230 elections they've entered, for slots on school boards, city councils, state legislatures, and so forth, in cities as diverse as Minneapolis, Houston, Madison, and Little Rock. In Arkansas, the New Party helped pass its own statewide campaign finance reform bill. The organization enters local nonpartisan races, supports progressive Democrats where appropriate, and works to create a force capable of compelling Democratic leaders to respond to the needs of those who aren't high-rolling donors.

Activists in Nebraska also used "village outreach" to dramatically overhaul the state's tax code. In the early 1960s, a group of University of Nebraska economists used the university's statewide network of adult education extension offices to organize workshops, county by county, at which people could discuss different ways to make the highly regressive state tax system more fair. The existing system had long weighed disproportionately on family farmers and low-income residents. Reaching out through the extension offices and through organizations such as the Farmers' Union, the Farm Bureau, and the Grange, the economists invited people to see for themselves how a range of approaches would affect them and their neighbors. "If people just really had a chance to look at the numbers," one of the faculty members recalls, "we felt they could come to an intelligent decision. But they had to have a context to analyze the system, and this seemed a perfect use of educational networks that were already in place."

The workshop leaders pursued their task without laptops, computerized spreadsheets, interactive Websites, or any of the other tools that would now make a comparable process far easier. But participants examined who was getting a free ride and how to make the system more equitable, and considered the likely results of specific policy changes. Local and statewide media covered the debates. It took a half-dozen years of follow-up education and discussions, but Nebraska finally passed a far more progressive graduated income tax.

ENGAGED COMMUNITIES

Mobilizing our villages to address larger issues can give us the strength to change political and economic policies. We also gain a community of support, which eases the inevitable frustrations of working for social change. When we don't act through organized communities, our voices are far less effective. It's instructive, in this regard, to view the difference between Newt Gingrich's successes in enacting highly regressive changes in tax and welfare policy and the relative frustration of his efforts to roll back environmental laws. The Gingrich Congress did indeed push through some destructive antienvironmental bills, such as the so-called salvage rider. This bill allowed widespread clear-cutting in major sections

of our national forests, by effectively scrapping environmental protections that activists had spent decades working to enact. But the
environmental movement convinced enough Democrats and mod-
erate Republicans to block most of the worst of the proposed dep-
redations, and did so through an organized presence in every
corner of the country.

Those who support more progressive welfare or tax politics
have been far less organized, and therefore far less successful. Even
when polls indicate solid support for specific policy changes, such
as taxing the wealthy at higher rates than the poor, ordinary citizens have few vehicles for presenting their message in a form that
will be heeded. Environmentalists have simply developed a more
extensive and stable network. And without such a network to enable us to act together, we end up like a technical editor I know,
who explained, "I cringed at the welfare reform, at the tax bill, at
Clinton's bombing of the Sudan. But I felt so busy and overloaded,
I didn't do anything. Maybe I just hoped Clinton would hear my
cringe."

Engaged communities can give us a way to do more than cringe
in private. They can help us speak with a common voice and put
up with the endless mailings, phone calls, meetings, and other
repetitive tasks needed to mobilize people to act. They can help us
exchange our own stories, so we remember why we take our
stands. They can help us develop and share a rich vision, and sustain our commitment and hope.

Mary Catherine Bateson describes how this process unfolded in
the feminist consciousness-raising groups of the early 1970s.
"Here, women gave one another mutual support and pooled their
experience, adding an analytical process of mutual comparisons to
move toward insight. . . . For many women, the greatest discovery
of these groups was that other women could be companions rather
than rivals. They learned the value of shared experiences and the
benefits of solidarity, becoming friends." A comparable process occurred in Latin America's Basic Christian Communities. Peasants
read the Bible together and discussed their common economic suf-

fering. These communities created profound democratic ripples both in the Latin American Catholic church and in their societies as a whole. The civil rights movement's Freedom Schools employed a similar model to teach people basic literacy and political skills and to nurture their spirits.

Perhaps the greatest immediate benefit of such communities is that they remind us that standing up for what we believe is a great deal easier when we're standing shoulder to shoulder with others. "How hard it is to go on singing when one sings alone," writes prison poet Tim Blunk. Challenging the presumption that our efforts are futile, engaged communities teach us that change comes only when we climb the mountain together. At their best, their purposefulness, generosity, and reciprocity anticipate the world we seek to create.

In a recent *Atlantic Monthly* article, Charles Trueheart examined the culture of America's new megachurches, which have congregations of two thousand, five thousand, even fifteen thousand people. These all-encompassing institutions satisfy nearly every conceivable human need, offering parenting groups, teen groups, singles groups, singing clubs, and soccer teams. They build a sense of broad purpose in a time when that feeling is scarce, and speak to people's longing for community.

Those who attend the megachurches experience the same time crunches as everyone else does in our society, but their religious village gives them practical support as well as spiritual nurturance. You have more free hours if you're part of a group that looks after your children, visits you when you get sick, picks up your kids from school when you're working, and shares a car pool on the freeway. We could view these institutions as larger and more spiritually oriented versions of the baby-sitting co-op. If the rest of us had such supportive structures, we'd be less likely to view political involvement as just one more imposition on our already overburdened and fragmented lives.

Much like today's megachurches, the political movements of the 1930s built a cultural infrastructure. This made it easier for people to participate, forming unions and winning major legislative victories like Social Security, unemployment insurance, a national minimum wage, and the eight-hour day. It helped them democratize America.

The history's been buried as part of our collective amnesia, but one of the major participants in the process was the American Communist Party. Despite its undemocratic internal structure and its subservience to the astoundingly brutal Soviet system, the grass-roots activists who joined its ranks played a key role in nearly every political fight of the time.

The Party flourished because it addressed urgent issues, but also because it helped its members fulfill needs for cultural expression and community cohesiveness within an activist context. Drawing on traditions developed by earlier populist and socialist movements, as well as by nascent labor organizations, members in New York and other key cities could conduct virtually every aspect of everyday life within the Party's institutional framework. As Richard Flacks points out, a person could read the Party's daily newspaper; go to work in a shop represented by a Party-allied union; participate in a Party-organized softball league, chorus, or theater group; send the children to a Party-allied summer camp or after-school program; get medical care through the Party-sponsored medical society; attend lectures, concerts, and rallies put on by Party-related organizations; read books by writers celebrated by the Party cultural magazine or published by the Party publishing house; vacation at a Party-owned resort; spend their retirement at old people's activity centers sponsored by the Party; and be buried by the Party-sponsored funeral society.

The downside, of course, was the Party's dictatorial treatment of its own members, its lock-step allegiance to the Soviet line, and its insular mistrustfulness. The moment they dissented, even the most dedicated members were attacked for undermining the cause. Most eventually quit, and many gave up on social change altogether. So I cite the Party not to excuse its moral blind spots, but to identify the characteristics that drew people in.

Throughout the civil rights movement, black churches met similar needs for a community base independent of the dominant culture. They offered activists a social and spiritual refuge during immensely difficult struggles. They provided a theology of hope, following a tradition rooted in the Exodus story, when the people of Israel were liberated from Egyptian bondage. When movement participants sang "Ain't gonna let nobody turn me 'round. I'm gonna keep on a-walkin', keep on a-talkin', marching up to freedom land," they made clear their links to the past.

The largely white youth movements of the 1960s also tried to build their own oppositional counterculture. We didn't sponsor old-age homes, but we did create countless co-ops and collectives. Given the relative affluence of the time, these efforts raised hopes that we could build a new world within the shell of the old. Our dreams foundered due to rifts between hippies and political activists, growing economic pressures, and the sheer absurdity of trying to build a revolution centered on a single generation. But the impulse to meet people's needs for community was sound.

Since then, religious social justice activists have had the most success in building subcultures that sustain the difficult work of healing the world. Churches and synagogues offer an institutional base, a common moral framework, and a community with the avowed goal of serving others. At their best, when religious activists take on social problems, they do so with a vision that sees God—and therefore hope—in every person they meet. "Going to church helps me reevaluate myself," says Virginia. "It reminds me why I'm doing what I'm doing, and gives me the strength that I need. If I wasn't close to the church, or to God, I don't think I'd be able to continue."

VIRTUAL VILLAGES

Secular activists, too, build communities—Sierra Club hiking groups, gay social and civil rights groups, emergent labor organizations, the politically edged 'zine and music scene, and informal friendship networks. But it's a consistent challenge to maintain these supportive structures in the face of a culture that constantly threatens to erode them.

Later I'll return to the subject of religious and secular frameworks of hope; but for now, I'd like to focus on a phenomenon that might be called the virtual village. I get regular e-mail from the National Writers Union: messages about pending congressional bills, updates on our local meetings, proposals for new tactics and strategies, and emergency action alerts. My friend Nick Licata, the newly elected city councilman, regularly sends out electronic mailings describing key issues before the council and explaining what active citizens can do: His mailings have already played a key role in mobilizing community activists on several major local issues. Freelance photographers nationwide recently organized on-line to secure an Associated Press contract that was better than the onerous original offer; without the Internet, participants say, success would have been impossible, given their dispersion throughout the country.

Just before the 1998 Congressional election, a Berkeley couple who ran a software business began circulating an on-line petition called Censure and Move On. Washington's obsession with scandal and impeachment, they felt, distracted America from far more pressing concerns. The petition asked Congress to respond to the Monica Lewinsky affair by formally censuring President Clinton, and then moving on to the real problems facing the country. They posted the petition form on a Website, e-mailed an explanation and direct link to their family and friends, and asked them to pass it from there.

Within a few weeks, Censure and Move On had generated over 300,000 on-line signatures and 3,000 active volunteers. The day before the election, the organizers sent an e-mail to all who had signed, encouraging them to get as many others as possible to vote and send a message "to pro-impeachment, investigation-addicted, scandal-blinded politicians that it is time to MOVE ON with the business of the nation." Given the election's low turnout, they may well have shifted some key races.

The new technologies help ordinary citizens all over the world communicate and work together. Chinese dissidents evade government blocks by e-mailing their newsletters to servers in Silicon Valley, which in turn e-mail them back to the individuals on the recipient list. Mexico's Zapatista rebels have garnered international media coverage by posting reports of continuing developments on the Web. The anti-NAFTA movement used electronic communications to coordinate grassroots efforts and bring together environmental, labor, human rights, and religious groups across national borders. "We literally can have neighborhoods in Chicago link with villages in India," writes David Morris of the Institute for Local Self-Reliance, "to try to understand each other's perspectives and, ideally, actually work together."

The Internet also gives worldwide access to alternative sources of information. Anyone with the right equipment can, from anywhere in the world, visit the site of the Seattle-based WebActive project and listen to the alternative radio news of Pacifica, the commentaries of Jim Hightower, and analyses by media action group FAIR, or browse an annotated list of 2,100 socially active organizations with accessible Websites.

Ginny Nicarthy, whose book *Getting Free* helped launch the battered women's movement, finds the Internet tremendously useful with respect to complex international trade issues, such as the Multilateral Agreement on Investments (a proposal, which critics call NAFTA on Steroids, to give the rights of multinational corporations clear precedence over those of local governments and communities), and the African Opportunity Act, which will have a similarly dangerous impact throughout Africa.

"I've seen nothing," Ginny says, "about the African Opportunity Act in the papers. But I can go to the Net and download the exact text of the bill, then read statements opposing it by African nongovernmental organizations and African American congresspeople. With a couple of clicks, I can forward important information to legislators who ought to know about these issues, but often don't. One of my favorite Websites lists the coalition of multinational companies pushing the bill, and their history on environmental and labor issues. It's a gold mine of information at the click of a key."

Ginny doesn't know all the ways the Internet will end up changing our lives, for good or ill, "but for now, I love the ability to pass on news and analysis instantly, knowing it will go out to hundreds or even thousands of people. Maybe the Internet will even bring us back to some of the feeling of the old town hall, where everyone has a voice. But at the least, it's a very useful tool."

Still, useful technologies alone can't change political climates or replace traditional face-to-face organizing. The Center for Campus Organizing received a great deal of media attention for using on-line discussion groups and e-mail networks to coordinate nationwide protests against Newt Gingrich and his policies. Colleges throughout the country participated, but the number of students they drew depended on how much additional grassroots outreach they conducted. Where organizers canvassed dorms, made announcements in class, and worked with sympathetic faculty and the campus press, large crowds turned out for their demonstrations. Where they relied solely on electronic notices, only a handful of people showed up.

The same is true of community groups. Now we can send e-mail messages instead of making a hundred time-consuming and expensive phone calls to tell our membership about a pending congressional bill. We can distribute programs, platforms, and pamphlets, and get near-instant on-line feedback to revise them. We can use our Websites to post arguments, position papers, and action calendars, so we don't have to repeat the same basic information time and again, and so visitors to our sites can easily forward the information to others. A group of high-tech workers in Seattle is even now using the Internet to do union organizing, in a software industry supposedly so hip and high-flying that its employees have no need for representation. "It's wonderful," says one of WashTech's cofounders, "to be able to send out a message and communicate with lots of people for very little money, which used to be something that only large media corporations could do. We need to use these new technologies if we're going to have a chance."

But our e-mail in-boxes can easily fill up, and our Web searches can become endless distractions. While on-line discussion groups can foster surprisingly productive dialogue, they work best as an adjunct to face-to-face engagement, not as a replacement for it. People still need to gather together, eat, joke, flirt, tell their stories, attach names to faces, and remind themselves why they joined their causes to begin with. "It's almost reassuring that we still have to do all the traditional things if we want people to respond," says a software editor who chairs her local Amnesty International chapter, "not just rely on the new technologies."

BOWLING ALONE

Creating any kind of activist community is harder when the civic associations and institutions that might once have offered a foundation have themselves eroded. In a much discussed article, "Bowling Alone," the Harvard political theorist Robert Putnam observes that during the past thirty years Americans have steadily reduced their participation not only in voting, but also in traditional forms of community involvement, such as the PTA, the League of Women Voters, unions, mainstream churches, the Boy Scouts and Campfire Girls, and service clubs like the Lions and Kiwanis. We've squandered the "social capital" that allows people to work together effectively to pursue shared objectives. As a strangely poignant example of this trend, Putnam notes that local bowling leagues have seen a 40 percent decline in membership since 1980. During the same period, however, the number of individuals who actually bowl has risen until it now exceeds the number who vote in congressional elections. These trends bode ill for American democracy, Putnam argues, because the more socially isolated our citizens become, the fewer chances they have for the kinds of civic conversations that fuel involvement in crucial public concerns.

Putnam's critics, like *Atlantic Monthly* writer Nicholas Lemann, have argued that citizens are still just as likely to get involved in community social networks, but that as America's population shifts toward the suburbs, the networks have changed form. Youth soccer leagues, in which parents participate on the weekends, are booming, he says. So are Internet discussion groups and self-help associations like Alcoholics Anonymous. Organizations from NOW and the Sierra Club to the NRA and the Christian Coalition have taken the place of the old political machines.

Such examples notwithstanding, I remain convinced by Putnam's basic proposition, that civic involvement has dropped off significantly. In a follow-up article, Putnam examines a number of possible causes for the decline, including suburbanization, the increased numbers of women in the workforce, and the general demands of modern life. While most of these factors seem to play some role, they don't account for the fact that the decline cuts across cities and suburbs, the married and the single, working men, working women, and stay-at-home moms. The key change during the past fifty years, Putnam concludes, is the steadily increasing influence of television. Regardless of background or current circumstances, the more people watch TV, he finds, the less they involve themselves in civic activities of any kind, and the more mistrusting and pessimistic they become about human nature. As their sense of connectedness and common purpose erodes, they find it easy to scapegoat others, to view the world in prejudicial and unforgiving terms, and to believe that ordinary citizens can do nothing to shape the history of our time. This is all the more troubling given that extensive TV watching now begins in early childhood, taking up as much time among average kids aged nine to fourteen as all other discretionary activities combined. For many

adults, TV has gradually replaced nearly every social activity outside the home.

It worries me that so many of us now sit alone for hours on
end, passive spectators, paying more attention to the strangers on
the screen than to the real people next door. What are the consequences for ourselves and our society? The greatest misfortune, in
my view, is that by focusing so much on stories scripted by others,
we forfeit the opportunity to create our own.

Fishing Together

Whatever the reasons for our declining civic involvement, we need
to rebuild local communities even as we work to expand their vision. Pete Knutson took this approach in working with his fellow
fishermen: First he helped create a cohesive community; then he
involved its members in larger public issues. Pete, the son of a
plainspoken Lutheran minister, grew up in the hardscrabble mill
town of Everett, Washington. He had a Barry Goldwater poster
on his wall, "because Goldwater spoke his mind." At first Pete
supported the Vietnam War, and even got a jingoistic letter published on the *Everett Herald*'s youth page. His views changed as
friends who'd enlisted came back, feeling betrayed, and told him,
"Don't believe anything the military tells you. They always lie."
Before long, Pete was organizing an antiwar moratorium at his
high school; then he went off to Stanford, and became the only
draft-age man to testify before Congress. He even got his fifteen
minutes of fame on the national news, after Strom Thurmond
stormed out when Pete had the audacity to ask a Senate committee,
"If you're so eager to fight this war, why don't you pick up an
M16 and lead the first wave?"

Pete began fishing to work his way through school. Soon, fishing
became a way of life, as he bought his own boat, with borrowed
money, to support his wife and two young sons. Because he knew

his fellow fishermen were powerless in isolation, he helped build the Puget Sound Gillnetters' Association, which enabled members to market fish jointly, lobby on laws that affected them, and gain leverage against the giant canneries. "I felt we had to trust each other," he says. "If we didn't, we had no chance." The association became a base through which fishermen gradually became conversant with large ecological issues, such as the destruction of salmon habitat, upon whose outcome their livelihoods depended.

Pete worked steadily to bridge the gap between fishermen and the generally more middle-class environmentalists. That was no easy task, given long-standing mutual mistrust fed by class divides and stereotypes. Yet a coalition did in fact emerge, and the fishermen brought a powerful blue-collar presence to issues like the Endangered Species Act and habitat protection. When President Clinton visited Seattle for a Pacific Rim trade conference, a parade of fishing boats joined with Greenpeace activists to challenge his environmental timidity. Both Pete's ethical stand and pride in craft were evoked by the bumper sticker on his truck: "Jesus Was a Gillnetter."

This hard-won and unexpected alliance proved critical when Initiative 640 threatened to shut down the gillnetters' operations by banning the nets they used. The fishermen held joint press conferences with the now-supportive environmental groups, picketed a pleasure-boat company that was a prime initial backer of the initiative, and generally refused to succumb quietly to their opponents' well-financed campaign. They survived because Pete, along with a few others, had helped change their vision from one of enlightened self-interest to a more complex and sustainable ethic, best summed up when he spoke of nurturing the salmon habitat "so my kids can fish, too, and everyone's children can inherit a healthy planet." First the fishermen learned to work together, then to reach beyond their own ranks. Building their association's internal cohesion made it easier for them to tackle difficult issues later on.

COMMUNITIES OF THE VOICELESS

The veteran community organizer Arnold Graf describes the challenge of trying to pull people together in a time when individuals are often isolated. "When I'm out organizing in a community, I always feel like I'm in a vacuum. There's nothing to hook up to." Graf works with the Industrial Areas Foundation (IAF), an organization founded by the legendary community organizer Saul Alinsky that promotes some of the most systematic attempts to practice village politics in low-income communities. "In places like San Antonio or Baltimore," Graf explains, "we are as close to being a local political party as anybody is. We go around organizing people, getting them to agree on an agenda, registering them to vote, interviewing candidates on whether they support our agenda. We're not a political party, but that's what political parties used to do."

San Antonio's COPS group, the IAF affiliate that so changed the life of Virginia Ramirez, began with straightforward issues like bringing more city services to the desperately underserved Latino neighborhoods. COPS then moved on to address education, job training, and community economic development. They focused in particular on the invisible leaders who'd long held together local churches and PTAs.

Other IAF affiliates in such places as Houston, Baltimore, and the Brooklyn neighborhood of East New York have experienced similar successes. Critics of the IAF note that local affiliates still hesitate to join national coalitions on issues that affect their largely low-income constituencies—budget priorities, equitable taxation, welfare politics, campaign reform, and environmental justice. And the affiliates have had a hard time enlisting people who don't already belong to existing institutions. So they embody some of the disadvantages as well as the strengths of village politics. But they've made tremendous strides in helping people like Virginia Ramirez reclaim their voice, change their lives, and empower their communities.

The most serious drawback of addressing only issues of immediate interest to our particular "villages" is parochialism, which can easily become complacency. We need to work with members of other villages if we're to meet our most fundamental challenges, like securing adequate employment, housing, and education. This means we need to reach beyond the domains where we feel most at home. Too often, our communities are separated from those of our fellow citizens. We need ways to leap the cultural, political, and economic firebreaks that stop the spark of moral commitment from spreading too widely and keep our social concerns safely private. When social justice groups from widely divergent economic circumstances begin to form alliances with each other, they gain both political strength and a sense of each other's worlds.

We particularly need to surmount these boundaries if we inhabit a comfortable professional environment and spend significant personal time only with others equally affluent. But there are other divides besides economic ones. Urban liberals are often profoundly estranged not only from rural NRA stalwarts, despite many issues where bridges could be built, but also from the more privatized culture of the sprawling suburban communities and so-called "edge cities," both blue- and white-collar, where America's key political battles are being fought. As Frances Moore Lappé and Paul Dubois of the Center for Living Democracy remark in *The Quickening of America,* public life requires us to engage people of differing views and experiences.

This dialogue may make us uncomfortable. As Cornel West points out, whites often say they want to hear what's on the minds of African Americans, Latinos, or other people of color, then complain that they feel psychologically unsafe if the responses they invite sound angry. We also need to acknowledge the equally destructive and tenacious divisions of class. If you're starting at the bottom of the economic pyramid, your wounds are likely to be more personal than those of individuals inhabiting what the veteran civil rights activist Jim Lawson calls "the middle-class community of goodwill." You labor under more constraints and more burdens, suffer more pressures to make a separate peace and escape the circumstances into which you were born. It's going to be your neighbor who dies of cold because her house isn't fixed, your child—or you yourself—who lacks adequate medical care, your community where the toxic waste dump is sited. The people you seek to involve—your friends and neighbors—face greater despair, wield less institutional power, and have less room to maneuver than individuals coming from more insulated circumstances. You're fighting for the future of people you know.

Those of us who are relatively comfortable can play a key role in making public the voices of people whose stories are rarely heard, if not actively silenced. We can bring these voices into institutions where we have access, lending our credibility to make sure they are heeded. This process is starting to occur through partnerships between affluent and low-income churches, and coalitions working to strengthen urban schools. It can also be seen in the new environmental alliances now challenging the staggeringly high rates of pollution and toxic dumping in the country's poorest communities. In another recent example, overseas development projects have begun to help tribal peoples build sustainable local economies that support their cultural traditions. In these and other instances, we first have to recognize the moral firebreaks before we can bridge them.

A Shelter for My Grandchildren

Ultimately, as former Speaker of the House Tip O'Neill said, all politics is local. But sometimes activism that remains too localized not only limits its effectiveness, but also lets the problems it seeks to address grow worse. A Stanford student once explained how he'd learned more from his community volunteering than from all his courses in school. "I hope that one day," he concluded, "my grandchildren will get to have the same experience working in the same homeless shelter that I did." Friends gently reminded him that

they were working for a future when people in a country this
wealthy wouldn't need to sleep in shelters. The student meant no
harm, but his words raised a question about the relationship between long-term change and the volunteer work that so many of
us do in our communities.

Millions of Americans participate in voluntary activities. In its
much-quoted surveys, the nonprofit institute Independent Sector
counts almost half the adult population as volunteers. But these
surveys include such activities as visiting a sick friend, taking out
the trash of a neighbor, and networking in professional organizations, so their estimates seem overly inclusive, and much too high.
There are, however, countless numbers of us who serve in soup
kitchens and shelters, conduct literacy programs, read to otherwise
isolated hospital patients or the elderly, work with Big Brothers,
Big Sisters, Boy Scouts, and Girl Scouts. We teach Sunday school,
coach Little League, work with our children's schools, and run
churches, temples, volunteer fire departments, and historical sites.
Some of our efforts are compulsory—college requirements or
court-ordered community service. But most often, our motivation
is the same as that of citizens involved in more political forms of
advocacy: We want to alleviate human pain and affirm a sense of
human connection. And we get back similar feelings of personal
meaning and common purpose. Clearly, America would be a much
harsher society without our efforts.

Yet most of us also find it easier to help our fellow citizens one
on one than to exercise our democratic voice. We're far more likely
to volunteer to meet a specific human need than to work to elect
wiser leaders or pressure major economic, political, and cultural
institutions to act more responsibly.

I'm troubled by the division between personal acts of compassion and human solidarity and the work that's necessary to bring
about more structural change. As Jim Wallis points out, "In any
good community center that deals with the problems of youth, the
youth workers will spend most of their time talking about how the
young people can get their lives together, find the spiritual and

moral resources to make responsible choices, and take control of their own futures. Self-respect and mutual respect, cultural identity, community spirit, and social responsibility are all central. . . . But when describing the wider society, those same youth workers often will speak about the economic, racial, and social oppression that lies at the root of the problems their kids face."

Certainly, as Wallis suggests, the lines between service and advocacy often blur. I think of David Lewis, whose life was saved by the volunteer community of AA, and who regularly journeys into hellish crack houses carrying a message of hope and redemption. Or Chris Kim, who began, modestly enough, by extending a hand to the young man who'd tried to steal from his store, and ended up creating a center for his community. Or Ginny Nicarthy, who listened to the women whose husbands or boyfriends had beaten them, then helped them free themselves.

Volunteer efforts can help us regain our sense of connection, offer lifelines to beleaguered communities, and change people's lives. Like Gandhi's "constructive program," they can create new ways to address urgent problems, such as the pioneering work by Habitat for Humanity in building affordable houses. For certain kinds of crises, like the situation of young men and women trapped in bleak circles of violence, the only solution may be the development of powerful relationships with people who can give them the sense of being cared for that they've been previously denied, and show them a different way to live. Indeed, I suspect that the best responses to many of our society's ills may be local and decentralized approaches that draw upon such spiritual virtues as love, generosity, a willingness to listen, and the capacity to see a divine spark in even the most desperate and self-destructive of our fellow human beings.

Yet most of these one-on-one approaches require institutional support. In his powerful memoir, *Always Running,* the poet Luis Rodriguez describes his journey into East Los Angeles gang life in the 1960s—and how he finally left, thanks in large part to the influence and example of a former gang member turned community worker. Now Rodriguez works with Chicago gang kids who feel similarly angry and trapped, running poetry workshops where kids get a chance to express and exorcise their pain. But without the resources that allowed the community worker to turn social intervention into a full-time job, enabling him to spend hours and hours with Luis and his friends, Rodriguez might never have left the gang culture in the first place.

Recently, I saw a Seattle theater group that performs plays using street youth as actors. Drawing on the approach of the Brazilian director Augusto Boal, participants dramatized situations common to their experience, from dealing with abusive and drug-addicted families to facing harassment for being gay. Audience members, including other street kids, were encouraged to stop the action at key points, then take over the roles of individual characters to act out choices potentially more empowering and see how the rest of the impromptu cast responded. It was powerful work. It gave the kids confidence and hope. It moved everyone present.

But this theater group barely survives economically. They scrape and beg for dollars even as Seattle foundations and wealthy donors pour several hundred million dollars into lavish new buildings for the symphony, mainstream theaters, and other cultural institutions that they frequent. The lack of resources doesn't completely stop the theater group's work. But it means that they reach far fewer kids.

We should work to heal the wounds of our culture whether or not government programs support our efforts. But we should realize that, for example, Los Angeles gangs and Seattle street kids need more than mentors and models. They also need jobs to teach them skills and a sense of possibility, and drug treatment programs to help them overcome their addictions, and schools where teachers and counselors can spend the time and energy it takes to stop them from joining gangs or becoming homeless to begin with. Our critical social problems demand both individual and structural solutions. To rely on volunteer efforts is to duck the basic issue of common responsibility, and to ignore the fact that individual crises are often the result of collective forces.

I see too many compassionate individuals trying to stem rivers of need, while national political and economic leaders open the floodgates to widen them. We distribute two dozen loaves of bread to the hungry in one neighborhood, while Congress makes a decision that robs each poor community in the country of five hundred loaves. We build five houses with Habitat for Humanity, while escalating rents and government cutbacks throw a hundred families into the street. We laboriously restore a single stream while a timber company clear-cuts an entire watershed. Peter Cucchino, who's worked with Fordham University's community service center, worries that volunteer efforts may ultimately produce "a dissipation of energy into all sorts of charitable activities, without a focus on any kind of reform," averting "people's attention from the real victimization going on." As the Reverend William Sloane Coffin once said, "Charity must not be allowed to go bail for justice." The behavior of society's major political and economic institutions is too consequential to ignore, even if we have to spend less time working one-on-one, so we can spend more on public advocacy and organization.

Take, for example, the all-too-brief and cynical debate over the 1996 welfare reform bill. The organizational leaders who challenged it, like Marian Wright Edelman of the Children's Defense Fund, and Sharon Daly of Catholic Charities USA, received too little citizen support. In response to the argument that benevolent churches would take up the slack, Daly pointed out that the total annual contributions to churches and nonprofit human-service groups nationwide would have to more than double to cover the $15.1 billion in annual cuts scheduled in the bill. Edelman called the reductions a moral disaster. But despite the profound consequences, there was next to no grassroots outcry from those most involved in local service projects.

Among all the people I've talked to who work with the country's poorest and most desperate populations, none believed the bill would do anything but hurt those it was supposed to help. Although all had criticisms of the old system, none favored cutting food stamps for millions of working families trying to survive on bottom-end wages. None wanted federal funding cut for social service and child nutrition programs, or Supplemental Social Security ended for nearly a million largely elderly and disabled legal immigrants. None saw any virtue in reducing support for welfare recipients attending college, their prime path to reasonable economic prospects. Yet few of these dedicated professionals and volunteers raised their voices, or helped mobilize those they worked with.

Imagine if people who lived and worked in impoverished communities had gathered in protest. What if they'd expressed their outrage at their churches and temples, PTAs and block associations, in every outlet for village politics they could find? What if they'd demanded that the voices and experiences of the poor and powerless be at the center of the dialogue on solutions?

Had the nation heard more from those most intimately affected by the welfare bill's actions, or at least from people who regularly work with them, we might have produced some genuinely constructive reforms. We might have made a serious national commitment to invest resources in the most effective solutions available. Instead, silence allowed policy to be made by those most morally removed from the realities of the poor.

Consequently, many of us who might otherwise be working for a more just social order are now spending more time than ever trying to fill the gap in basic services created by government cuts. Many of the liberal funders who once supported the activism of marginalized communities have spearheaded this shift—pulling away from efforts, for instance, to secure adequate funding for low-income schools, and instead using their resources to support a handful of individual programs. (I've seen some parallel shifts in environmental organizations, toward buying a handful of threatened watersheds or timber stands instead of working to challenge our culture's more general destruction of the earth.) Meanwhile, those most damaged by the welfare cuts must struggle even harder to survive, which leaves them even less time and energy to make their voices heard. Their needs will now be addressed, if at all, by already stretched charities and caring individuals, rather than by common social institutions and common resources. What once was a shared responsibility has now been made private—and voluntary.

THE POLITICS OF WITNESS

So how should we proceed if we wish to act on a more personal level, yet make our individual actions more productive on a larger scale? We can resolve to work harder, solicit more donations, and bring in more people to help. Much of the one-on-one work we do will always be necessary, even in the best of societies. But we also need to be part of a larger public dialogue about the roots of the problems we face.

Greg Ricks, former director of Boston's powerful youth involvement program, City Year, compared the situation of community service volunteers to people trying to pull an endless sequence of drowning children out of a river. Of course we must address the immediate crisis, and try to rescue the children. But we also need to find out why they're falling into the river—because no matter how hard we try, we lack the resources, strength, and stamina to save them all. So we must go upstream to fix the broken bridge, stop the people who are pushing the children in, or do whatever else will prevent the victims from ending up in the water to begin with.

How do we combine this with a more personal touch? The link, I believe, is the concept of witness, developed by people like Dorothy Day, who founded the Catholic Worker movement. We can use our service efforts to help cross daunting boundaries, like those of race and class. We can listen to those who come to the food banks, homeless shelters, and battered women's centers, and

learn how they got there. We can talk to those on the street, and
hear their stories. We can work to understand why our society
produces so much needless human pain.

Maybe we'll decide that the answer lies in the impossibility of
supporting a family on a minimum wage that has fallen further
and further behind the actual cost of living. Or we'll focus on cuts
in food stamps, on the lack of adequate child care and health care,
on the outmigration of jobs. Or on the endless waiting lists for
treatment programs that might offer hope even for those who've
collaborated in their own addictions. Appropriate solutions will
undoubtedly require supporting powerful local projects with common resources. But whatever stories we encounter, whatever conclusions we draw, we can't keep them to ourselves.

The politics of witness involves taking these examples and lessons to the village square—or its contemporary equivalent—and
then doing our best to convey them to as many others as possible.
It means using them to refute myths that justify callousness and
withdrawal. It also implies that we do all we can to help those
habitually ignored or silenced to find their own voices and platforms, such as the newspapers written by the homeless.

An ethic of witness affirms the bonds that link us. It helps us
avoid being so ground down by our efforts to ease day-to-day
miseries that we have no time to address their larger context. Given
the current drift of American culture, it's hard for those of us who
work in beleaguered communities not to feel defensive, on the losing end of history. We may even mute our voices, lest we offend
those whose financial and political resources our community institutions may depend on. Yet at least some of the energy we spend
on volunteering must be directed toward the political roots of the
crises we address. For if we don't challenge the meanness of our
time, we can hardly expect others to do so in our place.

"LET'S NOT TALK ABOUT THE BAD THINGS"

I've discussed ways everyday social networks can help us get involved. But they can also insulate us from others. They can suppress as well as expand civic dialogue, reinforcing our moral cocoons as well as dissolving them. In my time at Hanford, for instance, I visited churches and schools, bridge clubs and bars, virtually every domain of everyday life. Participants in the nuclear enterprise rarely discussed the downside of their work—neither the potential for global annihilation from bombs created with the plutonium they produced, nor their enterprise's horrific environmental consequences. As one Hanford wife said, when I raised these questions, "Let's not talk about the bad things."

Hanford may be an extreme example, but I see a similar culturally and economically reinforced silence in other domains. Corporate whistleblowers often risk their careers. Southerners resisting the civil rights movement fired blacks who spoke out, and used social pressure to isolate whites who supported integration. In Amarillo, Texas, the United Way cut off all funds to Catholic Family Services because Bishop Leroy Matthiesen had suggested that workers who assembled the final nuclear warheads at the nearby Pantex plant should consider the moral implications of their work.

The desire for community approval can make it harder to bring up urgent social concerns, sometimes especially among people who know and respect us. We may fear being branded as dissenters or outsiders, merely for raising controversial ideas. Occasionally our passivity is the result of misplaced politeness: We don't want to intrude on people we care about. We don't want to depress them. We fear the tension that emerges when we switch from discussing the latest movies or *Seinfeld* reruns to voicing emotionally loaded issues. We fear we'll trigger family fights or jeopardize our friendships.

"It's always harder to take a stand in your own neighborhood and community," says Suzy Marks, "to leaflet at your own local market or synagogue. Most of us got involved after being approached by someone we knew. But that doesn't make it easier. If I'm really brave, why was I so hesitant and ashamed to talk about these issues with my friends? It's simpler with people who don't know you. You can always raise hell in a strange town."

The French theorist Michel Foucault and other social philosophers in his tradition view daily life as a web of domination that suppresses critical dialogue at every turn and can only be challenged through "transgression" at the margins. I think the actual picture is more complex, and that we have more latitude to create change than such analyses acknowledge. Most of the networks and associations of civil society can either promote or hamper an ethic of common responsibility. To be sure, it's a risk, at least a psychological one, to "talk about the bad things" within these networks. But whether or not they become conduits for addressing our most critical public issues depends on what we do.

BEYOND OUR COCOONS

We should never underestimate the potential social power of our culture's existing villages, even those that appear, at first glance, self-absorbed or frivolous. In 1984, a computer scientist named Glenn Hening began worrying about the pollution and deterioration of the California beaches where he loved to surf. He'd just become a father and wondered whether, when his daughter grew older, she'd be able to enjoy them at all. He was also increasingly angry at the stereotype of surfers as dumb blond party guys "whose total vocabulary consists of 'hang ten,' 'cowabunga,' and 'far out.' " He decided to counteract that image by persuading his fellow surfers "to use their skills to protect the marine environment for all of us."

Glenn first talked to surfer friends who were similarly concerned. Their inaugural effort addressed the problem of a Malibu lagoon that the Parks Department was managing badly and whose spillage was gradually changing the shape of the waves on an adjacent beach. The group, now called the Surfrider Foundation, next challenged the dumping of contaminated waste into that same lagoon, and of sewage into Santa Monica Bay. Fellow surfers, delighted to find a way to fight to protect their beaches, enlisted in droves.

By the early 1990s, Surfrider won the second largest Clean Water Act suit in American history, stopping pulp mills run by Louisiana-Pacific and Simpson Paper from polluting northern California's Humboldt Bay. Members testified at hearings, filed lawsuits, educated schoolchildren about marine ecology, challenged destructive developments, and monitored coastal water pollution levels nationwide. They enlisted swimmers, divers, beachcombers, windsurfers, sympathetic environmental scientists, and others who love the marine environment. The organization now has 25,000 members in chapters throughout the United States, plus affiliates in Australia, Japan, France, Brazil, and Mexico. They've also initiated the Snowrider Project, which educates skiers and snowboarders about the links between the mountains where they play and the watersheds below, and encourages them to exercise a similar sense of stewardship.

Glenn believes he's helped change the culture of his community. "Twenty years ago, a beach full of surfers would end up being a beach full of trash. We let developers wreck some of the finest surfing areas on the planet—including one in Orange County right across from the national headquarters of Hobie Surfboards and *Surfing* magazine. That doesn't happen anymore. By now, the issues we've raised have gained the attention of surfers everywhere. They think about water quality, the impact of development, the need for government agencies to protect the environment. We created a new thread in the weave of what it means to be a surfer."

Chapter Nine

Widening the Circle

I do not forget that my voice is but one voice, my experience a mere drop in the sea, my knowledge no greater than the visual field in a microscope, my mind's eye a mirror that reflects a small corner of the world.

—C. G. JUNG

The line separating good and evil runs through the heart of every human being, and who is willing to destroy a piece of his own heart?

—ALEXANDER SOLZHENITSYN

Even when we build on the foundation of our existing values and knowledge, social involvement helps us enter new worlds. We take on new priorities, gain new skills, meet new people, hear and heed new stories. Issues once at the margins of our vision become the focus of our lives. Distractions that once consumed us become peripheral. Upon accepting the challenge of trying to shape a different future, we feel a sense of larger purpose. We become linked with others who share our vision.

If we're lucky, the activist communities we join or create can become places where we feel safe not only in talking about the issues at hand, but in admitting uncertainties and vulnerabilities. As Richard Flacks points out, America's most powerful citizen movements have flourished when the communities they built not only achieved tangible victories but also helped participants nurture their self-development. By the same token, they've crumbled when participants felt like mere cannon fodder for the cause.

At their best, these communities enable us to pool our individual energies into a single common power. They help us sustain our enthusiasm and remind us that we're not alone, even when expressing our most urgent concerns. Engaged communities provide opportunities for us to build deep friendships and to learn from inspiring mentors. Providing a sense of shared purpose and company for the journey, they're essential if we're going to remain committed over the long haul.

Yet activist communities, like any others, can easily become insular. It's tempting to share our visions only with those who already agree with us. But if M. Scott Peck is right, and I believe he is, that very impulse is counterproductive. "The great enemy of community is exclusivity," he says. "Groups that exclude others because they are poor or doubters or divorced or sinners or of some different race or nationality are not communities; they are cliques—actually defensive bastions against community." True communities are "always reaching to extend themselves."

When we're working to change society, it's tempting to retreat into isolated cliques. Reaching out to people who don't share our assumptions is definitely a risk. They might reject us, or challenge our motives or arguments. We might feel unprepared and inadequate, unable to change their minds. Our visibility might bring economic or social costs. It's safer to stay hunkered down with our fellow believers. After a while, we may regard ourselves as more noble, pure, and virtuous than those lesser souls who remain uninvolved. Why risk having our visions attacked?

In the words of a longtime peace worker, activists too often spend our time "haranguing each other on what we're doing wrong, bemoaning why no one understands our positions, clinging to our isolation as if it proved our rightness. If we want peace in the Middle East, we need to do more than berate the Jewish fundamentalists and Netanyahu. We need to reach new people and help them understand why we hold the views we do. We need to go out and speak at the synagogues and talk at the Hadassah meetings."

At its worst, insularity breeds a dangerous cultishness. I think of the Leninist sects that splintered the 1960s antiwar movement, and which persist to this day, with members selling their newspapers on city street corners and hectoring passersby with their bullhorns. The activists involved in such groups may be dedicated and courageous, taking on various worthy causes. More often, however, they act like malevolent wind-up toys, whose sole mission is to drive all other activists completely crazy. They browbeat people with their "correct line," disrupt coalitions, and relentlessly refuse to listen to the views of others. Their core sins are intertwined: an absence of democratic principles and a pervasive contempt for those who disagree with them.

Yet even activists with far more generous and ecumenical spirits can succumb to insularity. I've seen too many well-meaning groups whose members write letters, hold modest vigils, post fliers, and put together paper coalitions—yet never take the trouble to reach out and talk to anyone except those who already back their causes.

Granted, outreach is hard. It requires us to meet people where they live, not where we might like them to be. It makes us explain our perspectives, and sometimes our motivations. Outreach can lead to rejection, even in our own village networks. The nun from COPS who visited Virginia Ramirez after she'd stormed out of the meeting might have been turned away at the door. Alison Smith might have been ignored or ridiculed at the community forums where she made the case for campaign reform. When Bill Cusak continued to speak out at his South Carolina Rotary Club even after "they kind of treated me like I had the plague," he risked permanently losing close friends. Sometimes involvement requires taking physical risks as well, as when environmental activists in certain heated fights face the prospect of being attacked by police or right-wing vigilantes, or when David Lewis risks his life by going to crack houses, bars, and shooting galleries, to enlist desperate addicts in his Free at Last programs.

Without outreach isolation becomes self-perpetuating. Like *Dr. Strangelove*'s General Jack D. Ripper, who launches a nuclear attack because he fears the Russians are corrupting his "precious bodily fluids," activists caught in the enclave sensibility can become obsessed with purity, taking refuge within their movement's familiar language and values; fearing contamination from outside interlopers with less than perfect political consciousness; ending up, as a longtime Australian labor activist once said, "run by what we dread instead of by what we want."

ARMORED WITH LANGUAGE

The further we get into our causes, the more likely we are to believe that everyone shares our knowledge and assumptions, and that can be dangerous too. Often we armor ourselves with language, talking of hegemony and patriarchy, imperialism and oppression, as if everyone assigns the same meaning to these words that we do, and as if everyone enjoys wallowing in rhetoric. Used appropriately, the phrases and acronyms we adopt can serve as a useful shorthand among those already in the know, like the specialized language of scientists; if we're talking about the Multilateral Agreement on Investments (MAI) to people already working on the issue, there's no need to spell out its complex implications every time—not to mention that mouthful of a name. But our language can also exclude others who haven't learned the right words and feel less confident in their beliefs, and thus it can leave us more isolated from the rest of the world.

It's especially important to explain ourselves clearly to new people, to walk them through the process that produced our perspectives—as the COPS trainers did with people like Virginia—so they can reclaim their own voice and take their own stands. Often we fail to appreciate how foreign social engagement seems to those who've not yet made it part of their lives. We forget that we were hesitant at first, too, doubtful and confused. We risk portraying ourselves as the experts to whom others should defer, creating our own unreachable perfect standards.

The University of Nebraska student group that addressed the crisis of family farms worked hard at continually enlisting new members. Yet even there, a rift grew between initial participants, who quickly became highly knowledgeable about farm issues, and those who joined later on. "It becomes hard to relate to someone with a different level of understanding," says one of the founders. "Our efforts to educate people often blow them out of the water instead of painstakingly taking them along. It's almost like we have to create another organizational level for those just coming in."

Movements flourish, as I've suggested, when discussions in thousands of ordinary communities bring issues to public attention. And movements die out when activists talk with no one but themselves. But the conversations with "outsiders" must be real. They must be give-and-take exchanges, accessible and particularized. They must include the stories that impelled us to act in the first place, and not merely the abstractions and rhetorical shorthand that come to represent those stories.

THE LIMITS OF IDENTITY

A large part of the most energetic social justice activism in recent years has centered on the need to recognize and respect people's distinct experiences as women, African Americans, gays, or members of some other marginalized group. These movements raise vital questions and foster community for many whose voices have long been silenced. Their existence is cause for significant hope.

But focusing solely on the wounds and needs of our particular groups can leave efforts to bring about social justice fractured and divided, unable to support a common vision. As the African American student body president of New York's Hunter College said, lamenting the splits in a coalition against crippling tuition hikes, "I'm tired of Puerto Ricans who don't speak to Dominicans. Black people who don't speak to nobody who speaks Spanish even if they're blacker than them. And nobody speaking to whites. I'm just not into it."

In 1997, Washington State voters rejected, by a twenty-point margin, an initiative that would have protected people from being fired for being gay. Its passage would have been a major victory

for human dignity. For one thing, depriving people of their livelihood because of their sexual orientation is barbaric. For another,
if more gays and lesbians felt able to be out at work, their colleagues might better understand their lives and begin to feel a bond
of human empathy. But I believe the initiative's failure was due to
more than homophobia, particularly since pre-election polls suggested that voters agreed with its basic idea. In a time when all
manner of people are routinely laid off at the whim of managers,
owners, or stockholders, it's easy for the political right to play on
growing class divisions and economic uncertainty and use them to
scapegoat. In Washington, opponents of the initiative argued that
if you were gay and got fired for no apparent reason, you'd have
"special rights," a potential claim for redress, but if you were
straight, and lost your job under identical circumstances, you
would not.

It would have been hard to pass the initiative in any case, given
powerful sexual prejudices. Also, the campaign relied too heavily
on its core constituency in Seattle and failed to build an adequate
statewide infrastructure. But what ultimately led to its failure, I
believe, was the absence of enough strong, complementary efforts
that addressed the vulnerabilities that all people feel, gay or
straight, at their workplaces. If more activists were talking about
the need for greater workplace protection for *everyone*, and the
need for addressing the arbitrary exercise of power at its roots, the
right would have found it harder to scapegoat gays, or anyone else.

The lesson here is not to stop challenging injustices that arise
from people's particular identities and backgrounds. But to promote human dignity, we need to build coalitions that are as broad
as possible. In addition to the important task of staking out rights
for specific marginalized groups, we also need to organize around
issues that affect everyone, such as the unprecedented gap between
rich and poor, the corrupting influence of unaccountable wealth,
the threats to our environment, and the general sense of powerlessness that pervades America today. And we need to point out
that the same political forces that would send gays back to the

closet and that have attempted to end even the most modest affirmative action programs also consistently serve larger interests of wealth and power.

In the absence of inclusive alternative visions, the political right is free to use its own version of identity politics to whip up support, appealing to the beleaguered white men supposedly left out in the cold. Think of the Jesse Helms commercial that showed a pair of white hands crumpling a rejection slip while a voice-over explained how the man had lost out for a job to a less-qualified minority applicant. Unless we pay heed to the stories of all whom our society makes expendable, we set the stage for backlash.

People in marginalized communities do need to come together for support. "If I see Asian and Latino groups," says Sonya Vetra Tinsley, "or gays and lesbians of color, that's a sign of a healthy community. I started a black women's group at Emory, because our problems aren't always the same as those of black men, and they certainly aren't always the same as those of white women. Sometimes these groups work together. Sometimes they work apart. To me, that makes people stronger."

But Sonya also stresses the need to reach out, which is why she worked so hard building interracial coalitions. "There's so much mistrust these days," she explains. "But if people work together day to day, communication lines are created. When a crisis happens, they don't have to jump up and point accusational fingers at each other. They can talk and work things out."

A Good Atheist

Practically speaking, the key to successful outreach lies in finding perspectives and concerns we share with the communities we approach. The one-hundred-year-old environmentalist Hazel Wolf recalls a talk she gave at a Seventh-Day Adventist college. Immediately afterward, an audience member asked her why she was an atheist. "Why are you Christians?" she responded. "Because your parents were. If your parents were Moslems, you'd be Moslems. I'm an atheist because my parents were. There are some bad Christians. But most Christians are good. There are some bad atheists. But most atheists are good. I'm just trying to be a good atheist."

A good atheist, Hazel continued, is required to take care of the earth, just as a good Christian is. "And just in case I'm wrong, I have some insurance. Because Jesus said to the man, 'You fed me when I was hungry, clothed me when I was naked, visited me when I was in prison. If you've done this to the least of these, you will be on my right hand in heaven.' Well, I've worked for child welfare, worked for Medicaid to take care of the sick. The only other time I came to this town was to visit the prison up on the hill. So I just might be seeing you guys in heaven." The audience loved her, this fiery great-grandmother with her white hair, white blouse, lined face, and playful style.

Reaching out to bring people together came naturally to Hazel. In 1979, when she was only eighty-one, she organized a conference of environmental groups, church associations, and Native American tribes. When a Yakima Indian leader arrived late the first morning because his motel forgot to wake him, Hazel asked, in her most mischievous voice, "How come you noble savages are staying at a motel, when us whites have to sleep on the cold floor? You know, we're all nonsmokers," she added, "so it's no use dragging out the peace pipes." The two became instant friends, and they and the others at the conference joined to block a dangerously sited oil port on the Washington coast. "We've never needed to have another conference," Hazel says, "because now we automatically work together."

Hazel was born in British Columbia in 1898. Her father, a cook on freighters, died in an accident at sea when Hazel was eight. Her mother belonged to the Wobblies, the Industrial Workers of the World, and eked out a living scrubbing floors, working in an overalls factory, and taking in boarders. Hazel grew up strong and energetic, swimming in the slough near the house, playing basketball, outrunning the local policemen.

She also developed a sense of compassion. Early on, she was exposed to the harsh lives of people in her neighborhood, for instance the local prostitutes. There was an orphanage nearby, and when Hazel selected softball players for her team, she chose the orphans first—so, she says, "they'd feel wanted, reaching out to them in my childish way." One day Hazel and some friends threw snowballs at the windows of the local Chinese laundry, and took off running when one of the windows broke. Later one of the laundry workers returned a valuable brooch that the parent of one of the children had left attached to a piece of clothing, and Hazel felt terrible for having harassed them. "I realized how hardworking and honest they were, even when everyone taunted them."

The Canadian economy hit the skids shortly after World War I, so Hazel moved to Washington State. Her first job was pasting "Made in Japan" stickers on plastic Easter bunnies. Then one day a Communist Party organizer circulated a petition for unemployment insurance. The issue touched Hazel's heart, because she'd been in and out of work far more than she wanted, and was struggling to support a daughter from a brief marriage. So she signed the petition and joined the Party. Soon she was writing letters to politicians, demonstrating at the state capitol, carrying evicted families' furniture back into their houses, and occupying Seattle's city hall. She fought for food, housing, and clothing for the poor and unemployed. She also helped the Party organize a Senior Citizens Union, whose efforts helped secure the first public pension program in the country, a model for Social Security. Hazel considers this "one of the most exciting and delightful periods" in her life.

All the while she was raising her daughter and working as a legal secretary. Having never made it past eighth grade, she enrolled in night school and at age thirty-four entered the University of Washington. But adult students were rare at the time, and the school provided no support systems for single mothers like her.

Eventually Hazel dropped out and went back to work for a Seattle civil rights lawyer, with whom she stayed for more than twenty years.

She'd left the Party by then, frustrated at its insularity. "I liked them in the thirties, when they marched on the state capitol. But I've always been an action kind of person, and it changed when they just sat around talking about Karl Marx, who always bored me. I never got past the first chapter in that big book of his. So I gradually quit going to meetings and paying my dues. I just drifted away."

But Hazel was still a target for those who wanted to stamp out every hint of dissent in America. In 1958, when she'd been out of the Communist Party for thirteen years, the FBI tried to deport her. Hazel resisted, "while those stupid characters bent heaven and earth to send me back to Canada." Along the way, she stopped the deportation of radicals from England, Finland, Norway, and the Philippines, all of whom had committed the same unpardonable sin of speaking out. Finally, after sixteen years, the government caved in and let Hazel become a citizen.

Not until the 1960s (and when Hazel was in her sixties) did she take part in the environmental movement, but when she did it was with her characteristic passion and high spirits. A friend who belonged to the Audubon Society had long badgered her to join. Eventually she did, then went on an Audubon field trip to a local park. Lending her a pair of binoculars, Hazel's friend pointed out a small brown bird, which was pecking and eating as it made its way up a tree. "Suddenly I realized how much we had in common," she says. "He works hard for his living, for his food. So do I. He has his lifestyle and routine. He always goes up the tree, never down. He gets up in the morning and goes through his day, just like me. I'd never paid much attention to birds before, hardly even noticed them. But I felt something in common. I liked that Audubon was committed to protecting them."

It was a revelatory moment, unleashing what would become a burning concern for the natural world. Eager to do more than just watch birds, Hazel soon became the secretary of Audubon's Seattle chapter, a position she's held for the past thirty-five years. Living on Social Security and a Section Eight rent subsidy, she's founded twenty-one of the state's twenty-six Audubon chapters. She's built alliances, drawn new people into the organization, forged links between environmental and social justice activists. I remember her calling to enlist me in a Hanford coalition, explaining ever so persistently and teasingly why I needed to join. I routinely meet activists who mention similar experiences, describing how Hazel convinced them to lead a particular nature tour or speak out on watersheds or old-growth forests, and how they've been at it ever since—for five, ten, fifteen years, or longer.

"Obviously, I'm enjoying all this," Hazel told me in between taking phone calls to help set up a conference and checking the action alerts that came in on her fax machine. "When you don't get involved, you're missing something. I've learned to speak in public, which always terrified me. I've learned not to come on too hard, because no one listens when you're ranting and raving. I've met so many people I respect."

Throughout her life, Hazel's worked to broaden the constituencies for her causes. Most recently, she's worked to persuade environmentalists to support the organizing of California strawberry workers, because, she says, "even if they don't care about the labor aspects, they can understand the pesticides." By the same token, she's pushed unions to take on ecological issues. Middle-class environmental groups, she believes, need to take seriously the lives of those struggling to survive as carpenters or loggers, or raising their children near toxic dumps or noxious incinerators because those are the only neighborhoods they can afford. She's helped start a new environmental justice coalition, to forge links between these often contentious groups.

Coalitions form, Hazel says, "when different people come together, often for different reasons. If you want to get people to respond, to do things, it also helps to make them laugh. When people see me having such a good time with all this, maybe it inspires them."

BIRDS THAT NEED WATCHING

I've always felt that one of Hazel's most effective tools is her mischievous sense of humor. When the state legislature proposed an innocuous bill to give free fishing licenses to all visually impaired people, Hazel convinced a friend of hers to offer a brief amendment—"and hunting licenses." The legislators loved it. In her eighties Hazel repeatedly visited Nicaragua as part of her opposition to U.S. Central America interventions. One time a Republican congressman came up to her in Managua and said, in a tone that suggested she was either feeble minded or frivolous, "I hear you're a bird-watcher." "Yes," said Hazel. "And there are some birds in Washington, D.C., that really need watching."

Because we're so serious about our issues, we often don't realize that humor can be our most effective tool. A few years ago the Seattle city council wanted to ban all signs and posters on telephone poles. An ad hoc coalition of musicians, garage salers, community activists, and people worried about lost pets formed to oppose the ordinance. When the council finally held a public hearing, Pete Knutson testified that to get to his fishing boat he had to drive past commercial billboards selling him underwear and cigarettes. "Every day for six months I had to look at that baseball player Jim Palmer, stretched out on a billboard wearing nothing but his skivvies. Eight in the morning, every morning, you're trying to get on the freeway and hold your cup of coffee and here's some guy in your face, bulging out of his underpants. But that's okay. Someone paid big money to put Jim Palmer's crotch in my face." The hearing erupted with laughter. And, although the issue's still being debated in Seattle, humor enabled Pete to challenge the ban's unfairness in a manner that briefly reached even its proponents.

Here's another example: A few years ago, after extensive city-wide meetings, San Francisco's Tenderloin Housing Clinic prepared a rent-control initiative. When the measure was designated Proposition H, they took advantage of the name's similarity to that of the hemorrhoid cream by calling it "relief for rental pain" and distributing literature that included a picture of a female doctor prescribing it. The image stuck in the public mind. With the help of a tremendous mobilization of low-income tenants, the measure passed, although proponents were outspent by more than ten to one. Later the same group brought people in polar bear costumes to a board of supervisors hearing on the lack of adequate heat in residential hotels. Clearly humor can help us open both hearts and minds.

An Ethic of Listening

Whenever we reach across traditional boundaries, we create opportunities for learning and growth. In *Everyday Blessings,* Jon and Myla Kabat-Zinn advise parents that they can't simply repeat what "worked well" in their earlier child-rearing experience. Instead, they say, we need to stay in the present moment with our kids, "to meet it freshly" enough to understand their concerns and meet their needs. So, too, with social involvement. After a while, much of what we do will become familiar, even routine: calling those on our phone trees, posting our fliers, sending out our mailings, holding up the same kinds of signs at the same kinds of vigils. These actions are necessary, to be sure, but they rarely renew or expand our vision. That happens only when we place ourselves in circumstances that require us to view our efforts and ourselves with new eyes.

We can also stay fresh by reaching within. To hear others clearly, or to hear our own heart, we may need to momentarily still our own voice. In his essay "The Spiritual Heart of Service," psychiatrist William Deikman distinguishes between what he calls the "survival self," or "instrumental consciousness," by which we view ourselves as separate and distinct from our world, and the "spiritual self," or "receptive consciousness," by which we realize our connection to others and the world as a whole. "Both modes of consciousness are needed," Deikman explains. The virtue of instrumental consciousness is that it helps us focus, achieve material goals, carry out practical tasks. But it also limits our ability to be part of something larger, makes us feel more isolated and alone than we need to be, and, unchecked, leads to exploitation and greed. Receptive consciousness, taken alone, breeds passivity. It gives us no way to defend what we believe in against the all-too-instrumental predators of the world. But it helps us view ourselves as part of a larger life process. It gives us a sense of meaning and equanimity. It is the means by which we reach out to our fellow human beings. Without the spiritual self, in other words, we're left disconnected and mistrusting.

At its best, receptive consciousness encourages humility, reminding us both that we are imperfect and that others have much to teach us. It helps us to acknowledge that our positions on social issues may be flawed, and our own motives mixed. As Alexander Solzhenitsyn writes, "The line separating good and evil runs through the heart of every human being, and who is willing to destroy a piece of his own heart?"

Wholeness requires that we know our limitations. I once ate at a Chinese restaurant with paranoid fortune cookies. "Pay no attention to what others tell you," said one. "You know better than anyone." An ethic of receptivity is based on precisely the opposite assumption—that our knowledge and perceptions will always be partial, and that we learn best from dialogue with others. "I do not forget," writes psychologist C. G. Jung, "that my voice is but one voice, my experience a mere drop in the sea, my knowledge no greater than the visual field in a microscope, my mind's eye a mirror that reflects a small corner of the world."

This perspective, says Ginny Nicarthy, is consistent with Quaker and Gandhian views of humanity. "You try to recognize the good in every person, and try to speak to that, while maintaining your own values, goals, and autonomy. My vision of the world is more than the good guys and bad guys, friends and enemies, just and unjust, because all of us have good and bad elements within us. We have to work to understand all people from their own perspectives."

Ginny applies this philosophy to the abortion debate. "My friends tend to bristle when I say that some antiabortionists are decent people who truly believe abortion is morally wrong. They say that opposition to choice is just one more way to push women back into traditional roles in the kitchen, bedroom, and nursery. That's certainly true for many of the right-to-life activists. But I know that others are taking a position that from their perspective is defensible and even humane. Whatever their motivation, their campaigns damage women's lives. But we can't create a just world unless we're willing to work at listening to each other. Or being open to changing our minds on some issues. Or at least searching for common ground. It's hard to seriously consider ideas that seem to threaten our values, but we have to try."

This doesn't mean letting go of our sense of urgency. When our heart cries out against injustice, it's wise to pay heed. But we would also do well to cultivate a bit of humility. We can only hear the souls of others if we silence the clamor of our own obsessions and our assumptions about how the world should be. If we truly listen to those who don't share our beliefs we may build unexpected bonds.

When Alison Smith took on the issue of marine oil recycling, she joined a committee that drew together different constituencies: environmentalists, representatives of state and local government, wharf owners, the petroleum industry. "And as we worked together, I developed a growing respect for the people. One guy came off at first like a stick-in-the-mud. But then I realized he always showed up at meetings, which is the first step. We got past the sneering cynicism that you'll never get this person on board because he's a bureaucrat, or she works for an oil company. We were working with a petroleum industry representative who seemed like such a pill. She never contributed one positive word. But in the end she got on board and supported our plan—I think because we'd heard her out often enough to reassure her that our bill wasn't some horrible thing that was simply aimed at shutting business down. In the end, she testified for us, as did everyone else we enlisted."

Listening carefully can create powerful personal transformations, which in turn can bring about profound social changes. The corporate culture of Inland Steel didn't shift until general manager Steven Bowsher attended the Atlanta seminar, and found himself the sole white upper-management person listening to what it means to be black in America. Deborah Prothrow-Stith found her impetus to act after listening to the young man on her operating table. John Weeks made it his mission to link the world of alternative medicine with the vastly different world of health care's financial gatekeepers, the HMOs and insurance companies. The more we listen to those whose experiences and perspectives are unfamiliar, the more we realize what draws us together.

COMMON AIR, COMMON GROUND

Alliances that emerge from this process can be as powerful as they are unexpected. In *The Activist's Handbook,* a terrific study of strategies and tactics for social change, longtime housing activist Randy Shaw describes a coalition that fought a proposed garbage incinerator in the Brooklyn navy yard for fifteen years. The fifty-five-story incinerator was supposed to convert garbage into electrical energy, but it would also have produced toxic emissions, including a half-ton of lead per year, further saturating already polluted neighborhoods like Williamsburg.

Leaders in communities adjacent to the navy yard quickly opposed the project. But they'd long been at each other's throats, the hostility being especially fierce between the Hasidic members of the

United Jewish Organization (UJO) and the Puerto Ricans and Dominicans, who worked together in an organization called El Puente. They'd fought over subsidized housing (the Hasidim occupied
a disproportionate share), control of local public schools, and com-
parative levels of police protection. They'd traded accusations of
bigotry and anti-Semitism. In the process, they'd built up a tremendous—and seemingly insurmountable—legacy of mistrust.

But they came together for the health of their children—first in
a fight to limit emissions at a local toxic waste facility called Radiac, and then in opposition to the incinerator. When a Hasidic
rabbi, David Niederman of UJO, walked into the offices of El
Puente and offered to help lead a march against Radiac, he inau-
gurated a historic rapprochement. El Puente's founder, Luis Garden Acosta, responded by reaching out not only to the Hasidim
but also to the Poles, Italians, and other white ethnics in the area.
Incinerator opponents then brought in additional allies, such as the
environmental activists of the New York Public Interest Research
Group (NYPIRG). Coordinating joint responses, coalition members raised complementary issues and spoke from complementary
passions.

Though they had no history of working together, the groups
continued to mobilize their constituencies and continue their protests. In time, Brooklyn borough officials joined in. The coalition
even enlisted American Legion posts and historic preservation organizations after discovering that the incinerator would pave over
a burial ground for Revolutionary War prisoners. It continued to
organize and demonstrate, despite hostility from such major media
outlets as the *New York Times*, reversals of support by elected
officials including Mayors David Dinkins and Rudy Giuliani, and
opposition from most of the New York City power structure. Finally, in July 1996, NYPIRG worked out a deal in the state legislature, which ended the incinerator project for good. As Garden
Acosta said, "In our common air we have found our common
ground."

Pete Knutson built a similarly disparate coalition that extended from Sierra Club activists and Native American tribes to highly conservative Pentecostal churches of which fishermen were members. When a local affiliate of the fundamentalist Trinity Broadcasting Network broadcast a segment supporting Initiative 640, a gillnetter named John, who belonged to a local Assemblies of God church, called up the reporter and asked, "Do you know who Jesus's disciples were? They were fishermen. What do you think Jesus is going to do when he comes back and finds out you've stopped people from making a living by fishing? He's going to rip your head off."

Taken aback, the reporter apologized, as did John for losing his temper. The two prayed together, and Trinity gave the fishermen a half hour to make their case on the show. John also talked about the initiative with his minister, who decided, after dreaming about a related passage from Isaiah, that it was indeed a pressing moral issue. The minister in turn helped shatter stereotypes of who does and does not typically support environmental concerns by giving invocations against greed at fishermen's rallies and sending out fliers to the state's three hundred Assemblies of God congregations, endorsing the gillnetters' cause.

"We've got to keep approaching the Pentecostals," Pete says, later on, thinking back on the campaign. "Lots of their members are getting economically screwed. They mistrust the giant corporations. But if we don't reach out to them and establish some dialogue, they're going to be pulled into the right-wing coalitions."

An important element in maintaining complicated alliances like Pete's anti-640 group is recognizing that certain subjects need to remain off-limits. Former COPS lead organizer Ernie Cortes bluntly confronted a priest who wanted to raise the issue of school vouchers during a discussion COPS was leading about public schools. The issue would have fractured their coalition, Cortes told him. COPS was committed to public schools and would have to fight him if he raised it. The priest agreed to table the matter.

Though it's hard to reach beyond the "usual suspects" in our activist communities, it can't be avoided. As the singer and civil rights activist Bernice Reagon, of Sweet Honey in the Rock, points out, "If you're in a coalition and you're comfortable, you know it's not broad enough." We need this necessary discomfort both to achieve success and to renew our vision.

Unlikely Allies

The discomfort is never greater than when we create coalitions with people with whom we disagree on more issues than not. For example, when I look at the policies of the current Republican leadership I see mostly bullying and greed. But even among the most conservative people in Congress are some who've resisted being mere hired guns for the wealthy and powerful. I was infuriated by Orrin Hatch's dismissal of Anita Hill during the Clarence Thomas hearings. Yet as a staunch Mormon (a religion historically friendly to neither women nor blacks), Hatch has relentlessly challenged the tobacco industry and made unlikely alliances with people like Ted Kennedy and Tom Harkin to put more money into children's health care and support research into alternative medicine. Former congresswoman Linda Smith, in my state of Washington, is a hardcore fundamentalist whose positions on most social and economic issues I abhor. Yet she's gone to the mat repeatedly for campaign finance reform, bucking her Republican colleagues. She also helped defeat Clinton's attempt to extend the NAFTA trade agreement. This outcome, in my view, was a major victory for environmental and economic accountability, and for the right of local communities to determine their destiny.

When I look at the ordinary followers of the right-wing agenda, the picture gets more complicated still. I believe many in the religious right's core constituency have dangerous blind spots on issues like abortion and homosexuality. They've failed to grapple, I believe, with the complex human stories behind the behavior they demonize. Yet when the Pew Center for the People & the Press has surveyed the conservative religious constituency they call "the moralists," they've found that a solid majority mistrust corporate power, support environmental protection and regulation, and believe the government should take an active role in improving health care, housing, and education for low- and middle-income families. This means there's common ground, plenty of it, even among people of widely different ideological perspectives. Coalitions can be formed around certain basic issues of concern to all communities.

Examples abound of such productive bridging. The Green Scissors Coalition brings together environmental groups like Friends of the Earth with the conservative National Taxpayers Union, and targets ecologically damaging corporate welfare projects. Recent coalitions against granting China favorable trade status have included not only representatives from labor and human rights groups, but also people like Gary Bauer, Reagan's former chief domestic policy advisor. Bauer now heads the conservative Family Research Council, and has been outraged by China's persecution of religious Christians. Among the staunchest supporters of the successful UPS strike, in 1997, was a group of highly conservative former military officers from the Independent Pilots Union: They held firm and risked their $80,000-a-year jobs by refusing to cross the picket line of $8-an-hour UPS part-timers. The community of radical evangelicals who publish *Sojourners* fought the 1996 "welfare reform" as hard as they could. Founder Jim Wallis was arrested while demonstrating in the halls of Congress. But when the measure passed, *Sojourners* convened a "Christian Roundtable" on ways churches could respond creatively to the new urgencies created by the bill. Participants talked and prayed with groups as diverse as the National Council of Churches, the U.S. Catholic Conference, the National Association of Evangelicals, the Family Research Council, and the Promise Keepers.

In the words of Don Snow, who's long campaigned for a sustainable regional economy through Montana's Northern Lights Institute, "Strange bedfellows make interesting kids. To listen to people who you disagree with most ardently, you come out changed from the experience, from understanding their different beliefs and perspectives."

Sometimes the search for justice requires us to reach out to people whose actions appall us. In the late 1980s, the human rights lawyer Julia Devin joined with the Quaker physician Charlie Clements and the activist Seattle congressman Jim McDermott in an effort to negotiate an agreement for medical neutrality in El Salvador. It was the height of the Salvadoran terror; the U.S.-trained military had just brutally murdered six Jesuit priests at the University of Central America, as well as their housekeeper and her young daughter. Yet Julia and the others met with the colonels and generals to persuade them to allow people to give and receive medical care in all areas of the country, from the government zones to those controlled by the opposition FMLN guerrillas.

"Many of my friends who worked for Central American peace were outraged that we even talked with the military," recalls Julia. "But we weren't naive. We knew the generals would use any agreement to look good in Congress and try to get more money in the face of our efforts to cut off the aid that kept them going. But the peace process had to start somewhere. This seemed a logical place. If they went back on their word, we'd have a huge report that we could wave in front of Congress describing all the violations."

Some of the generals gave Julia the chills. "You walked out feeling like you'd just encountered pure evil. Maybe others were doing the best they could, based on their experience and value systems. They'd still done horrible things, helped kill thousands of people. I tend to believe that everyone has a spark inside them that's redeemable, even if they've never done a single decent act in their lives. Maybe I was trying to speak to that, although there are some people who for all practical purposes can't be reached or redeemed. Mostly, I kept coming back to the sense that we had to try, and the possibility that this might help end the war. You don't have to like people to talk and negotiate."

Much as Julia hated what the generals had done, meeting with them offered "a way to draw them in, to give them a stake in the peace process, and to build a connection on other issues, like not bombing hospitals. We kept coming back to our priorities, what people in the Salvadoran villages said would help their situation. Working out agreements like this with both sides seemed a first step, a piece of the puzzle toward something larger." As it turned out, the medical neutrality agreement they helped negotiate became a key building block in finally achieving peace in El Salvador.

Julia's belief in a "redeemable spark" may seem like wishful thinking, but people who've done terrible things reverse course often enough that we should never lose hope that a particular person can change. We never know when someone whose past may seem abhorrent will nonetheless surprise us. C. P. Ellis joined the Durham, North Carolina, Ku Klux Klan because he had worked hard, gotten nowhere, and wanted someone to blame. Blacks were a natural target. Ellis's father was a Klan member who taught him, he says, that "it was the only organization in the world that would take care of the white people." Ellis soon rose to the high rank of Exalted Cyclops.

He particularly fought to prevent public schools from being integrated, organizing angry youth groups and packing city council meetings with his fellow Klansmen. But after a while, as he tells Studs Terkel in *American Dreams: Lost and Found,* Ellis began to feel used. City council members called him up when they wanted someone to shout down blacks at public meetings, yet avoided him when they passed on the street. He felt the people with money liked having low-income whites and blacks spend all their time fighting with each other. It helped them keep control.

Ellis received little sympathy when he raised this misgiving at Klan meetings. Nevertheless, he says, he began to "look at a black person walkin' down the street, and the guy'd have ragged shoes or his clothes would be worn. That began to do something to me inside."

Then the state AFL-CIO received a federal grant to address racial tensions in the school system. The labor organization invited

Ellis to a public meeting. And he accepted, wanting both to see what was going on and to speak his mind. "If we didn't have niggers in the schools," he told the group, "we wouldn't have the problems we got today."

To his surprise, a black activist praised him for "being the most honest man here tonight." Ellis left confused. He felt even more mystified two meetings later, when a black man nominated him to cochair the group. Worse yet, he'd have to work with Ann Atwater, "a black lady I hated with a purple passion" for leading civil rights boycotts and protests.

But Ellis "was tired of fighting." At least, he thought, his position in the group would give him an opportunity to speak his point of view. The committee gave the improbable partners a common project, and for all their mistrust, they began "to reluctantly work together," setting aside differences when they could. After both their kids came home crying because classmates had accused their parents of collaborating with the enemy, Atwater and Ellis began to recognize a deeper commonality, and eventually became close friends. Ellis found a new career as a union organizer, bringing poor blacks and whites together against employers who had long exploited their mutual mistrust. He was even elected business agent of a largely black local of the Operating Engineers. This former Klansman had completed one of the longest journeys imaginable— and had done so largely because someone had extended a hand and said, in effect, "There's a more hopeful way to live."

DRAWING THE LINE

It's essential not to dismiss potential allies, or even negotiating partners, because of their lifestyles, belief systems, or the political configurations with which they may have aligned themselves. But we also need to hold political and economic leaders accountable for the damage they cause. Too often, wealthy and powerful interests create sham coalitions of so-called stakeholders, whose pronouncements and reports justify clear-cutting forests, coddling dictators, or dismantling institutions like the Social Security system. In the face of such destructive actions, sometimes, as Virginia Ramirez says, we have "to learn to be rude."

Washington State timber companies have recently run a series of TV and newspaper ads urging that local salmon be exempted from the Endangered Species Act. Once again they insisted that their position would benefit the environment, reclaiming habitat management from distant federal bureaucrats. Yet as Pete Knutson said at a meeting of local environmentalists, "Everyone wants to hold hands and pretend we're all interested in preserving habitat. But we don't all have the same interests here. Weyerhaeuser says they're interested in preserving habitat. They've sure shown it with their clear-cuts. Trillium [another giant company] also says they want to preserve habitat but they're been just as bad. ITT Rayonier has the largest Superfund site in the state, and they say they want to preserve habitat too. Maybe we'd better look at their track record."

This time, instead of being humorous, Pete expressed moral outrage. Executives of the companies he attacked might consider his words rude. But gross abuses of power must be challenged head-on. When lives or land are destroyed by needless violence or greed, we need to be outraged. Otherwise we contribute to a climate of complacency. "There are moments," writes Charles Simic in *Harper's,* "when true invective is called for, when it becomes an absolute necessity, out of a deep sense of justice, to denounce, mock, vituperate, lash out, in the strongest possible language."

We live in a world where evil exists, where the rich and complex lives of individuals, neighborhoods, communities, entire species, and ecosystems are continually ravaged because of human callousness, ambition, and fear. Such destructiveness can't be erased by wishing it away or giving it a politer name. Quite the contrary. Tobacco companies may have sophisticated rationalizations for their deliberate targeting of teenage kids and their use of ammonia to make the nicotine in cigarettes more addictive. But they're ultimately responsible for the death and suffering of hundreds of thousands of people. When corporate or political leaders make deals that damage communities and lives, they must be held accountable for their actions.

In my opinion, many of the most powerful men and women in our society are addicted to greed. Their addiction stems from conditioning, education, and character. The culture they inhabit tells them that wealth and control are the ultimate good. It encourages them to believe they deserve all the material riches they can amass, and more. Most are unlikely to cease their destructive actions voluntarily, certainly not if the only payoff is that children can eat, families can have a roof over their heads, or remnants of the American wilderness can be preserved for future generations.

The religious notion of hating the sin while loving the sinner can be helpful in this context. True, it's sometimes used destructively, as when preachers tell gays that God wants them to be straight. But it's also a way to challenge unjust political, cultural, and economic systems—what the Bible calls "powers and principalities"—without dehumanizing those who participate in them. Like batterers in an abusive relationship, these individuals may cause human harm because of how they were raised, or because of wounds they inherited and now are passing on to others in cycles they feel helpless to break. They may support unjust systems out of habit, fear, blindness, or the limits of their experience. Their all-too-human flaws deserve our sympathy, even as we do everything we can to oppose their actions.

To use a domestic metaphor, if one member of a family is consistently bullying, abusive, or destructive, he or she must be made to stop. Sometimes patient explanation will suffice. More often, however, other family members have to learn to cease excusing or tolerating behavior that damages the group. The same is true of people whose actions damage the larger human family or despoil the earth. Bearing in mind that, as Julia Devin says, everyone possesses a redeemable spark, we shouldn't give up on them. But we nonetheless need to acknowledge their destructiveness and refuse to cooperate. We need to draw a clear line and abide by it, setting limits to their behavior and stopping them from creating further harm.

A POLITICS OF FORGIVENESS

The moral imagination required to picture the redeemable spark is an acquired skill. For most of us, our instinctive response is a desire for retribution. "I just hope there is a hell," said a South Carolina textile worker I once interviewed, "because that son-of-a-bitch foreman will get his." Think of Pirate Jenny's classic song from Brecht's *Threepenny Opera,* in which the hotel maid scrubs the floors under the scornful stares of the rich. Jenny dreams of "the ship, the black freighter," whose pirate crew will burn and ransack the town. Then they'll bring the well-fed gentlemen to Jenny in chains, "Asking me 'Kill them now—or later?' Asking *me*. 'Kill them now—or later?' " It's a powerful vision. We all know the feeling. We long for the avenging angel to strike down all who've wronged us. The urge is stronger still when those we love have been harmed.

Yet as Alcoholics Anonymous reminds us, holding on to resentments is like drinking poison, day in and day out. Eventually it will destroy us. We need forgiveness to avoid being eaten up by bitterness. As the Catholic theologian Henri Nouwen writes, "To forgive another person from the heart is an act of liberation. We set that person free from the negative bonds that exist between us. We say, 'I no longer hold our offense against you.' But there is more. We also free ourselves from the burden of being the 'offended one.' The great temptation is to cling in anger to our enemies and then define ourselves as being offended and wounded by them. Forgiveness, therefore, liberates not only the other but also ourselves. It is the way to freedom of the children of God."

Approaches that mix forgiveness with accountability, like South Africa's Truth and Reconciliation Commission, can offer unexpected hope. "To pursue the path of healing for our nation," writes Archbishop Desmond Tutu, "we need to remember what we have endured. But we must not simply pass on the violence of that experience through the pursuit of punishment. We seek to do justice to the suffering without perpetuating the hatred aroused. We think of this as *restorative* justice." Rather than being idealistic or naive, this path, Tutu argues, was "thoroughly realistic," perhaps the only way to heal a profoundly divided nation.

Restorative justice. That's an extraordinary notion, don't you think? Fairness *plus* forgiveness. Moral courage *plus* mercy. How can we Americans practice restorative justice, reuniting our own profoundly divided nation? Perhaps by letting go of some of our long-drawn-out resentments. By focusing less on the evils of our enemies and more on the world we would like to build—with their cooperation if possible; without it, if necessary. And by remembering that even those whom we mistrust most profoundly are capable of good—perhaps even of radical shifts of heart.

At a Seattle conference called Body and Soul, Marianne Williamson led a seminar at which she spoke of the need to heal America's long-festering historical wounds, and offered a prayer requesting forgiveness in particular for our deep racial divisions. She warned of the dangers that arise when forgiveness disappears, citing the example of Benjamin Netanyahu's seeming inability to view Palestinians without seeing the face of his brother, a soldier killed in the Israeli commando raid that freed the Entebbe airport hostages. At one point a gray-haired man in a suit raised his hand.

"I know this will probably push a lot of people's buttons," he said, soft-voiced and hesitant, "but my name is Egil Krogh. I was the lawyer who headed the 'plumbers' group' in the Nixon White House, hired G. Gordon Liddy, and coordinated the break-in at the office of Daniel Ellsberg's psychiatrist, Dr. Fielding. I pleaded guilty and went to prison for it. I've apologized to Ellsberg and Fielding. We've met and talked. But those apologies aren't complete enough. I want to apologize publicly now, for what we did and what it caused."

The seminar participants were stunned. Krogh went on to make a full confession, unexpected and unsolicited. This was something rare. Even former Defense Secretary Robert McNamara hedged when he reassessed his role in the Vietnam War. He had the courage to admit that the war he helped promote was a terrible mistake, and to use lessons from its failures to argue for nuclear disarmament. But McNamara also insisted that he had done the best he could at the time with flawed information. "We made an error not of values and intentions," he wrote, "but of judgment and capabilities."

Unlike McNamara, Krogh didn't hedge or equivocate. He'd helped demonize the Democrats and those who protested the war. He'd made them into enemies, he said. This was wrong, and it damaged the country. "I spent a long time at the Vietnam Memorial, thinking about my actions. Those of us involved have a responsibility to help America heal." He hoped that we could forgive him.

Neither I nor any of the other participants had anticipated Krogh's apology or even his presence. I felt humbled by his words, shaken by his vulnerability. He'd served a Nixon administration so sure of its own righteousness that it waged war on American democracy itself. The president and his advisors launched the secret bombing of Cambodia, disrupted Democratic campaigns, attacked domestic opponents as "vultures" and "parasites." "Anyone who opposes us, we'll destroy," Krogh told the head of the University of Chicago psychiatry department in 1969. "As a matter of fact, anyone who doesn't support us, we'll destroy."

"We kept files on all of you," Krogh said with an apologetic smile to the one-time peace activists who came up at the break in the seminar. Now he was asking strangers to forgive him.

Afterward, Krogh told me how disturbed he had been when prosecutor Leon Jaworski compared his excuse—that he was just following orders—to the one Albert Speer and other Nazis had used when Jaworski helped prosecute them at Nuremberg. Convicted and sentenced to a six-month term, Krogh was surprised by how generously his black fellow prison inmates responded. "We'd played racial themes so often in the White House. But they protected me. They said I stood up for my beliefs, even though I actually hadn't. I'd failed to ask, 'Is this right?' " Later, in California, Krogh heard a talk by Ram Dass, whom he'd previously mistrusted as a frivolous psychedelic promoter, and found "such a generous and forgiving sensibility," he again had to rethink his assumptions. He felt that Watergate had left people with a deep mistrust of their country—and that he and his cohorts were responsible. Except in his personal meetings with Ellsberg and Dr. Fielding, he'd not raised these issues in public. But Williamson's message about the power of forgiveness had compelled him to come forward and speak.

Krogh's public apology helped other seminar participants reassess their own relationship to history and their moral choices. One woman recalled marching against the war, then working in a refugee camp with Vietnamese boat people. "I was right to work for peace," she said, "but wrong to romanticize the North Vietnamese and Vietcong." She thanked Krogh for his courage and candor. So did other people, including particularly ones who'd also challenged that war and were now teachers, prison counselors, clinic nurses, therapists of abused children, or environmental or community activists. More than two hundred people witnessed Krogh's confession, and all seemed moved.

Krogh's gesture helped us feel more generous—less ready to demonize our enemies and make our fellow humans fodder for our own causes, however urgent. He reminded us that individuals and institutions can change, and that when we voice difficult but important truths, we can never know who may hear them and respond. He led us to unexpected common ground.

Chapter Ten

Coping with Burnout

Burnout only really begins to heal when people learn how to grieve.
—RACHEL NAOMI REMEN

Without *forgiveness, hurts grow unchecked and we recycle failures, resentments, bitterness, and mistrust in our lives. With forgiveness, hurts are acknowledged and healed, and we are able to break a mindless cycle of retaliation by saying that the decisions of human life, even when they turn out badly, are not beyond repair.*
—DORIS DONNELLY

For years I've gone to my friend Ruth's New Year's party. I think of the people in her circle as members of my tribe. They came of age opposing the Vietnam War and working for civil rights. Since then, they've challenged the nuclear arms race and U.S. support of Central American dictators and death squads. They've founded tenants' unions, low-income medical clinics, community development corporations, and major environmental projects. They've been involved in almost every significant cause I can imagine.

But a few years ago, I noticed that something had changed. The people at Ruth's party still viewed themselves as activists, even radicals. But only a fraction were still directly engaged. Many of those who had stayed involved did so through their jobs, like the political director of the Washington state teachers' union, a community organizer turned county councilman, an ACLU staffer, gay activists involved in local community foundations, an energy conservation consultant, and a couple who made public-interest documentaries.

Except for modest local involvements, like being part of a block association or occasionally volunteering at the neighborhood school, most of the rest had withdrawn into private life. They worked in emotionally draining human service jobs or the lucrative but soul-devouring software industry. They pursued hobbies like gardening, fixed up their homes, spent time with friends, tried to save a few dollars after years of living on the edge. A few had all they could handle with young children, but most had older children or none at all, so their family responsibilities were light. Yet by and large this once tremendously active group was doing little to shape the political culture of their time. Instead, they'd become political spectators, mournfully watching from the sidelines of public life, even as the Republican wrecking ball steadily demolished sixty years of social programs.

POLITICAL SPECTATORS

What creates this revolving door, through which citizens take powerfully committed stands, and sometimes help change history, then withdraw in isolation and despair? What happened in the 1990s that turned so many once-engaged people away from the fray, even as others opened up new areas of hope? What is the difference between those who find ways to persist and those who do not?

Social movements inevitably surge and recede. Activists come and go, following the rhythms of their lives and the political rhythms of their time. When there's a sense of crisis, as was true during the peak of the Vietnam War or the height of the Reagan-era nuclear arms race, millions put aside their ordinary concerns and take on causes they'd never otherwise have considered. Sometimes they do the same when they see new opportunities, like those presented by the civil rights and feminist movements. When the emergency is over or the reform movements slow their pace, many return to more private lives. And clearly such mobilizations are more likely to happen in the face of immediate, large-scale conflagrations, such as foreign wars, than in response to the slow-burn violations of human dignity and routine pillaging of the earth that characterize our current time. But when large numbers of people pull back from social involvement all at once, the consequences are damaging. Understanding why so many once-staunch activists have withdrawn in recent years is important for several reasons, not the least of which is that their retreat makes it all the harder for the rest of us to act.

Let me describe some moments in this process of withdrawal, as they've been played out in my own community of Seattle. On the eve of the 1991 Persian Gulf War, thirty thousand people—more than attended any national anti–Vietnam War rally before 1967—marched in our streets in protest. A year and a half later, local activists turned out by the thousands to volunteer in the November 1992 election, with the hope of ending the Reagan-Bush era. We helped carry Washington State for Clinton and Gore, elect our first woman senator, capture eight out of nine House seats for the Democrats, and elect a strong populist governor. On election day, I joined five other volunteers to help get out the vote in a precinct of a swing congressional district twenty-five miles south of Seattle. A coordinated campaign produced similar efforts, saturating the state's most populated areas.

By the next year, however, things had changed. A regressive tax-limitation measure, Initiative 601, qualified for our statewide ballot. This time, no volunteers worked the outlying areas. The opposition campaign was so poorly staffed that it didn't have enough people to distribute literature even in Seattle's most liberal neighborhoods. With the state's sizable progressive community largely uninvolved, the get-out-the-vote effort was minimal, and turnout abysmal. Even then, the initiative passed by only a 2.5-percent margin. Ever since, despite a boom economy and a budget surplus, the measure has choked the state's ability to meet fundamental needs in such areas as education and social services. Had progressive activists volunteered in numbers even remotely comparable to those of the year before, Initiative 601 would almost certainly have been defeated.

The same phenomenon occurred across the nation in 1994, the

year the Republican Party captured both houses of Congress. I was on a promotional tour for my book on student values, *Generation at the Crossroads,* staying at the houses of friends who'd long been involved with social causes. Everywhere I visited, critical races would be decided by the narrowest of margins. Yet my friends seemed strangely detached from the process, as if the political sphere had become so corrupt, it would soil them to so much as go near it. Seven of the nine Washington State congressional races were won by Republicans, each more right-wing than the last, and voters reelected a senator known for baiting Native Americans and environmentalists. According to polls by CNN and Gallup, the 42 percent of the country's registered voters who stayed home leaned Democratic by a wide enough margin that they would have reversed the electoral outcome, had they only gone to the polls. And that doesn't take into account the equally large number of mostly low-income people who weren't registered to begin with. Even a modest volunteer effort would have prevented the Republican sweep. The same was true in 1996, when Republicans won two Washington congressional seats in races that weren't determined until the final absentee ballots, captured another two in victories only slightly more substantial, and again actually trailed among registered voters nationwide, but won by less than 1 percent among those who turned out. Even in the more hopeful election of 1998, turnout was the lowest since 1942, and a higher percentage of Republicans than Democrats still voted. But the gap narrowed in part due to volunteer get-out-the-vote efforts that swung the balance in some key races.

Electoral campaigns are hardly the sole way to participate in the public arena, or even necessarily the most important. Candidates and politicians rarely represent our highest values. Money and manipulation predominate, and high-tech consultants dismiss grass-roots efforts as irrelevant. Yet elections like these have had tremendous consequences. And despite important and hopeful efforts like those I've profiled in this book, too many once-committed citizens have withdrawn in recent years not only from formal electoral politics but from virtually all public involvement.

We saw this in the nondebates over the Gingrich-Clinton welfare bill, and over the recent regressive upper-bracket tax cuts. Longtime activists said they were distracted by other concerns. What discussion did occur seemed remote from their lives—a faint echo from a distant shore. They didn't think the bills would pass, and had come to doubt that their voices mattered. They didn't want to fight to save flawed systems, even when they believed the proposed "reforms" would make matters worse.

In fairness, I should say that many who've withdrawn, like my friends at Ruth's party, haven't wholly abandoned their values. They may still watch political events with interest, if from a distance, following them on NPR or CNN, tracking each twist and turn, much as they might the fortunes of a baseball team. They may still bemoan perceived political betrayals, like Bill Clinton's habitual subservience to the powerful. They may still read alternative publications, purchase environmentally friendly products, and write modest checks to Greenpeace, NOW, Citizen Action, or sympathetic political candidates. They may occasionally attend demonstrations or volunteer for community projects. They still try to do useful work that doesn't violate their souls.

Yet once their ambitions were much greater. They envisioned a more generous, just, and inclusive society, and worked long and hard to realize that vision. Now they do not. Once they reached out to their fellow citizens. They've stopped doing that as well. And the more they pull back, drifting ever further from public life, the less they believe their actions can make a worthwhile difference.

CYCLES OF DISAPPOINTMENT

Individuals who've dropped out of social involvement have different perspectives than do those just beginning. They've endured cycles of hope and disappointment specific to their causes, and to the larger project of working for social change. Their stories may seem like a detour in a book about empowerment. But understanding why people burn out *is* empowering, and crucially so. The more we know about the obstacles that lie ahead, the better equipped we'll be to surmount them.

Let's begin with dashed political expectations. Since Bill Clinton first took office, I've watched countless individuals who'd been involved for years withdraw from public engagement, and do little except condemn Clinton's failures, or hope, more and more forlornly, for his better instincts to prevail. Abandoning the very kinds of public involvement that might have pushed Clinton to take more courageous stands, they have created a self-fulfilling prophecy.

I saw a similar process occur during Jimmy Carter's presidency. Exhausted by years of fighting the Vietnam War and by the ruthlessness of Richard Nixon, progressive activists were relieved to have the presidency finally occupied by a kindhearted human being. So they brought little moral or political pressure to bear on Carter, pressure that might have persuaded him to take more socially committed stands. Meanwhile, the political right went on the offensive, supported by key corporate interests. Carter responded by appointing hawkish conservatives like Zbigniew Brzezinski and James Schlesinger to key policymaking positions, and then, unfortunately, heeding their advice. Once he left office, Carter acted courageously and effectively on a variety of issues, but his lackluster presidential tenure, coupled with the passivity of once-active citizens, brought mostly disappointment.

The comparable activist reaction to Clinton's presidency has been compounded by his lack of personal integrity, which surfaced long before the Monica Lewinsky soap opera. From the outset of his first term, people involved in progressive social movements were sharply divided. Some damned Clinton right away, but did little except gripe from the sidelines as he made one disappointing move after another. Others vested modest expectations in his victory, hoping he'd finally set America on a course away from greed.

They applauded a few modest gains—family leave, "motor voter" registration, and a higher earned-income credit for the poor. But they never mobilized the sustained grassroots pressure that might have forced Clinton to fulfill his far-reaching original promises.

On the whole, both groups watched silently while Clinton backed off on campaign reform, failed to invest in America's desperate urban ghettos, and proposed a baroque and compromised health care package that collapsed of its own weight. The only time he went to the mat and risked his political capital was to support NAFTA—a dubious victory indeed. Then the Republicans rode in on a wave of discontent, helped by the near-total collapse of volunteer participation in the Democratic Party. Suddenly facing a hostile Congress, Clinton caved in on welfare, equitable taxes, and practically every other issue that might give him even the slightest apparent lift in the polls. Individuals who'd first drawn back from involvement because they'd hoped Clinton would solve America's problems now withdrew further because he'd dashed their hopes. For many who'd long fought against the Reagan-Bush administrations' subservience to greed, Clinton's cravenness proved the last straw. In their eyes, he became the personification of cynicism, a man who'd exploited their hopes to get himself elected, then behaved exactly like those before him.

Even those who stayed involved felt dismayed. "What a disappointment," says one woman who'd been active in social causes since the 1960s. "He's bright. He's younger than I am. He plays a pretty good blues sax. I feel sad that he squandered so much hope."

A more general collapse of the liberal center also hurt. "Under Reagan and Bush," adds one of her friends, "at least you had Democratic congressmen and senators challenging greed. Now, with Clinton, there's hardly anyone. Most of the Democrats go along for fear of dividing the party. The Republicans invite corporate lobbyists to write legislation. The news media treats the few dissenting senators almost like crybabies. It makes it that much harder to act."

Yet despite an ambivalent political mood and the lack of strong moral leadership from Washington, D.C., plenty of opportunities for humane social change still exist, and citizens could have been taking advantage of them. Roosevelt enacted his pivotal New Deal reforms only under pressure from massive grassroots organizing, like that of Hazel Wolf and her radical cohorts. It took a popular movement to convince John F. Kennedy (belatedly) to support civil rights legislation. By constantly articulating their vision, the radical right has dramatically reshaped the mainstream Republican agenda. Whatever Clinton's core belief system, or lack thereof, progressive-minded citizens could have demanded a wiser and more compassionate course for the American ship of state.

Standing Against the Storm

We can't wholly blame Clinton for activist withdrawal, however. The demoralization of far too many social justice activists started several years before he took office. Even had Clinton taken more courageous stands, he couldn't have provided easy, instant solutions to the careening and all-leveling power of a runaway global economy, the staggering pace of technological change, or the more general erosion of community in America. And those movements for human dignity that have attracted significant numbers of participants have often been isolated from each other.

Although seemingly remote to most Americans, certain global events have fed the sense, for many who were once active, of feeling uncertain and adrift. Large numbers of citizens felt outraged, for instance, when Ronald Reagan and George Bush followed a long tradition of U.S. intervention in Central America by backing brutal military regimes in El Salvador and Guatemala, and arming the Contras to attack the Nicaraguan Sandinistas. Many also got excited by the Nicaraguan revolution's early promise, as they saw formerly powerless people fighting to create a better society.

"There was a sense of hope and possibility, separate from ideology," says a friend of Ruth's named Kraig. "The government ran pioneering literacy and health programs. We felt they were trying to forge their own alternative to a world based on greed. Even the little old ladies in the pensions where I stayed were singing Sandinista songs."

But after a half-dozen years of the Contra war, the mood in Nicaragua had turned bleak. "The picture was incredibly grim," Kraig continues. "They'd been ground down by all the fighting. There was hardly anything left to hope for." Eventually, the Nicaraguans voted for the Sandinistas' opponents. They did so, I believe, because many feared that otherwise the U.S.-backed war would never end, which meant that the bullies had won, that Reagan and Bush had successfully bent the Nicaraguans to their will. And because key Sandinista leaders had themselves grown arrogant and remote from ordinary citizens, lusted too much for power, and in general exposed too many human flaws. Whatever the precise mix of external pressure and internal disappointment, the results were demoralizing.

Bosnia and Rwanda added to people's uncertainty. Lifelong peace activists were themselves divided over how to respond to "ethnic cleansing" and genocide. They'd challenged CIA coups and undeclared wars, and ended U.S. support for apartheid-era South Africa. But despite the geopolitical origins of the atrocities in these small and beleaguered nations, they couldn't be ended simply by bringing pressure to bear on the American government. These conflicts seemed at least as terrible as other ones that American peace activists had challenged, but more intractable.

Though brief, the Gulf War also left lasting scars. With respect to Central America, peace activists could always take some comfort in the fact that more than three-quarters of the American public disagreed with U.S. policy. In this instance, the numbers were reversed. With polls registering overwhelming approval of our war against Iraq, many who opposed it felt betrayed not only by their government but by an American public they'd expected to respond differently. They knew Saddam Hussein was a murderous thug.

But America had supported him for years, and helped arm his military. Our ambassador had told him that how he responded to his conflicts with Kuwait was none of our affair. Given the autocratic corruption of the Kuwaiti and Saudi governments, and how often Bush squandered opportunities for a negotiated settlement, those who opposed the war viewed it as rank hypocrisy.

Making matters worse, opposition voices were drowned out by coordinated media cheerleading that literally showed the war from the point of view of the bombs. Images of immaculate surgical strikes played on TV day and night, as if the networks themselves were public relations firms working for the Pentagon. A quarter of a million people marched opposing the war in Washington, D.C. More than a hundred thousand did the same in San Francisco. But the same networks devoted as much airtime that day to a group of less than one hundred of the war's supporters, who stood by the D.C. march holding signs. Those who challenged Desert Storm quickly felt helpless and isolated. They forgot how long it took for the anti–Vietnam War movement to gain momentum. They didn't anticipate the dampening effect of freezing winter weather on their marches and rallies. They failed to consider the difference between a six-week war and one that lasted decades.

For most Americans the war was a flicker on the TV screen, scattered fireworks over Baghdad, a parade when the troops came back home. It was easy to forget. For many who fought in it, however, the memories linger, as do the medical consequences. Memories also linger among the peace activists. Surprising numbers continue to be plagued by a sense of isolation and futility that first emerged in its wake. As a Seattle nurse involved in antinuclear civil disobedience says, "Many of us never did take the time to grieve and heal and confront our sense of isolation and loss." They kept their despair largely private. As a result, those most demoralized not only dropped out of the global peace movement, they abandoned social involvement in general.

NO MAGNETIC NORTH

This is a confusing historical time for all of us. Vast new techno-logical forces transform our lives. Traditional communities are eroding. Increasingly our fortunes are tied to an unstable but all-consuming global economy. As a friend says, "I don't think even the people in power know where they're headed."

Many longtime social activists face an additional challenge: the collapse of radical belief systems—in particular those of the Marx-ist tradition—that once challenged the rule of the dollar, and in-spired many to fight for a more just world. Just mentioning this tradition, I realize, is controversial and, perhaps, confusing, be-cause the Communist states that claimed to embody it were as soulless and soul-destroying as one can imagine. But communism's well-deserved collapse has left many who found that system pro-foundly abhorrent unexpectedly confused. They're unsure just what alternatives they can now offer to our own system's most destructive aspect: the role of unchecked corporate global power.

In the next chapter, I'll talk more about these potential alter-natives, including ways to craft compelling visions of change in a time when long term certainties are elusive. For now, I'd like to focus on that significant group of social justice activists who've found themselves adrift and unsure about just what they want to fight *for*. Make no mistake: Activists like those in Ruth's circle had no love for the Soviet Union's stultifying police state, or the coun-tries that followed its model. They applauded the dissidents of Prague Spring, Polish Solidarity, and Tiananmen Square. They cel-ebrated the collapse of the Soviet bloc and the tearing down of the Berlin Wall.

But many also hoped that despite the brutality and blindness of the Communist regimes, their attempts to take collective respon-sibility for the economic welfare of their citizens might offer some hopeful lessons. Sadly, the eastern bloc nations seem even worse after their fall than many of us could ever have imagined. Witness their terrible ecological devastation, persistent economic stagnation, and utter failure to create a more participatory and socially responsible culture. Their devolution into nationalist factions and economic Darwinism dominated by mafias and cartels has further tainted the tradition of radical social change.

I recently gathered together a half-dozen of Ruth's friends to discuss their withdrawal. They talked about their disappointment in Clinton, the Gulf War's demoralizing impact, their cumulative exhaustion from years of juggling work, kids, and the uphill fight for change. They talked of the difficulty of creating engaged moral community in a time when community itself is eroding. But mostly they felt uncertain of their vision, and viewed current issues as too limited to get them excited.

"It's not that we liked the Soviet Union or Eastern Europe," said Ruth. "But we had a sense of an alternative out there that had tremendous problems, moral and practical, but also represented a tradition that asked some of the right questions. We hoped it might evolve into something else or be replaced by something better. Now there's no alternative, just the global rule of corporate capitalism.

"I feel like the political ground's shifted and grown slippery," Ruth continued. "I'm uncertain about what direction to go." As a teacher in her circle put it, "It's like trying to steer by a compass when there's no longer a magnetic north."

When these activists took stands in the past, it was with a sense that they could dramatically change the world for the better, and that history was on their side. They acted not only from anger but also from hope. Now they're unsure about precisely what kind of future they want to propose, and wonder whether all their previous assumptions made sense. They feel confused and adrift. "You start working on very local issues like the drug house across the street," said an environmentally oriented architect named Anne. "Then you realize how separated you are from any larger context. How hard it is to get your bearings or even to discuss how your work links to that of people elsewhere."

A librarian named Geri, a former tenant activist, described the political paralysis created by her own uncertainty. "I see people selling their sectarian newspapers in front of the university library or when people bring in a speaker," she said. "I want to take these poor misdirected souls in hand and say 'Hey, you're wasting your time acting in this way. You should be doing *this* instead.' But the lack of the *this* embarrasses me. Because I don't know what they really should be doing, or what they should fight for."

The absence of a clear overarching vision has left many of us hesitant to enlist even in direct and pragmatic efforts whose merits seem obvious, such as working to reform campaign financing, resisting the dismantling of social support systems, or challenging environmental degradation. We could act on any of these questions without having a blueprint for the ideal society, but too many once-active people have given up.

This paralysis has affected secular social justice activists to a far greater extent than those from religious communities. That's why I focus on more secular groups in this chapter. But involvement among religious activists has dropped off as well. Even if they've continued to work in one-on-one community service efforts, many have pulled back from addressing the kinds of larger political choices that profoundly affect the communities they serve. In both cases, the political silence of so many committed, compassionate, and thoughtful individuals has created a dangerous void.

"Most Americans have a sense that our fundamental situation is on the slide," says my friend Charley Meconis, a former priest whom I first met when he was blockading Trident submarines. "Things may not be as good for our children or grandchildren as they were for our parents. Religious conservatives say going back to the Bible will solve this. That everything will be fixed if we just return to their definition of private morality. That's a vision to fight for, even if it's false and simplistic. It gives a sense of promises that can still be kept if people only live up to the values they prescribe, or if we return to some ideal previous time. The economic conservatives don't need a vision of justice. They can just work for self-interest, or a belief that the market and technology will solve all our ills. Most don't worry much about the destruction of community."

Activists on the political right have been steadily organizing, often with backing from powerful economic interests; so, if the rest of us stay silent, their views will prevail, whether or not they represent a wise national course. Those of us on the left or liberal end of the political spectrum may, as Charley says, have a much less clear vision of our ideal society. "But even though we don't know where everything is heading, our choices do make things better or worse—and we've been letting worse ones be made in our name. We don't have to accept this, even if there's a lot about which we're uncertain."

Charley makes a crucial point. Whatever our uncertainties regarding our ultimate political goals, we can still respond to current abuses of human dignity and assaults on the earth. Individuals fighting for the survival of their own communities, like Virginia Ramirez, David Lewis, and Pete Knutson, may appear to have a stronger sense of direction these days than those whose involvement has focused on the wounds of others. But those at the economic bottom also have a greater sense that the deck is stacked against them. And both groups face the same fundamental challenge of building momentum in a difficult time. Both struggle to find their magnetic north—the point on the horizon to aim for.

What activists like Virginia haven't lost, however, is heart. Their stories offer a lesson that all of us—burned-out activists or not—should heed: Even when we can't envision the ideal future, we can still recognize callousness, shortsightedness, and injustice. And we can still challenge it with compassion, vision, and courage.

For a number of reasons, progress for justice may be slower in this particular historical period than in others. We may have to rebuild people's basic sense of human connection at the same time as we encourage their voice. Our activist communities may have to offer even stronger models of conviction to attract people living more isolated lives. And we may have to be more humble than usual about our visions, and act despite a greater quotient of uncertainty. Yet as the stories I've recounted have suggested, even modest common efforts can lead to unforeseen but profound social changes. The challenge is to take the initial step, whether we're doing so for the first time, or reemerging after a period of demoralization and retreat. And to take that first step we must believe that our actions can matter.

RADICAL IDENTITIES

In *Beyond the Barricades,* a study of former Vietnam-era activists at U.C.–Santa Barbara, Jack Whalen and Richard Flacks write, "Disengaged radicals are disillusioned, not with the values espoused by the movement; rather, they have lost faith in the possibility of changing society so that those values can be fully realized." The same could be said of Ruth's group. Their fundamental values are the same today as they were years ago, even if they might propose some different political solutions. But they've lost faith in activism. And even though their particular experiences are distinct, the dilemma created by their uncertainty resembles that of countless other active citizens who've burned out. Just as important, the means by which they and others overcome their disenchantment and regain their faith provides a model for those of us for whom participation in public causes is new.

Before those in Ruth's group can once again act, they need to shed a definition of political commitment that excludes any public involvements except those that seem likely to transform the world completely. When I was talking with the group, the subject of welfare came up. A computer programmer named Gary said Gingrich's supposed reforms were awful, then explained why he'd not spoken up to challenge them. "We all know the welfare system is screwed," he said. "This will make it worse. But saving that system's a liberal fix. We're radicals. I want to do more than just work to save what Newt Gingrich is attacking. We're supposed to offer an alternative to the welfare state and the market economy, not just offer Band-Aids."

Poverty, Gary acknowledged, is "a real issue. But most of us here grew up middle-class. If we got everyone to that level, we'd still have problems like overwork, overconsumption, and our destruction of the environment. What's the point of helping the poor achieve gains that we ourselves have turned our backs on? I want to build a society that benefits the poor and middle-class alike."

For all the real issues Gary raised, his sentiments seemed dangerously aloof. It makes a tremendous difference in the character of our society whether we do our best to give those at the bottom a chance to lead healthy, reasonably comfortable lives—even if they risk being caught in the same binds as the rest of us—or ignore their plight, whatever our rationalizations for doing so. What I detected in Gary's response was yet another version of the perfect standard, one that too many former activists apply to all causes: Because none promises sufficiently dramatic change, they decide, none is worth joining. "We have to be hard-nosed," Gary said, repeatedly. "Radicals shouldn't just fight defensively, to save a bunch of liberal programs that are way too limited from the start. There are lots of places where people are hurting, but I want to act where I can raise fundamental issues. I want to act where there's real hope for change."

When I next ran into him, Gary wondered whether his comments might have reflected "my being in a particularly sour mood that day." But his responses seemed to arise from something deeper than a particular mood or even his temperament. Burnout has made some of us withdraw from involvement, he said. But it's made others start going through the political motions without thinking, repeating stale solutions. "Thought is activism," Gary said, "discussion is activism, education is activism, every bit as much as licking stamps at campaign headquarters."

True enough. Yet I've seen few burned-out activists flocking to study groups to rethink the premises that once supported their involvement. Mostly, those who've turned their backs on larger public concerns in recent years have done so quietly and privately. And like Gary, some remain so bound to the image of themselves as keepers of the radical flame, and to all-or-nothing visions of social change, that they can no longer imagine how they might address issues about which they still care profoundly.

The mechanism that underlies such attachments is one we all share. As the psychologist Lillian Rubin points out, during the evolution of the individual self, one identity doesn't replace another. Rather, our definitions of self rest upon each other in successive layers. "Thus," Rubin says, "the radical or deviant identity we adopt in our youth remains with us, part of the experience and definition of self, even when we no longer act on the values it embodied, sometimes even when we no longer believe in them."

In effect, too many onetime activists have become prisoners of earlier identities, unable to see beyond them to the possibilities of a very different time. Like my friends in Ruth's circle, or Geri the librarian, many of us who came of age in the Vietnam-era movements would still like to view ourselves as heroic agents of change. We want to speak truth to power, struggle mightily for human dignity, create a new and better society. These are all worthy goals. We may even believe that we're staying true to our principles simply by maintaining a desire for justice. But the more we cling to our earlier radical identity, the more we prevent ourselves from creating public expressions of who we are today, and from responding to the complex political challenges of the present. In the name of radical change, we end up changing nothing at all.

No Room for Doubt

As I mentioned, the bind that's trapped these and other once passionately committed activists is the familiar perfect standard. It can sabotage not only those just beginning to get involved, but also individuals with long experience of social commitment. A former Greenpeace staffer I know dropped out of the environmental movement to focus on paying off his student loans. With his financial affairs in order, he considered getting reinvolved, but none of the issues at hand seemed important enough. "I was waiting," he said, "for something that would really change the world, the ultimate dramatic cause." Five years passed before he realized that the ideal moment was never going to arrive. He decided it was time to reinvolve himself, then see where his involvement led.

If we don't acknowledge our doubts about particular approaches or causes, the gap between our internal psychological state and our outward allegiances will eventually erode our will to act. The former Vietnam-era activists interviewed by Jack Whalen and Richard Flacks consistently cited ways that the movements they'd joined had discouraged them from expressing fears, misgivings, or feelings of inadequacy. "If one's collective embarked on an organizing project," write Whalen and Flacks, "members expected each other to become instant organizers, free of anxiety about talking to strangers, confidently able to argue a position publicly, perfectly at ease in roles that most people would find intimidating. . . . Activists who had belonged to such collectives are likely to recall the experience as painful because of the unacknowledged gap between public profession and private feeling—and the shame and guilt that resulted." When movements don't allow hesitation, uncertainty, ambivalence, they make it almost impossible for many of their most dedicated participants to continue.

Doubt and ambivalence are precisely the lessons many activists from the 1960s drew from their experiences. By the time the Vietnam War wound down, many of its opponents were exhausted by years spent opposing it while more people were needlessly being killed, wounded, and driven from their homes every day. Peace activists were also exhausted by the movement's own factional divisiveness. Uncertain what to focus on next, they wanted a respite from constantly trying to shape history. And many needed time to rebuild stable personal lives. As the years went by, individuals who'd once envisioned radical commitment in terms of dramatic confrontation found it hard to act in more low-key political styles. U.S. military interventions became more covert, and therefore harder to challenge. Activists who'd built a vision on critiquing the limits of abundance watched in puzzlement as that abundance, for most Americans, began to slip away. Pressures of family, career, and day-to-day survival steadily mounted; so did the sense of isolation, as attempts to maintain supportive political communities proved difficult. While many 1960s activists continued to take public stands on a variety of issues, others became disenchanted with the very process of political commitment.

Now, in a seemingly less receptive time, those of us who've left the fray tend to forget how long it took to convince people to oppose the Vietnam War, challenge the nuclear arms race, or begin to act as stewards of the earth. We look back with longing on an era when we seemed to be part of close-knit communities, passionately committed to the work of social change. Instead of drawing strength from these memories, we use them to excuse inaction. We compound the paralysis of impossible standards by wallowing in nostalgia.

But it doesn't have to be this way. The route back to involvement parallels that by which people get involved in the first place. Burned-out activists can renew their commitment one step at a time, working with specific communities to which they have access. They can relinquish the search for the ideal political blueprint, instead basing their visions on people's immediate needs and on the stories that touch their hearts. They can learn from their own history, reminding themselves that even seemingly quixotic efforts can bear unexpected fruit. The cure for doubt isn't certainty, it's commitment.

WE NEVER CELEBRATE OUR VICTORIES

Much social change work is necessarily difficult. It can leave us feeling, in the words of the writer Anne Lamott, like "Sisyphus with cash-flow problems." There's no way to get around it: Repeatedly sending out the same mailings, making the same phone calls, distributing the same fliers, attending the same meetings, and navigating the same endless grant applications is wearisome. That's one of the reasons former activists talk again and again about having felt a "lack of traction" in their efforts.

"I took my Central American slide show to all these Kiwanis and Rotary clubs," says a lawyer long involved in human rights work. "I gave my talk, showed my slides, and looked out toward a sea of blank faces. People didn't ask questions. They didn't even argue. They just didn't respond. My experience in Central America was so intense, dealing with war, pain, and all of people's hopes. Then I came back and felt no one wanted to hear about it. After a while I stopped trying to reach out."

That someone might grow demoralized in the face of such resistance is easy to understand. Few of us are capable of taking on highly difficult tasks without being rewarded somehow. We need approval, gratitude, a feeling of accomplishment, some indication of success. Too often social activists overlook the need to renew our spirits, and so get overrun by pessimism.

Yet a sense of futility can hit even when we've achieved profound victories. When the Vietnam War ended, I was editing a small political magazine called *Liberation*. We ran a special issue on the legacy of the war, including articles about returning vets and a long essay—written well before *Apocalypse Now*—that compared it with the madness Joseph Conrad described in *Heart of Darkness*. In a brief introduction, I offered the opinion that the story would not be complete until we explored how ordinary citizens had successfully shifted America's course. My fellow editors and I planned to do that in a later issue. But we never did, nor did most peace activists of the time ever step back to reflect upon having finally stopped the war. Not taking the time to draw out the meaning of that achievement, to savor and take heart from it, made their subsequent political retreat far easier.

The recent student anti-apartheid movement followed a similar pattern. Participants helped bring about an astonishing victory. Yet most scarcely paused to note their accomplishment. In fact, groups at schools like Columbia quickly disintegrated as they argued bitterly over what to do next. Given the number of disappointments we're likely to experience in life, to say nothing of that frustrating and challenging part of life called social activism, how can we afford not to make the most of the satisfactions that come our way?

Inflated expectations can obscure our successes. A friend of Virginia Ramirez's works on problems of domestic violence. "When she started," Virginia says, "no one wanted to work with her. The issue was too controversial. Now it's changing, even on the state level. There are so many places where people can go to get help, and before there were none. Even in the traditional Hispanic community, things are different."

But Virginia's friend, she says, feels she hasn't done enough. "She told me, 'Virginia, things are not how I wanted them to be. I only got this much change. They didn't pass the law that would have given women more support.'

"So I said, 'Think about where we were seven years ago.' She wanted a hundred percent, but she got fifty percent. That's good. That's a big start. She's changed things. I don't think we'll ever get a perfect world, but we have to work the best we can."

"It's useful to be self-critical," says Julia Devin, the lawyer who helped negotiate the Salvadoran medical neutrality agreement. "But we don't stop and celebrate our victories. We don't stop and say, 'It's really amazing what we've achieved.' Perhaps that's because what we win is so often mixed. Or we feel we should already live in a just world, so when change comes it seems long overdue. But when we take major steps toward justice, we take them for granted."

Mr. Liberation

Sometimes we have to throw ourselves into political causes—perhaps a crisis suddenly emerges or a new opportunity arises. Certainly, for short periods, we can sacrifice sleep, exercise, family relationships, and every other personal aspect of our lives. But if we work only in crisis mode, sooner or later we'll burn out. Commitment can be sustained only when we continually renew our reserves of physical energy and spiritual and psychological strength.

I've mentioned the magazine, *Liberation*, that I edited from 1974 through 1976. It had been around since the mid-1950s and had an inspiring history. Nelson Mandela had written for it, as had Albert Camus, Bertrand Russell, and James Baldwin. Martin Luther King, Jr.'s "Letter from Birmingham Jail" had appeared in its pages. The social critic Paul Goodman and the civil rights leader Bayard Rustin were founding editors. But that time was long past when I arrived, at age twenty-one. Within six months, I'd become the senior person on staff, working desperately to keep *Liberation* afloat.

Miraculously, my five equally inexperienced coworkers and I began to pull it off, despite the crumbling of the Vietnam-era movements, skyrocketing paper and postage costs, and a shortage of the experience and connections necessary to raise the funds that independent political magazines constantly need. We enlisted new writers and financial supporters. We sent out mailings and appeals. We even increased our circulation. Because I felt the magazine's survival was at stake, I put in sixty hours a week, soliciting and developing articles, designing promotions, and raising the $60,000 a year in grants and donations that kept us going. When a piece of junk mail arrived one day addressed to "Dear Mr. Liberation," the other staffers handed it to me, explaining with a smile, "Of course they mean Paul."

But the work and circumstances ground me down. We earned $60 a week, and didn't always get that. Even though my rent in a shared Brooklyn house was only $85 a month, what I earned didn't cover my needs. The other staffers worked hard as well, but they logged fewer hours and were able to supplement their meager salaries by outside freelancing—indexing, proofreading, graphic design. They stayed financially afloat, albeit precariously, while I steadily depleted the money I'd saved from working my way through college as a bartender. A number of times I thought of asking for a bit more salary, both as compensation for my extra time and because I brought in the bulk of the magazine's budget. Had I received even another $500 a year, I might have been able to stay. But I never asked. Instead, when my savings ran out, I had to leave, financially and emotionally drained. Two years later, *Liberation* folded.

If we're to stay involved we need to set boundaries, so our lives don't get so consumed by the cause that we're forced to drop out entirely. In part, this means that we should pay attention to important personal concerns, making sure we vest enough time and energy, for instance, in our basic economic survival. An activist who's continually suffering financial crises is less than optimally effective. Eventually, he or she burns out and becomes no activist at all.

It's also important to avoid being psychologically blindsided. The week after a nonviolent small-boat blockade of America's first Trident submarine, a group of participants sat talking outside the courthouse where several were being tried. A woman from Malibu, dripping in Santa Fe silver and turquoise jewelry, had come up to watch the spectacle of the blockade. Now she began a conversation with a bus driver who'd marched in Vietnam-era protests. "You get involved as you go," she explained, as if a teacher outlining a lesson. "First sign a petition, then write a letter, do support, and the next thing you know you're blockading. You should join the next blockade."

"Right," said a listening blockader named Chris, very quietly. "And then the Coast Guard is shooting you with water cannons."

Chris wasn't cynical, just shaken by the massive Coast Guard response, and by a feeling of being in over his head. He'd given up his San Francisco apartment, sold his books, left a graduate program in English, and prepared himself for jail. When the charges were dropped, he was free to go where he chose. But the experience left him dislocated and uncertain.

I'm not suggesting we shy away from commitment just because our actions may carry a cost. We need all the courage we can muster to make our society more humane, and this often means stepping out of our comfort zone. But we can also think through our choices, prepare ourselves for the consequences, and remember that, in any event, we're in it for the long haul.

Gloria Steinem grappled with these questions of balance and boundaries as she realized how often she played the quintessential woman's role as sacrificial nurturer to the movement. Often she'd noticed herself going through the motions, as she says, "doing over again things I already knew how to do . . . saying things I'd said before . . . reacting more than acting." The reason, she believed, was the classically female "disease of being empathy sick," of always heeding the feelings and needs of others before her own. Steinem concluded that the classic golden rule needed to be read both ways. "The traditional sequence assumes a healthy self-esteem and asks for empathy: 'Do unto others as you would have others do unto you.' But for many people whose self-esteem has been suppressed, the revolution lies in reversing it: *Do unto yourself as you would do unto others*." This doesn't mean withdrawing from the world, but refusing to cannibalize ourselves for the sake of our commitments.

READY TO TAKE ON EXXON

The trick to succeeding in any high-stress situation is to find ways to nurture ourselves, even as we maintain our commitment. This is how Susan Butcher repeatedly won the twelve-hundred-mile Alaskan dogsled race, the Iditarod. In an intensely competitive situation, Butcher won, in part, by caring for her dogs. At every rest stop in one race, her prime rival left early, while Butcher attended to her dogs for the full four hours allotted. By the end of each lap, Butcher's dogs were forging ahead of his. "My dogs just kept getting stronger and stronger," she told the *Boston Globe*. "They gained in power the further along we got." By the last stop, her lead became unbeatable.

It helps to maintain a similar balance in our political commitments. Sometimes this means varying the work that we do. "I like to have one big project, and one small one," says the Sierra Club's Adam Werbach. "Last week I was tracking marbled murrelets in an old-growth redwood forest near Big Sur to see how many are still there. It's very concrete and practical. I compare that to other work I'm doing on the post-Kyoto negotiations on global warming. I like shifting between big and small issues, local organizing and huge international questions. On their own, either one can be extremely frustrating. But the combination reminds me why I'm involved in the first place."

A sense of balance also requires letting go of the assumption that we have to do everything. This means gently turning down the tenth or twelfth request to join a committee, call a phone tree, canvass a neighborhood, draft a letter, speak at a program, or march for a cause. Often we can do more than we think. But at some points we need to draw the line, and say we can do this much, but no more. We need time to play with our children, read a book, go to a movie, dance to good music, or soak in the bathtub and do nothing. "There are days," says Pete Knutson, "when you just have to drop everything, take the dog down to the woods or the beach, and simply take a break." If our causes call for more, and they always will, we can find other people to participate, or take on fewer projects. One way or another we need to stop before we're so spent, exhausted, and bitter that we feel no choice but to retire permanently.

"You can't solve all the world's problems," Hazel Wolf reminded me on the eve of her hundredth birthday. "You have to

guard against taking on more than you can do and burning out
with frustration. But you can take on one project at a time, and
then another. You can do that your entire life."

Steven Levine grew up in gangs, spent time in jail, then found
a new career teaching meditation in prisons and hospices. At one
of his seminars, a man who had survived family violence described
his current work, counseling and playing basketball with gang
kids. The kids were troubled, challenging, inspiring. "Sometimes
their energy threatens to blow my head off," he told Levine. "I feel
exhausted trying to keep up." He worried whether he could continue carrying the load.

Levine asked the man whether working with half the kids would
be enough to fulfill him. "More than enough," the man said with
a laugh. Levine suggested he find other activities that would channel the kids' creativity and slow their pace, such as creating a group
garden. Maybe, he suggested, the man could also shift his work-
load to include some other less desperate kids. Levine thought it
would be better for him to back off a bit so he could keep doing
his important work.

Think about the difference between physical and psychological
exhaustion. "Classical physics has taught us that energy is finite
and conserved," writes Mary Catherine Bateson, "but when we
use terms like 'energy' in speaking about human potential, we are
into another area entirely. . . . One person can 'energize' or 'empower' another without any transfer of physical qualities. The energy to write this page is released by metabolizing food—it comes
from my breakfast. But the 'energy' to write this page depends on
my state of mind, and such 'energy' can come from a sunset or a remembered smile. During the worst periods at Amherst [where Bateson was a dean trying to challenge a resistant old-boy culture] . . .
I learned to keep books of art and poetry in my office, giving myself three- and five-minute breaks to look at an African mask or
linger over a verse and be refreshed. . . . An activity that affects
vitality is not directly competitive or subtractive from other activities—on the contrary, it may enhance them."

If we save time for contemplation and rejuvenation we'll be better equipped to keep on. "You get out of the city," says Hazel Wolf, "you hike, run a river, or watch birds in a park. With all the things to observe, there's less room for worry. Your mind gets a rest. You come back ready to take on Exxon."

GETTING PAST BETRAYAL

I've described how movements bloom when they provide emotional support for their participants and encourage self-development along with social awareness. Conversely, nothing burns out activists faster than feeling that the movements we've joined have betrayed us. In the early 1970s, I worked in a Queens, New York, bar alongside a Greek immigrant in his early thirties named Charley. Bitterly right-wing, he supported every military escalation by the Nixon administration, and said that protestors and dissenters should be shot. He was a good man, but I cringed every time we got in a discussion, as our political values seemed radically opposed.

My final day on the job, Charley told me that he'd been a member of the Greek Communist Party. He'd resisted the brutal regime of the colonels who ran the country following their 1967 coup. As a result, he was jailed and tortured. When he was released, he discovered that some of the party leaders were wealthy doctors who survived the oppression untouched, safe in villas on the coast. In the wake of his sacrifice, something snapped.

Charley's backlash was more extreme than that of most disillusioned activists. But when our efforts already subject us to difficult circumstances, and when community is essential if we're to keep on, it's profoundly damaging when our comrades violate our trust.

We've all met individuals who espouse lofty ideals, then treat their fellow human beings with contempt. In *For Your Own Good,* psychologist Alice Miller describes parents who wreak hatred, intolerance, neglect, and abuse on their children, all in the name of love. Given how much our culture teaches us to treat people like objects, and given our inherent propensity to hunger for power, it's not surprising that our emotional flaws affect every sphere of human activity, including valuable social change efforts. When people work to create a more just world, but treat their fellow human beings unkindly—or, worse, as expendable for the cause— even their victories may leave behind a legacy of resentment.

Pete Knutson backed off for a time after his activist days at Stanford. He'd learned the power of his own and others' voices. He'd seen people respond in an inspiring way. Yet he couldn't shake his memories of sectarian manipulation, especially the actions of a campus Maoist group whose members strutted around the quad, wore red buttons with pictures of AK-47 rifles, and labeled those who disagreed with them "racist sissies." Every time someone started something politically worthwhile, they'd try to take control of it. The group even sent a voluptuous female member to visit Pete in his dorm room. "You know I'm very attracted to you, Pete," she said, "but I could never get involved with someone who isn't a member of a revolutionary organization." Nearly a decade later, Pete recounted their factional craziness, laughed bitterly, and shook his head in disgust. It took the community of his fellow fishermen to help him find a way back to social involvement.

Factionalism develops when we feel most powerless. In the wake of the Gulf War, human rights lawyer Julia Devin visited Iraq with a group of water and sanitation experts. "It was awful seeing children dying of hunger and needless sickness," she recalls. "I remember sitting in a New York apartment typing up testimonies of Iraqi women while a ticker tape parade marched by, celebrating the war. But what was worse was tearing each other apart in our delegation because of our pain and sense of helplessness. We argued over everything. We almost broke down into lawsuits. If we can't deal with our own community, how are we supposed to help people halfway around the world?"

The more desperate we feel, the more easily we blame those closest to us. When Saddam Hussein invaded Kuwait, my friend Glen Gersmehl had just taken on the job of directing Washington State SANE/Freeze, the state's largest peace organization. He'd grown up poor, worked low-level jobs (as a security guard, for instance) until he got a master's degree at Harvard's Kennedy School of Government, and then ran the peace studies program of a Massachusetts college. He left that position for SANE/Freeze. As the buildup to the Gulf War escalated, Glen threw himself into coordinating volunteers, bringing in new members, forming new coalitions, and organizing press conferences, rallies, and speakouts. He did a terrific job.

But the war severely strained the organization. Staffers who were supposed to be raising money over the phone took off to protest at the federal building. Peace activists in general felt isolated, confused, and dislocated. By the time the war ended, many despaired at the seemingly overwhelming popular support for it, and at the apparent futility of their opposition. In the wake of all this, SANE/Freeze board members, who were themselves struggling with doubt and self-blame, suddenly panicked at the organization's chronic financial crisis, and targeted Glen's leadership as the source of the problem. In a rushed and contentious meeting they forced him out of the job.

Glen was already exhausted from eighty-hour weeks spent in crisis mode. Being scapegoated made him feel worse still. For a while he retreated to the books that had always sustained him. He read about how people had acted for change in the past, and what kept them going in difficult times. He spent time expanding what had been a side project—a Peace and Justice Resource Center where he served as a consultant to libraries on books about social change, and sold these kinds of books to grassroots activists at conferences and through periodic mailings. Despite his wounded feelings, he also stayed active in SANE/Freeze, developing a model effort to challenge the U.S.'s role as the world's leading arms trader. And to pay the rent, he lived off a modest grant he'd secured for the arms trade project and worked for SANE/Freeze's phone bank. Eventually he found a job he loved, coordinating the national Lutheran Peace Fellowship.

But Glen had been treated badly. Although he never completely dropped out of the peace movement, he had to overcome his hurt before he could return to full-time work on the issues he passionately cared about.

I recently invited Glen to a discussion group on what sustains commitment. Those just beginning, he stressed, "say they're in it for the issues: homelessness, the Gulf crisis, the global arms trade, whatever." But the long runners, he said, "talk about finding a caring community." That's why Glen worries most about the breakdown of activist communities. "If you did exit polls of people who left after peace and justice meetings and didn't come back, most would be for that reason. Someone talked to them in the wrong tone of voice, cut them short, turned on them, failed to care about them enough to respect them."

Another woman in the group agreed. "When someone quietly drops out," she said, "we rarely take time to find out why. But we need to see whether it was something personal, or their feeling underappreciated, or whether we might be able to help them be involved in a different way, perhaps at a less demanding level of commitment."

Too often, those of us who are activists fail to treat our colleagues in the cause with the compassion we extend to those targeted by the policies we wish to change. During the discussion, I thought of Glen's ejection by SANE/Freeze. He received strong encouragement to persist from the woman who later became his wife, and from a loyal circle of friends. This was no small thing. Sometimes the difference between staying in a movement and dropping out can be as simple as people who believe in us. Glen also drew strength from his Christian faith, which, he says, "if you take it seriously isn't about trying to minimize the difficult moments in your life, the painful aspects, but about engaging them, making them sources of strength—making a priority out of our relationships, our compassion, and using our intelligence and skill to challenge what's destructive." In other words, Glen was fortunate enough to have multiple sources of personal support. Someone who didn't, who was a little less certain about his or her commitment, might have been discouraged enough to leave social involvement forever.

"When I work with churches," said Glen, "I'll tell them that I've been wrestling with forgiveness. 'I'd like to be able to love my enemies,' I'll say, 'but as an intermediate step I've decided to try to act lovingly toward everyone I serve on a committee with.' They'll break up laughing when I say this, because they know how rarely it happens. Maybe we should invest just two percent of our organizational budgets in finding the best people possible to teach us how to work together and express legitimate disagreements without backbiting and blaming. We'd spend it in a minute on mailings or phone bills. But we're afraid to invest it in ourselves."

Saints or martyrs might find such concerns beneath them. But for the rest of us, how we're treated by our fellow social activists can be critical. So we need to find ways to express disagreements without either censoring ourselves or demonizing those we're arguing with. If our fellow citizen activists are sometimes disappointed by the process of social activism, we need to convince them not to abandon their basic commitment, much as we'd tell a friend not to give up on a marriage merely because of an occasional argument or frustrated desire. Members of our groups won't always agree. That's a given. But we need to build communities in which we actively support each other, instead of dragging each other down with petty bickering.

THE PAIN OF THE PAST

Often we speak first of political burnout in physical terms, as a deep exhaustion. But physical exhaustion can be remedied by sleep, exercise, vacation, or the passage of time. Much harder to overcome are memories of doing too much and feeling isolated, un-appreciated, and let down by people we counted on. Indeed, a sure gauge of the seriousness of our burnout is what happens when, even years later, we so much as think about resuming social activ-ism. If we once again feel overwhelmed by apprehension, weari-ness, and powerlessness—by the feeling that we have no more to give—then our burnout is severe.

These negative feelings resemble the experience of veterans with post-traumatic stress disorder. The visible scars heal, but the invis-ible ones don't. Years later, related images can bring back all the old fear and confusion. As our mental and emotional circuits short out, the pain of the past overwhelms the possibilities of the present.

Evolutionary biologists have suggested that human beings may well be hardwired to relive painful memories. Our brain replays trauma so authentically that it triggers a full response from our involuntary nervous system. Among other things, breathing and heart rate accelerate and stress hormones are released. That's why the feelings seem so real. Fortunately, we're not completely at the mercy of this brain chemistry. Studies of abused children have shown that strong interpersonal bonds and intense positive emo-tional experiences can overcome the handicaps caused by violence. Obviously, recovery from political burnout is easier. But it, too, depends on acknowledging our unseen injuries, building supportive relationships, and allowing ourselves to be challenged and excited by new involvements.

FORGIVING OURSELVES

Making matters worse for those of us who retreat from social en-gagement are the guilt and shame we often feel afterward. When people slip in their personal lives, relapsing into addictions like alcoholism, smoking, or binge eating, their self-esteem often plummets as well. Absent a supportive community like AA, their picture of themselves as weak and worthless makes it all the harder to begin again. When we abandon social movements that once stirred our souls, a similar process can occur. It's only going to be temporary, we say at first. Then withdrawal becomes a habit, a way of life reinforced by cultural and economic pressures. In time we actively avoid opportunities to rejoin engaged communities, because we don't feel up to the challenge and don't want to be forced to explain ourselves. The very prospect reminds us of our failings. More than anything, we want to avoid our shame.

I've talked about the need to forgive our enemies, to liberate both them and ourselves from self-destructive impulses toward vengeance. It may be even harder to forgive ourselves for not winning every battle, salving every wound, and instantly changing the world—or for temporarily falling back. Granted, it's useful to re-examine our work, as COPS members do routinely, and determine whether particular efforts serve our goals, affect their intended targets, and continue to involve new people. But we help neither our spirits nor our causes by perpetually beating ourselves up for the shortcomings of our efforts. "*Without* forgiveness, hurts grow unchecked and we recycle failures, resentments, bitterness, and mistrust in our lives," says the writer Doris Donnelly. "*With* forgiveness, hurts are acknowledged and healed, and we are able to break a mindless cycle of retaliation by saying that the decisions of human life, even when they turn out badly, are not beyond repair."

It's easier to forgive ourselves if we acknowledge our fallibility from the start. All of us have been wrong; all of us will make mistakes again, in all domains of life, public and private. Whenever possible, we should learn from our past. But it doesn't help to obsess endlessly over what we should have said or done, how we could have changed things, or how we were wronged. It's better to continue to move forward, not waiting for the perfect circumstances but instead expanding our sense of possibility as we go.

None of us is perfect. A wise person is one who acknowledges imperfections and mistakes, does her or his best to make amends, and then tries again.

Going It Alone

"I've felt for a long time that people have had less and less energy," said my friend Ruth. "That's made it harder for me to act. Just before the 1992 elections, I sent out a hundred letters to friends, asking them to hand out literature during the final four weekends for a candidate of their choice. Only two responded, even though lots of other people were volunteering, and there was a whole slate of pretty good Democratic candidates who ultimately carried the state. Then I tried to put together a book group just to talk about some of these big-picture issues of all these global changes and how we might respond. I couldn't even get people for that. Maybe that was the last straw."

The more we expect people to reject our calls for involvement, Ruth's example suggests, the harder it becomes to keep on. As other activists drop out of the fray, we lose our faith in them. If we do persist, we begin to expect that we'll have to do so alone. Yet we also end up needlessly overwhelmed and isolated when we bury the pain that comes from taking on difficult issues of human destructiveness. As psychologist Joanna Macy writes, "Many peace and environmental advocates, exposed to terrifying information by the nature of their work, carry a heavy burden of knowledge. It is compounded by feelings of frustration, as they fight an uphill battle to arouse the public. Yet they view their own despair as a sign of weakness that would be counterproductive to their efforts. In their roles as mobilizers for the public will, they don't feel they can 'let their hair down' and expose the extent of their distress about the future. The consequent and continual repression of this despair takes a toll on their energies that leaves them especially vulnerable to bitterness and exhaustion."

In their studies of therapists who counsel abuse survivors, the psychologists Laurie Anne Pearlman and Lisa McCann have developed the concept of secondary or vicarious trauma to account for a parallel process. Therapists working in such situations hear story after story of human suffering. At first the stories inspire sympathy, generosity, and a passionate commitment to reducing human violence and destructiveness. But if they witness too much pain for too long, therapists who work with people who've been abused can themselves become hopeless and despairing. We've all met social workers, teachers, and counselors whose work has left them hollow-eyed and listless, just going through the motions even in situations of the gravest human consequence.

Yet Pearlman and McCann discovered an alternative. When practitioners meet regularly to sigh together, complain together, even shed a few tears together, and also to share their successes, they usually feel stronger. The support participants receive from such communities isn't technical. Their support circles have more in common with feminist consciousness-raising groups than with academic seminars. They provide a sympathetic forum, in which participants can share the most difficult and most rewarding aspects of their work. And the very act of discussion transforms interactions that would otherwise be draining and overwhelming into ones that feed participants' souls. In her work with physicians who attend dying patients, Rachel Naomi Remen notes a similar process. She concludes that "burnout only really begins to heal when people learn how to grieve."

Directors of community service projects and longtime political organizers also see the value of such intimate conversations for relieving stress and reinforcing camaraderie. If people do nothing but work in shelters and soup kitchens day after day, or fight protracted, piecemeal battles with entrenched institutions, they can quickly be overwhelmed. But if they have the chance to talk with each other and process what they experience, they tend to maintain their confidence and hope. They pass on stories and jokes, reflect on why they got involved to begin with, think about how they've changed along the way. Creating this kind of community not only reenergizes activists, it's also a central satisfaction of joining social movements—or it should be. Working for social change in solitude is a contradiction in terms.

SHARING THE JOURNEY

We often isolate ourselves more than necessary. A couple of years ago, I found myself weighing whether to attend Seattle's Hiroshima Day commemoration, an annual event coordinated by local religious, peace, and environmental organizations. I was feeling very down that day. The Republicans were busily dismantling sixty years of social reforms. The movements that should have offered an alternative seemed silent. I'd just received a batch of rejections on the initial proposal for this book, after editors who loved it lost out to marketing people who said, "Politics doesn't sell." At first, I thought I wouldn't go. I knew more than enough about the horror of the bombs. Why bum myself out any further? Although I certainly intended to stay engaged in some fashion, that particular day I was depressed, and depression is the polar opposite of engagement.

Nevertheless, at the last moment, I decided to go. I hoped seeing friends would cheer me up. When I arrived, hundreds of people were gathered by a lake to float paper lanterns with candles inside. Calligraphers decorated the lanterns, and people folded paper cranes to attach to them. Musicians played taiko drums and shakuhachi flutes. A children's peace choir sang, accompanied by young dancers. A Buddhist minister gave a benediction and spoke of a world in which children would no longer be killed by weapons of war. Some activist doctors spoke, as well as other veteran activists. People filed slowly down to the lake and launched their lanterns, which floated across the water, creating glowing trails of light.

As I listened to the music, and visited with people I knew, including a wonderful retired teacher in her late seventies and the college-age daughter of my next-door neighbor, I felt cleansed and calmed. The ceremony melded spirit and politics. It reminded me that isolation amplifies our impulses toward fear, resignation, and despair, whereas community helps us overcome them.

In his book *Why Marriages Succeed or Fail*, the University of Washington psychology professor John Gottman observed that in successful relationships, daily words and deeds that affirm the fundamental bond outnumber those that erode it by at least five to one. I'm skeptical of attempts to reduce love to mathematics, but the principle holds: The more relationships are nurtured, the stronger they become; the more they're neglected or undermined, the more likely they'll collapse.

The way people participate in social movements may follow a similar pattern. We act not only out of altruism or a sense of duty but because of what we get back—both the sense that our efforts can matter and the feeling of shared purpose with others who struggle alongside us. As the African American sociologist-turned-comedian Bertrice Berry says, "You want to make your movements so good they're like a party where people want to come and join in, feel left out if they're not taking part." Whether we persist may well depend on the relationship we create between these moments of solidarity and hope, and those of despair and alienation.

Lifelong commitment requires that the balance consistently tilt toward the former. In plain terms, this means that we need communities to sustain us. We need to find them, or create them, then labor continually to keep them vital and alive. Virginia Ramirez loved COPS's mix of celebration and struggle. Ginny Nicarthy had friends like Jane Klassen, who helped make her book on battered women possible. Scharlene Hurston joined with her fellow black employees at Inland, and together they changed the corporate culture. Adam Werbach laughs when he talks about "Sierra Singles" groups, but says they're a powerful way to support the needs of the club's members.

"I have friends," says Dave Hall of Physicians for Social Responsibility, "who'll say 'I don't go to church, I go to PSR meetings.' We've developed a common vision. But we also really like each other. The work matters, but also the chance to do it together." It's no accident that I and most of my friends have found their true loves through their social involvements.

When activists take care of each other, they can surmount the most difficult personal situations. I know a carpenter and dedicated peace and justice activist whose van was recently stolen. Inside were all his tools. He already lived on the financial edge. The theft threatened to push him over. But a friend enlisted enough support from friends, acquaintances, and others who respected his work that he was able to survive. Another man in the same circle suffered a series of life-threatening illnesses. Again people rallied around him with physical, financial, and emotional assistance. They helped make it possible for him to pull through.

Just as people who deal routinely with human trauma and pain talk among themselves to avoid being overwhelmed, we all need opportunities to share our concerns and apprehensions, our hopes and desires. When I organized discussion circles among people who'd pulled back from public engagement, something surprising happened. The very act of exchanging stories over a potluck meal created this kind of opportunity. Simply talking and thinking about the process of withdrawal made people want to get involved again. My friends in Ruth's group were typical. Even though they'd continued to see each other socially, they'd never discussed or acknowledged their common experience of disengagement. Maybe they felt ashamed of not staying true to dreams that were once the wellsprings of their lives. Whatever the reason, it soon became clear that they hungered for a chance to talk about their lives, choices, and uncertainties.

Near the end of the discussion, I asked what drew them to social involvement to begin with. The answer was always specific human stories, and my friends recounted them with passion: "It made me furious that we were dropping bombs on innocent people in Vietnam." "I had a black friend and she got treated so badly." "I knew someone who had an illegal abortion and nearly died." "When I lived in a Guatemalan Indian village, I learned what it's like to haul water by hand every day." "When I was an eighteen-year-old North Dakota farm girl, I helped smuggle an injured Native American activist out of Wounded Knee, and his courage totally inspired me." Without exception, their initial commitments had been sparked by specific examples of strength or of suffering. Only later did their experiences lead them to embrace and construct the larger political visions whose ambiguities now seemed to paralyze them.

As they described people they'd worked with, and their sense of common purpose, my friends became more animated. They stopped slouching. Their faces lit up. Exploring the taproots of their commitment gave them a renewed sense of hope and possibility. They began to shake the despair that had cast such a cloud over their souls.

Chapter Eleven

Pieces of a Vision

What is hateful to you, do not to your fellow man. That is the entire Law;
all the rest is commentary.

—*RABBI HILLEL*

Which issues should we take on, in this complex and demanding time? The answer will vary according to our different perspectives and backgrounds, of course. Some of us may be just beginning to wrestle with these questions, unsure of how to get engaged in our communities. Others who have been involved for years may feel disoriented and estranged, following the collapse of the grand paradigms of social change that once helped guide their commitments. Still others may continue to take important and challenging stands, yet long for a stronger sense of purpose. Whatever our situation, however, it would be easier to act if we had a compass to steer by.

Of what would this compass be composed? Where would it lead us? That's what I'd like to explore now. Even if there's no magnetic north, no blueprint for the ideal society, there are, I believe, some overall goals worth working toward, as well as others that should be avoided. I hasten to add that what I'm about to propose is not a formula for solving all our planetary ills. No such formula exists. And if it did, trying to describe it in the space of a single chapter would be absurd. Nor am I offering a compendium of specific policies and programs. A number of the books in my Resource Guide take up that matter, and I urge you to consult those that dovetail with your interests.

Meanwhile, think of my remarks here as a set of notes based on thirty years of watching citizens I admire struggle to make the world a better place. Taken together, these notes outline the beginnings of a direction. But even so, I offer them as suggestions, not prescriptions. This is not a manifesto, heavy with declarations and conclusions. It is, instead, an invitation, the jumping-off point for another facet of our conversation, one that I hope will help you think about the future, even if you disagree with my particular passions and priorities.

It's useful at this point to remind ourselves again that the issues and actions that appeal to us are inevitably personal. We each heal from physical illness in our own way, Rachel Naomi Remen explains. "Some people heal because they have work to do. Others heal because they have been released from their work and the pressures and expectations that others place on them. Some people need music, others need silence, some need people around them, others heal alone." Similarly, we each have our own approach to healing the world. We find particular ways to make our voices heard, and follow paths appropriate to our unique character, as well as to our circumstances. Ideally, we'll link seemingly disparate causes in service of a larger vision. But we can begin almost anywhere, and act in a way that matters.

VALUES TO FIGHT FOR

Let's think first about the kind of world we'd like to see, postponing for the moment the means by which we might bring that world into existence. Simply unleashing our imaginations can be empowering. And even if what we envision seems hard to achieve, the firmer our grasp of what we want, the more effectively we can work to make it a reality.

In a troubled time like ours, much can be learned by examining what's wrong. As writer Susan Griffin says, "There is a resemblance in the look and feel of a field that has been polluted with chemical waste, a neighborhood devastated by poverty and injustice, a battlefield." All are products of similar dehumanization, greed, and neglect—in other words, of an ethic of disconnection that makes people and places expendable. They're the antithesis of what results from an ethic of care. Carol McNulty's observation is worth pondering: It's hard to find inner peace when people are starving, the air is polluted, the water is filthy, and companies make money from the suffering of children.

To begin to sketch an alternative vision, then, we can look at all our economic, political, and cultural decisions, and ask whether they respect human dignity and nurture a more sustainable relationship with the earth. "We're living in an imperfect world," says Pete Knutson. "We have to make choices and judgments that aren't always easy. But you start with basic ethics, like truthfulness, fairness, equity, reciprocity, and sharing, that are at the core of our species nature, what makes us human. You reject the PR-firm notion that truth is a disposable commodity. If powerful economic interests are backing something, you don't shy away from naming them. These are very simple things, but they've become radical concepts in today's political reality."

At the heart of the ethics Pete describes lies the principle of mutual respect. "What is hateful to you, do not to your fellow man," said Rabbi Hillel, two thousand years ago. "That is the entire Law; all the rest is commentary." Hillel's words define a standard to live up to.

At a minimum, I'd argue, this standard calls for a world in which everyone has access to food, housing, and medical care; in which no one beats, shoots, evicts, tortures, or otherwise degrades their fellow human beings; and in which individuals can express what they believe without fear. Though honored far too often in the breach, most of these rights were enshrined fifty years ago in the United Nations Universal Declaration of Human Rights, signed by the major nations on earth.

For Virginia Ramirez, such a vision of human dignity is embodied in the ways we treat our children. "I'd like to see a world," she says, "where every child has the same opportunity. I see children suffer from hunger, sickness, cold, and lack of education. Or they're abused, humiliated, or whatever. That's the hardest thing to take, to see children suffer. To me, there would be justice if every child in this world got treated well. I don't know if that's ever going to happen. Maybe it won't. But for me that would be perfect justice."

A good society, I further believe, creates a sense of economic security for all its members—so that, in the words of songwriter Bruce Cockburn, "nobody has to scrape for honey at the bottom of the comb." It damages us all that the United States leads the industrialized world in rates of homelessness, child poverty, lack of health care, infant mortality, inequality of wealth, and nearly every other index of desperation among the voiceless and vulnerable. Even if we own our own homes, have decent jobs, and possess a modicum of financial comfort, we're demeaned by our society's radical economic polarization. Having to avert our eyes on the street, avoid certain neighborhoods, and mistrust other human beings who might take what we've got is "tacky," as preacher Will Campbell would say, and we know it. "We are going to have to develop a concept of *enough* at the top and at the bottom," Marian Wright Edelman writes, "so that the necessities of the many are not sacrificed for the luxuries of the few."

A good society gives us opportunities and resources to shape our common future. "What we're trying to do," says Ernie Cortes, the former lead organizer of COPS, "is to draw people out of their private pain, out of their cynicism and passivity, and get them connected with other people in collective action." In this sense, the very act of taking responsibility for our communities embodies the vision we seek. It makes democracy not a vague slogan masking manipulation and greed, but rather a living process by which all citizens participate in the creation and governance of society. The public arena should be the property of everyone.

A good society also helps each of us fulfill the full bloom of our uniqueness, the "acorn" of our character to which James Hillman referred. It honors our individual gifts and encourages our particular callings. It gives all its inhabitants the economic, emotional, and spiritual support needed to follow their dreams. An unjust one, in contrast, starves hopes, aspirations, and possibilities. It stunts lives and potentials.

And because we realize ourselves fully only through interaction with others, a good society fosters community in all its forms. It nurtures rich and vibrant places to live, where we are surrounded by friends and acquaintances, feel a sense of belonging, look out for each other's children. Such communities once existed in our small towns and urban neighborhoods. Efforts like Rebecca Hughes's baby-sitting co-op are an attempt to revive them. The longing most of us have for places where intimate connections are commonplace makes clear how deeply we need the company of other human beings if we are to feel at home in the world.

But wherever we reside, we'll realize neither our individual nor communal selves if we're totally consumed by our work. That points to another feature of a good society: We should be able to earn a living wage without sacrificing our psychological, spiritual, and sometimes even physical well-being by giving over our entire lives to our jobs. The bumper sticker "The Labor Movement: The Folks Who Brought You the Weekend" is more than a joke. For generations, citizens struggled to shorten the hours they worked—in part because democracy is impossible when employers control our every waking minute. But during the past few decades, the time we spend on our jobs has been steadily increasing, even though American industrial productivity has more than tripled since 1948. As Juliet Schor suggests in *The Overworked American,* we could reverse this trend by pushing for flextime that's fairly compensated or for cutbacks in the workweek, or by adapting Western European standards for paid vacation and parental leave. A good society allows citizens time to think and reflect, to be with their families and friends, and to engage themselves in their communities.

Finally, if we're to have a society in which good endures, we're going to have to do a better job of nurturing our sense of the sacred and honoring the complex web of life that supports us. We did not create the earth, as Adam Werbach stresses, so we have no right to play God by destroying it. We need an ethical vision that helps us slow down the pace of global change, challenge the idolatry of mindless consumption, and wield our awesome technological capabilities with humility. "We can start with the basics," Adam says, "like protecting food that's safe to eat, water that's safe to drink, air that's safe to breathe, and a little more wilderness than our parents left us."

WHAT DO WE VALUE?

Aristotle once said that a barbaric culture consumes all of its resources to support itself in the present, whereas a civilized culture preserves them for later generations. Many of our society's most destructive actions yield consequences whose gravest implications aren't immediately apparent. That's true of our casual destruction of the planet. It's true of our writing off entire communities of young men and women who will grow into adulthood bereft of hope and skills. It's true when we say, in one of the richest countries in the world, that we can't afford to address our most pressing common problems.

The alternative, as environmentalist David Brower says, is to act so that "the new child or the new fawn or the new baby seal pup that's born a thousand years from now . . . opens its eyes on a beautiful, livable planet." Virginia Ramirez touches on this in explaining why it's important to persist. "Maybe the things we're working on today," she says, "won't bring about changes for years. But it's just as important that we do them."

Working for the future requires a vision of accountability, by which we hold individuals and institutions responsible for the impact of their choices, and by which we link seemingly disconnected actions and consequences. Novelist Ken Kesey's son died when the ramshackle bus carrying him and the rest of the University of Oregon wrestling team skidded off an icy mountain road. After-

ward, Kesey wrote Oregon senator Mark Hatfield, explaining that
his first response was to turn the other cheek, to accept the tragedy
as fate.

"But what," he continued, in a letter printed in the *Whole Earth*
magazine, "if the other cheek is somebody else's kid? In some other
slapdash rig? On some other ill-fated underfunded trip next wrestling season? Or next debate season? Or next volleyball season?
Moreover, what if this young blood has been spilled not merely to
congregate people and their feelings, but also to illuminate a thing
going wrong?"

Kesey considered blaming the Oregon coach "for driving a borrowed rig over a treacherous pass without snow studs, or seatbelts,
or even doors that closed properly"; or the state of Oregon for not
better funding the program; or the NCAA, for "fostering a situation where more energy is devoted to monitoring the ethic of the
few 'stars' in the sports firmament than to the actual welfare of
the untold thousands of unknown athletes traveling to their minor
events all across the nation."

He mentioned other accidents on similar trips by other schools'
athletic teams, then added, "But what can they do? . . . It's hard
enough to pass a school budget in Oregon without asking for fancy
protection. Just not enough money in the communities. Nobody
wants to increase property taxes, not even for safer playgrounds,
let alone for safer activity buses.

"Then, the other night, as I watched the national news, it came
to me. We were lobbing those 16-inch shells into the hills of Leb-
anon. The Pentagon spokesman said he wasn't certain exactly
which faction we were hitting, but he reassured us that we were
certainly hitting *somebody*. Then he was asked what each of those
shells cost. The price was something enormous. I can't remember.
But the spokesman countered by saying that the price for national
defense is always high, yet it must be paid.

"And I began to get mad, Senator. I had finally found where
the blame must be laid; that the money we are spending for national defense is not defending us from the villains real and near,

the awful villains of ignorance, and cancer, and heart disease and highway death. How many school buses could be outfitted with seatbelts with the money spent for one of those 16-inch shells?"

Expressing a similar sentiment, Congressman Ron Dellums once said that we know the state of a nation's soul by looking at its budgets. In Dwight D. Eisenhower's classic words, "Every gun that is made, every warship launched, every rocket fired, signifies in a final sense a theft from those who hunger and are not fed—those who are cold and not clothed." Over the years, I've seen this statement on so many posters, banners, T-shirts, and signs, that now I barely notice it. But it remains truer than ever in a post–Cold War world. We continue to spend $300 billion a year on what we call defense—as much in real dollars as during the heart of the Cold War, and a figure that, when added to costs still being paid from past wars and weapons buildups, accounts for nearly half of all discretionary federal spending.

We need to talk honestly about the human toll of such choices, asking specifically who benefits and who pays. When a nurse I know was conducting physical exams of inmates in Seattle's county jail, she discovered that a huge percentage had chronic ear infections. That prompted her to wonder about the implications of young kids with untreated earaches: It's hard to hear what the teacher is saying. Maybe they feel angry and edgy. Soon they drop out, start stealing to survive, and end up in jail. My friend wondered how many of these men might have followed a different path had their families had access to decent medical treatment.

We're often told that we can't afford to provide health care for all of our children, can't afford to ensure that they attend adequate schools or have a roof over their heads. We can't afford to fund adequate youth employment programs, though we somehow find the money to continue building prisons. Nor, we're told, can we afford to protect our environment, the world our children and their children will inherit. "We can clone animals," points out David Lewis. "We can send rockets into space. But we can't give young people anything better to believe in than worshipping the god of money. We can't even make drug treatment programs available to everybody who wants and needs them. I would like to see that same kind of effort applied to saving people's lives."

David's point hits home to me. Enough resources exist in America to meet our public needs. But we must reform the policies and institutions that allow our society, in the words of economist John Kenneth Galbraith, to be dominated by "private affluence and public squalor." While writing *Generation at the Crossroads* in the early 1990s, I interviewed students protesting tuition hikes at New York City's mammoth 200,000-student CUNY system. Most came from impoverished backgrounds. The families of nearly a third lived on combined yearly household incomes of less than $14,000. The students went on strike and occupied campus buildings after New York State cut $92 million from the budget line that supported their colleges—in the process hiking tuition, cutting financial aid, and slashing faculty and support staff. The legislators said that the state simply lacked the money.

Shortly afterward, the investment firm Goldman Sachs, headquartered in New York City, announced a good year. It paid out bonuses to its 161 partners that totalled over $800 million. Ten percent of just this tiny group's yearly bonus would have just about covered the entire CUNY budget cuts for that year. But throughout the 1980s, the Goldman Sachs partners—and others equally affluent—had all seen their federal and state taxes cut repeatedly, producing major shortfalls in government revenue. Now the legislators said they no longer could afford to maintain the right of 200,000 students to receive an education. Their financial priorities reflected their values, and they deemed it most important to make sure their wealthy contributors were contented.

Budget numbers seem abstract until we realize that they represent the common resources of our society—resources that could support better schools, efficient mass transit, low-income housing, community investment corporations, inspiring arts programs, universal health care, or a serious investment in repairing the environment. If the most successful attempts to heal our society's ills and promote human dignity are often local grassroots efforts, like David's Free at Last project, imagine the impact if we gave these groups enough resources to do their work as well and powerfully as they could, instead of forcing them to scramble constantly for crumbs.

Lest you think I'm making too much of this, consider the following examples: For less than half of the tax cuts that Congress gave corporations and wealthy individuals in the 1990s alone, we could bring the health, nutrition, and education standards of every child in America up to European standards. If corporations paid the same federal tax rates as they did in the high-growth 1950s, we'd have balanced our federal budget years ago, and would be making major strides toward paying off the national debt—just from that one source alone. But few political leaders are willing to propose this, any more than they're willing to challenge our $170 billion a year in corporate welfare, or to examine the difference between legitimate defense spending and pork-barrel projects like the Lockheed-Martin plants in Newt Gingrich's home district of Marietta, Georgia. A remark attributed to the late Republican senator Everett Dirksen wryly sums up the scale of the problem: "A billion here and a billion there," Dirksen said, "and pretty soon you're talking about real money."

To borrow a phrase from the ecologists, we need a full-cost accounting of our political and economic choices. We need to realize what we're losing: When kids grow up in poverty, many end up in jail; when watersheds are devastated on speculators' whims, salmon runs dwindle; when people like the Goldman Sachs executives get tax breaks for making millions, students can't afford to go to school; when corporations lay off employees, institute speed-ups, and reduce benefits, families disintegrate and communities erode. We need to think about all the deferred, denied, and unintended consequences that ripple out over time, including opportunities lost and potentials unrealized. Only when we are honest about the consequences of our choices can we begin to move forward.

BEYOND MCWORLD

Changing how we make our public decisions would also help. As Alison Smith says, broad-based citizen participation is itself an "antidote to cynicism." "I'd love to see a more humane society," she stresses, "but to get that, we're going to have to have a much greater level of involvement, across economic lines, across racial lines, across every line that divides us. We have this two-hundred-year-old experiment in self-governance. I think it's a worthy experiment. But it won't work if we're passive. One of the great things about the reforms we passed in Maine is that they require citizen participation. I want to see people running campaigns without fund-raising pressures, and serving in elected office knowing their only debt is to the voters. Imagine a political system where the worthwhile things people do in their communities count for more than the size of their wallets. Imagine people actually participating."

Efforts like the Maine initiative could make a major difference if we pursued them nationwide, persistently enough to succeed. But challenging as it might seem to bring our political process back into line with democratic principles, it's an even more daunting task to gain a greater say in the economic decisions that most affect our lives and communities. Politics and economics are linked, of course. Consider again the role of money in campaigns, or the influence of well-funded lobbyists and right-wing think tanks in promoting the agendas of the affluent, or the degree to which the media skew reporting to favor powerful financial interests. While clear paths exist to reform electoral mechanisms, however, it's not at all apparent which steps would bring about a truly just and democratic economy. Many of us would like to work toward something better than a world ruled by the likes of G.E., Mitsubishi, Microsoft, and Rupert Murdoch. We believe that unaccountable corporate power and a correlate ethic of greed create many of our most significant national and global problems. But we're not sure just what could replace our present system. Unable to come up with a clear alternative, too many activists have withdrawn from civic involvement, while others hold back because they don't know where to begin or how to proceed once they've started.

Our cultural gatekeepers are so adamant about this being the best of all possible systems—past, present, or future—that I hesitate even to question their triumphalism. But whether you agree with my particular criticisms of what political scientist Benjamin Barber calls "McWorld," I think it's worth briefly looking at the radical approaches that once claimed to represent a different path. There are lessons here for all of us, about power and its abuses and dreams of justice gone awry.

As I've mentioned, the nations that once prided themselves on carrying the torch for the Marxist tradition have now seen their systems ignominiously collapse, as in the Soviet Union and Eastern Europe; have transmuted themselves into a depressing mix of marketplace exploitation and political repression, as in China and Vietnam; or have been isolated and marginalized, like Cuba. The United States has fed this process by making war on democratic alternatives. Our government has attacked a succession of reformist governments in countries from Iran, Indonesia, and Guatemala to Brazil and the Congo. In Chile, the Nixon administration helped overthrow Salvador Allende's democratically elected socialist government in favor of the brutal dictator Pinochet. But the Soviet-style regimes basically fell of their own weight—their brutal oppressiveness, profound inefficiency, consistent stifling of the human spirit, and pervasive ravaging of the earth. This occurred even as economic globalization exported the most all-consuming and rapacious aspects of market approaches to every corner of our planet.

Marx's early writings, in particular, reflected a powerful hunger for justice and some compelling visions of a better world. My gut sense is that he would have been appalled at the brutalities later perpetuated in his name. But he created a dangerous precedent when he, and especially Frederick Engels, argued that their particular version of socialism embodied the ultimate "scientific" approach that enabled those who adopted it to finally understand the forces of history and steer it toward their desired ends. It was then but a short step for those who took up their legacy to justify immensely destructive actions under the banner of historical inevitability.

We can see this in Marxism's Leninist stream, which, by equating Lenin's Bolshevik party with the embodiment of the promised future, betrayed the cause of freedom from the beginning. In 1917, the workers and sailors of the city of Kronstadt helped spearhead the new Soviet revolution. Four years later, they demanded that the Bolsheviks fulfill their promise of establishing a worker's democracy. Trotsky's Red Army attacked and slaughtered them ruthlessly, setting the Soviet pattern of crushing all dissent.

Conservatives have used the violence and bleak authoritarianism of the states that emerged from these unhappy events to tar all alternative economic visions and embrace the universal rule of the market. In the process, they've raised valid moral and practical points about the dangers of centralized economic and political control, and of the belief that we can engineer human nature, ridding it of the lust for power and other corruptions. Most important, they've questioned making lives and liberties expendable in the name of revolutionary necessity.

These flaws, and others, led to the end of the major state Communist regimes, which was a profound victory for human dignity. For many, however, this collapse has also spelled the demise of a worldview whose proponents claimed it was the prime historical opposition to the destructive aspects of global corporations. Yet even this notion, that the Communist systems were the sole political alternative to the most damaging aspects of multinational capitalism, is itself a dangerous myth. Efforts to create societies in which money isn't the measure of all worth go as far back as recorded civilization, millenniums before Karl Marx was born. The state Communist experiments lasted only seventy years, or less than the lifespan of Hazel Wolf. Despite the immensity of their failure, their example hardly seems basis enough to pontificate about the course of all pending human history. Nor does it invalidate the larger challenge of creating economic and political systems in which people have a say in key decisions that affect their lives.

If we seek an alternative to an economic philosophy based on the unchecked pursuit of more, we could start with biblical passages, like those studied by the COPS members. Think of the Prophet Isaiah's scathing depiction of a land "filled with silver and gold, [where] there is no end to their treasures," but because people make idols of material creations and turn away from compassion, they fight, "one against the other, neighbor against neighbor, city against city, kingdom against kingdom." Think of the Old Testament's Jubilee Year, when debts were forgiven and land redistributed. Think of Jesus kicking the money changers out of the temple, and telling them to "stop using my Father's house as a market." Think of the description from the book of Acts, explaining how, among the company of Christian believers, "Not a man of them claimed any of his possessions as his own, but everything was held in common. . . . They had never a needy person among them, because all who had property in land or houses sold it, brought the proceeds of the sale, and laid the money at the feet of the apostles; it was then distributed to any who stood in need."

In his classic *I and Thou*, the Jewish theologian Martin Buber examined the process of dialogue between an individual and other human beings, or an individual and God, as an ideal moment of mutual recognition and respect. It's the polar opposite, he says, of more narrow and instrumental approaches that reduce other people to things, whose value resides only in their usefulness, not in what they are in themselves. Buber found the political expression of this impulse toward mutuality in the traditions of community-based socialism that Marx first embraced, then later scorned as "utopian," but which Buber believed offered a humane alternative to the Soviet Union's oppressive path.

Such visions aren't merely theoretical. In his brilliant *Homage to Catalonia*, George Orwell portrayed anarchist workers and farmers during the Spanish Civil War; they ran complex industrial and agricultural enterprises under the most difficult circumstances. Eventually, their efforts were destroyed by Franco's troops and betrayals by their Stalinist supposed allies. After the war ended, however, a Basque priest who'd supported the Spanish Republic and barely survived Franco's jails began a small cooperative stove factory in a remote town called Mondragon. Today, more than fifty years later, the interconnected Mondragon cooperatives include 29,000 people, who together own, manage, and operate a highly successful community development bank; an insurance company; agricultural co-ops; Spain's largest manufacturer of refrigerators, stoves, and electrical appliances; a factory that makes computer-controlled machine tools; a chain of supermarkets; a joint co-op/government university; and a vocational school and occupational retraining system. Industrial sales alone have grown to nearly $5 billion per year, 40 percent of which comes from exports. Mondragon is a powerful example of a successful cooperative model.

Speaking more generally, a just economic order would almost certainly include many of the advances in preserving human dignity enacted by the Western European labor and socialist parties, which have come out of what's known as the social democratic tradition. As I've suggested, decent health care and child care, adequate vacations, and retirement security should be part of any good society. Movements based on the social democratic tradition have made major strides in ensuring that these support systems are available to all. As I write, parties coming out of this tradition have recently recaptured power in most of Western Europe. Granted, they don't guarantee universal justice and happiness. Nor have they solved all the global economy's complex problems. But the principles they fight for are well worth considering, along with others that are emerging, piece by piece, from ecological research, religious traditions, and a wealth of creative local initiatives across the globe.

AMERICAN ALTERNATIVES

Though you won't often find them in standard history books, America has its own tradition of attempts to create a more democratic economy, the legacies of which remain relevant today. In the view of Thomas Jefferson, for example, economic imbalances threatened the foundation of democracy. Inequality, he wrote, produced "so much misery to the bulk of mankind, legislators cannot invent too many devices for subdividing property." "I hope," he warned, "we shall crush in its birth the aristocracy of our monied corporations which dare already to challenge our government to a trial of strength, and bid defiance to the laws of our country."

Lincoln had similar reservations about the damaging effects of gross inequality of wealth, proposing instead that we favor "the man before the dollar." "Inasmuch as good things are produced by labor," he said, "it follows that all such things of right belong to those whose labor has produced them. But it has so happened, in all ages of the world, that some have labored and others have without labor enjoyed a larger proportion of the fruits. This is wrong and should not continue. To secure to each laborer the whole product of his labor, or as nearly as possible, is a worthy object of any good government."

The populist and socialist organizers of the late nineteenth and early twentieth century took up these themes in a context of rapid industrialization and emerging corporate monopolies. Their agendas included a powerful mutual-aid component, whereby small farmers worked together to market their crops and challenge the stranglehold of powerful railroad and banking interests in favor of what they called "the cooperative commonwealth." They talked of ways that workers could run major enterprises. Though ultimately these movements were defeated, their egalitarian philosophy led to the creation of successful institutions that persist to this day, like North Dakota's state-owned bank, Wisconsin's state-owned insurance company, and, later on, hundreds of rural electrical cooperatives.

The principle of using common resources for the common good reached fruition in Roosevelt's New Deal, and the policies that emerged from it. Howard Zinn recalls coming back from the Second World War and working as a waiter, a ditch-digger, and a brewery worker while trying to support two young children in a rat-infested Bedford-Stuyvesant apartment. Then he got the chance to go to New York University, with expenses paid for by his veteran's benefits. His education and the educations of millions of other vets helped fuel the longest-sustained growth period in American history. "Whenever I hear that the government *must not* get involved in helping people," writes Zinn, "that this must be left to 'private enterprise,' I think of the G. I. Bill and its marvelous non-bureaucratic efficiency."

Our historical amnesia makes it hard to draw practical lessons or moral strength from such traditions. Because we're poorly informed about the effort that went into such socially progressive victories as Social Security, Medicare, the forty-hour workweek, and the right, however constrained it now is, to organize unions, we're ill-equipped to defend them, much less to comprehend the principles they represent and their relevance to contemporary issues. Even if our vision of a truly just society is hazy, however, these advances should be preserved and strengthened, not eroded. For they help answer Jefferson and Lincoln's concerns about democracy's vulnerability to unchecked economic forces.

I'm not suggesting that we automatically embrace every social welfare or public investment program placed before us. Whatever organizations and institutions we believe in, it's worth asking which of their approaches effectively serve a greater common good, and which do not. This applies to government projects, public schools, community development corporations, and common support systems like welfare and disability compensation. It also applies to nonprofit agencies and unions, churches, temples, the Salvation Army, and homeless shelters. And it applies to the private sector—specific workplaces, industries, and the market as a whole. Regardless of our political allegiances or fears about giving ammunition to hostile critics, we help nothing by cultivating blind loyalty. Our challenge is to encourage the institutions to which we belong to fulfill their potential, and to make sure that their actions strengthen democracy, not weaken it.

Although participatory economic forms are far from the norm, some contemporary American examples suggest some potential directions. Pittsburgh's nonprofit Steel Valley Authority recently used money from banks, churches, unions, local government, and a community development corporation to establish a successful community-owned bakery called City Pride. Majority worker-owned companies now employ between two and three million people, and include corporations as large as United Airlines, Publix Supermarkets, and Science Applications, a thirty-thousand-employee research and development corporation that recently bought the R&D subsidiary of the Baby Bells.

Even when workers aren't also owners, they can participate more often and more directly in corporate policymaking, thereby building real democracy. Germany requires worker representation on the boards of major corporations, and Genoese longshoremen have long managed their own operations while running one of the busiest ports on the continent. In this respect, the United States has much to learn from Europe. Nevertheless, at GM's unionized Saturn plant in Spring Hill, Tennessee, workers have the final say on day-to-day hiring decisions, and their twelve- to sixteen-person teams have authority over purchasing, budgeting, and maintenance. The Spring Hill operation has remained profitable during a number of periods when other GM factories suffered losses and layoffs. According to a recent study by economists Lisa Lynch of Tufts University and Sandra Black of the Federal Reserve Bank, American factories that are unionized and offer such participatory programs are 20 percent more productive than the average for their industry.

Another model for economic democracy can be found in partnerships between private corporations and their surrounding communities. COPS and its sister organizations in other cities have generated commitments from major companies to invest in long-neglected neighborhoods, and to provide resources so high school students with good grades and regular attendance records will be guaranteed financial access to college. In 1989, the Vermont National Bank established a Socially Responsible Banking Fund. Depositors can assign to it any of their conventional bank accounts, receiving standard interest while also supporting housing co-ops, environmental education centers, organic farms, and an energy recycling business that recovers methane from the Brattleboro landfill. During the past ten years, a period when total Vermont bank deposits shrank, the fund has grown to $87 million.

Building on Jefferson's ideas of a nation of freeholders—citizens who control their own livelihoods—economist Gar Alperovitz suggests that communities develop their own locally controlled enterprises, so their residents will be less vulnerable to the caprices of the global economy. Markets and trade would still exist. Technology would still develop. But communities would have greater control of their regional economies, and would keep as many resources as possible circulating indigenously. It's hard, Alperovitz says, for people to be full and active citizens unless they enjoy enough independence to speak out without fear of reprisal by powerful economic and political institutions (factories, for instance, may threaten to shut down or move if their workers organize a union, or owners may pressure their workers to lobby for pork barrel contracts). Alperovitz believes the more control we have over our local economies, the more we can promote genuine liberty.

Likewise, Pete Knutson considers independence a virtue of his local fishing economy, whose roots go back thousands of years. "We face lots of frustrations," Pete says, "like dealing with corporate domination of our markets and the destruction of the watersheds. We'd have a much better situation if we didn't. But we also have a lot of individual autonomy. We're out there in nature, relying on a few other people, so there's a sense of camaraderie.

We're doing environmentally sustainable work, harvesting a wonderful regional food source in a way we can continue, so long as
people monitor the salmon runs and fight to take care of the habitat. Those are qualities of responsibility. You want them in any
kind of work and any society."

Local self-reliance also make communities far less vulnerable to
the potential breakdowns of interconnected global technologies.
I'm thinking now of the three lines of faulty computer code that
repeatedly disrupted ATT's long-distance lines in 1990, and the
1998 shutdown of most of America's pagers by the failure of a
single satellite. Not to mention the "millennium bug," also known
as Y2K, the problems anticipated from older computer programs
and microchips that are unable to handle dates beyond 1999. As
long as we're linked to ever more complex and interconnected technological systems, such problems will affect us. But we can blunt
their impact by increasing our capacity to meet basic needs with
resources from our own region, and by creating strong, participatory communities that can respond quickly when breakdowns
and other crises occur.

We may disagree on the desirability of any of these approaches,
or on whether they're feasible. But my aim, again, is not to convert
you to specific prescriptions but simply to suggest that alternatives
to the most destructive aspects of our current economy do exist,
or can be created. As American citizens, we must remember that
many of these alternatives are homegrown. We should also remind
ourselves that whatever our vision of the ideal world may be, there
are more than enough things we can do to improve the one we
live in.

DEFENDING THE EARTH

We also possess the means to rein in the power of our own technical inventiveness and to challenge environmental despoliation.
Nature cannot defend itself against the damage we create, though

it may exact a toll through flood, drought, desertification, and famine. This means it's up to us, as ordinary citizens, to speak for an imperiled biosphere and to help chart wiser paths.

We could begin by replacing the ultimately self-destructive economic ethic of perpetual growth with principles more consistent with natural ecosystems. This means valuing the notion of limits, and the virtues of balance, differentiation, and interdependence.

The socially responsible business executive Paul Hawken asks us to consider the "income derived from a healthy environment: clean air and water, climate stabilization, rainfall, ocean productivity, fertile soil, watersheds, and the less-appreciated functions of the environment, such as processing waste—both natural and industrial." A sustainable economy, he says, lives off this income, which we inherit simply by virtue of residing on the planet. By preserving and replenishing natural systems, we can continue to draw this income indefinitely. Our current American economy, by contrast, is nonsustainable. It consumes not only the income, but also the basic natural capital from which the income is derived, and it passes on the consequences to future generations.

Yet examples exist of sustainable economic practices, and we can learn from them. In an essay on Peruvian mountain farmers, Wendell Berry describes agricultural traditions so rich and complex that even the least-skilled individuals do not erode the fragile land they work. Some intensively cultivated English farms have been worked for thousands of years, yet the soil has grown steadily richer. These practices are guided by cultural ethics that make accommodating nature a matter not of extraordinary skill, intelligence, or moral development, but of habits and cultural frameworks woven into the daily lives of ordinary citizens.

To move our economy toward this kind of sustainability, environmental activists have proposed several basic reforms, beginning with the elimination of public subsidies of enterprises that damage species, habitat, and the planet as a whole. "We provide price supports to sugarcane growers," Hawken points out, underscoring the contradiction in current economic policy, "and we subsidize the restoration of the Everglades (which sugarcane growers are destroying). We subsidize cattle grazing on public lands, and we pay for soil conservation. We subsidize energy costs so that farmers can deplete aquifers to grow alfalfa to feed cows that make milk that we store in warehouses as surplus cheese that does not get to the hungry."

Hawken and others suggest that instead of subsidizing ecologically destructive activities we should be collecting "green taxes" from them, while simultaneously offering commensurate credits for businesses that restore the environment and invest in human capital. This means encouraging state-of-the-art insulation and efficient lighting instead of additional power plants, organic and bio-intensive agriculture instead of chemical-dependent monocropping, and effective public transportation systems and fuel-efficient cars instead of massive highway subsidies. It means supporting closed-loop manufacturing systems that reuse materials and energy to avoid waste and pollution in the first place, or that create durable consumer goods with repairable components. It means continually asking, once again, how our actions today will affect generations to come.

Environmental economists have made other suggestions along the same lines, such as levying additional "social tariffs" on imports that depend on starvation wages or environmental pollution. Some have even drawn inspiration from the biblical Jubilee Year, suggesting that certain Third World loans be forgiven so that countries aren't driven to abuse their populace and ravage their environment to pay off bills incurred by corrupt, lavishly spending former governments. None of these approaches will cure all our environmental ills. They are pieces of a larger vision whose contours are still emerging. But they provide a significant start.

WE BUILD THE ROAD AS WE TRAVEL

A patchwork, partially constructed vision may strike exactly the balance between humility and boldness that's needed in these unpredictable times. Like the ragpickers I mentioned earlier, we may proceed best, as Mary Catherine Bateson writes, "by improvisation, discovering the shape of our creation along the way, rather than pursuing a vision already defined." So long as we stay open to new information, learning as we go, not allowing ourselves to be distracted by the search for absolute certainty, we can continue to work toward goals we can feel proud of. We can conduct what Gandhi called "experiments in truth," or as the priest who founded the Spanish Mondragon co-ops once said, "build the road as we travel."

As I've said, I can't emphasize strongly enough the importance to this journey of learning from the stories of our fellow citizens. This means listening to people, like Virginia Ramirez and her San Antonio neighbors, who live on crumbling streets and send their children to underfunded schools. To those who grow up unable to acknowledge their sexuality frankly, for fear of being beaten or scorned. To those who earn decent pay and live in comfortable surroundings but are ground down by endless commutes, sixty-hour workweeks, and a sense that their jobs lack meaning. And even to those who strongly disagree with the political solutions we may offer.

To be sure, these stories may offer conflicting lessons. Each of us may interpret them differently. That's to be expected. Our visions may be pieced together and subject to constant modification, but the more they're based on the specific details of individual lives, the more we can trust them. This requires that we pay close attention to the actual circumstances under which others live, to the specific problems they face, and to their basic needs.

Such attentiveness, for example, was key to the National Labor Committee's successful Gap campaign as well as to related successes, as when the NLC persuaded the Liz Claiborne and Kathie Lee Gifford companies to demand that their contractors treat their workers with greater respect. After consulting with local religious, labor, and community groups in towns where the clothing factories are sited, the NLC has mobilized public pressure to insist that companies not just close down their factories or those of their contractors, but instead stay, paying living wages, allowing unionization and independent monitoring, and ending the pollution of their surroundings. This approach gave Latin American workers leverage both to achieve some modest economic gains and to begin building democracy. It also made it harder for corporations to blackmail U.S. workers by chasing ever-lower wages and worse working conditions in other countries.

Campaigns like these pay close heed to the communities they work with, while also raising deeper principles of human dignity. They combine the pragmatism of learning as we go with a larger vision of justice. In his classic *Strategy for Labor,* the French social theorist André Gorz distinguishes between reforms that democratize power and those that mask fundamental inequities. When considering any present or proposed institutional and individual choices, he suggests we ask whether they will increase human dignity or diminish it, embolden people's voices or stifle them, give ordinary citizens more or less of a say in shaping their world. As Wendell Berry writes, good solutions recognize that they are part of a larger whole, while bad ones assume we can isolate discrete elements. If proposed reforms increase democratic rights, respect people's lives, contribute to a sense of individual power and community possibility, and increase the likelihood of a sustainable future, they are worth supporting. They are elements of the road that we build as we go.

Even in the most difficult situations, we can construct such self-made routes toward freedom and justice. In his book on Poland's Solidarity movement, Lawrence Weschler describes how the Poles took on, as a new principle of action, the task of creating for themselves what they wanted for their society. They wanted free elections, so they freely elected individuals; wanted free speech, so spoke freely; wanted a trade union, so founded one. Leaders of KOR, the workers' support movement, routinely risked job loss or prison by printing their names and phone numbers on the back of each mimeographed sheet describing incidents of police harassment against then unknown activists like Lech Wałesa. "It is as if," Weschler comments, "KOR were calling out to everyone else, 'Come on out! Be open. What can they do to us if we all start taking responsibility for our true dreams?' "

"We're often told that politics is the art of the possible," says Elaine Bernard, of the Harvard Trade Union Program, an intensive training school for union leaders. "But democratic politics isn't the art of the possible, but of constructing what's possible. People have been convinced that they can't hope for anything beyond their own individual mobility and the survival of their families. We need to offer an alternative vision."

This vision may be even more important than the critiques that we offer. As the Surfrider Foundation's founder, Glen Hening, said, "We have to fight what's wrong, like challenging environmental pollution. But we also have to act from more than anger or fear. We have to make clear that we can do better."

Whatever issues we take on, we should assume that we'll be living with imperfect societies, imperfect human beings, and imperfect solutions, for as far into the future as we can imagine. But this doesn't justify retreat from the admittedly difficult challenges of working for a more humane world. Whatever our approaches to change, and whatever political ambiguities we face, we can't let the apparent limits of our present time prevent us from articulating the very perspectives that might open up new possibilities later on.

AN ETHIC OF CONNECTION

Even a patchwork vision is more than platforms and programs. It's a picture of ourselves, of the world, and of the relationship between the two. As a Lakota Indian activist once said, "If you think you're related to the stars, you'll have a different view of your responsibility." In isolation, it's easy for our vision to fail and our heart to grow cold. When we cultivate a sense of broader connection, however, we see further, we take more of existence into account. In short, we find our place in the world. "The time has come to lower our voices," writes Thomas Berry, "to cease imposing our mechanistic patterns on the biological processes of the earth, to resist the impulse to control, to command, to force, to oppress, and to begin quite humbly to follow the guidance of the larger community on which all life depends. Our fulfillment is not in our isolated human grandeur, but in our intimacy with the larger earth community, for this is also the larger dimension of our being. Our human destiny is integral with the destiny of the earth."

It's also integral to the destiny of our fellow human beings. In both cases, we must choose between a constricted and disconnected self and one that embraces life's richness, including moments of difficulty and sorrow. As the naturalist Terry Tempest Williams writes, "If I choose not to become attached to nouns—a person, place, or thing—then when I refuse an intimate's love or hoard my spirit, when a known landscape is bought, sold, and developed, chained or grazed to a stubble, or a hawk is shot and hung by its feet on a barbed-wire fence, my heart cannot be broken because I never risked giving it away. A man or woman whose mind reins in the heart when the body sings desperately for connection can only expect more isolation and greater ecological disease. Our lack of intimacy with each other is in direct proportion to our lack of intimacy with the land. We have taken our love inside and abandoned the wild."

When we retreat from this demanding intimacy, we lose our sense of who we are. Elie Wiesel retells the expulsion from the Garden of Eden in the words of a wise Hasidic rabbi, who explained that when God asked Adam, "Where art thou?" God knew where Adam was, but Adam did not. "Do we know where we are?" Wiesel asks, and then explains, "My place is measured by yours. . . . My place under the sun, or in the face of God, or in my own memory is measured by the distance it has from you . . . if I see a person or persons suffer, and the distance between us doesn't shrink . . . my place is not good, not enviable."

Our identity, as I've said throughout this book, is discovered and realized only within the context of community. In *Emotional Intelligence*, Daniel Goleman talks of deriving our core moral sensibility from our ability to understand the emotions of other human beings, to sense their needs, and to care about how our choices will affect their lives. This is the essence of compassion, "to suffer with." Compassion asks us to enter places of pain, write the theologians Henri Nouwen, Donald McNeill, and Douglas Morrison, "to share in brokenness, fear, confusion, and anguish. Compassion challenges us to cry out with those in misery, to mourn with those who are lonely, to weep with those in tears. Compassion requires us to be weak with the weak, vulnerable with the vulnerable, and powerless with the powerless." Requiring "full immersion in the condition of being human," it's an ethic essential to reclaiming our souls.

If we want to create a just world, we must affirm these fundamental ties. Desmond Tutu celebrates "the rainbow people of God." "An injury to one is an injury to all," states the classic labor maxim. "We need to remind people," explains massage therapist and children's advocate Corrine Kelly, "of our common humanity. That we're all in this together. When we disown a part of that humanity, when we walk on another person, it comes back to haunt us."

Whatever our particular visions, we renew our souls in the company of other human beings. "Hatred tries to cure disunion by annihilating those who are not united with us," wrote Thomas Merton. "It seeks peace by the elimination of everybody else but ourselves. But love, by its acceptance of the pain of reunion, begins to heal all wounds. . . . Consequently, we can only be happy in this world in so far as we are free to rejoice in the good of another: specifically in so far as we are free to rejoice in the good which is God's."

Essentially, Merton's describing an ethic of connection. It's based on our willingness to look past our limited interests, appetites, and needs to embrace a world that will always be imperfect, will always contain suffering and pain, but is nonetheless worth working to redeem. If that sounds like spiritual language, so be it. In my view, any hopeful social movement has to be based in the elusive and perhaps unknowable forces that join us together. For in honoring these fundamental human bonds, we begin to embody the vision that we seek.

Chapter Twelve

The Fullness of Time

The difficult—I'll do right now. The impossible—will take a little while.
—SUNG BY BILLIE HOLIDAY; LYRIC BY BOB RUSSELL

It is not up to you to complete the task. Nonetheless, you are not free to desist from it.

—RABBI TARFON

However we promote social change, we do so in time: We link past, present, and future in our attempts to create a better world. Some historical eras, however, seem more pregnant with possibility than others. A few years ago, I saw a British art exhibit about Sergei Eisenstein, the great Soviet director, who in the 1920s and 1930s made films like *Battleship Potemkin* and *Alexander Nevsky*. The exhibit surveyed his work, his times, the history he helped shape. It conveyed the atmosphere of a period when everything seemed to be breaking loose—politically, technologically, and artistically. One room of the exhibit re-created Eisenstein's office, spilling over with artifacts given to him by such friends as Pablo Picasso, Georges Braque, Fernand Léger, the muralist José Clemente Orozco, and the photographer Edward Weston. There was a bust of the composer Prokofiev (Eisenstein's frequent collaborator), and signed photos of James Joyce, Albert Einstein, Charlie Chaplin, Walt Disney, Harpo Marx—and Lenin. The exhibit was a metaphor for a time of dramatic promise, when people believed they could reinvent the world. Whatever their illusions, they rode an exhilarating wave of hope.

The 1960s were marked by a similar sense of urgency and creative ferment. Ordinary people worldwide challenged entrenched institutions and policies. They talked of realizing a more humane and generous future. These movements then collapsed because of powerful opposition, their participants' exhaustion, and some dangerous moments of arrogance. But for a time, people unleashed powerful dreams.

Our lives today are hardly stagnant. We have access to a world of food, music, sights, sounds, and healing traditions. We can log onto Websites from Bangkok and Reykjavík to Nairobi and Calcutta. As technology changes by leaps and bounds, it alters our lives and the earth at an almost incomprehensible pace. So does the relentless global economy. Change happens so fast we can barely keep up.

But politically, we often feel powerless, incapable of moving forward. We may have witnessed citizens fighting for democracy in the streets of Prague, Berlin, and Moscow, Tiananmen Square and Soweto, Manila, and Jakarta. But we saw them from a distance on TV. People risked their lives to have a say in their common future, but the lessons seemed remote from our world. They didn't apply to us. Not here, and certainly not now.

It's tempting to gaze back longingly toward the most dramatic periods of history, while disdaining our own era as unheroic and meaningless. "People seem so stuck these days," says Ginny Nicarthy. "But things looked pretty grim in the late 1950s too, when I first got involved. A dozen of us would picket the bomb shelters or stores that were racist in their hiring, and people would yell at us, tell us to 'Go back to Russia,' 'Go back to your kitchen, where you belong.' There were no clear reasons to believe that we could change things, but somehow we did. We leaped forward, started the ball rolling, and built enough political mass that it kept going. Maybe we need to do that again."

Seeding the ground for the next round of highly visible social progress will take work. Yet major gains for human dignity are possible, even in seemingly resistant times. Indeed, our efforts may be even more critical now than in periods when the whole world seems to be watching.

THE TURNINGS OF HISTORY

Historical contexts can change shape suddenly and dramatically. As Václav Havel wrote before the epochal Eastern European revolutions, "Hope is not prognostication." Richard Flacks remembers visiting Berkeley in September 1964 and hearing members of the activist student group SDS complain that their fellow students were almost terminally apathetic, uncaring, and passive. They said that nothing they could try would work. A few weeks later, the free speech movement erupted.

We can never predict when a historical mood will suddenly shift and new hopes and possibilities emerge. But we do know that this shift won't occur unless someone takes action. Recall the struggle of Susan B. Anthony. She labored her entire life for women's suffrage, then died fourteen years before it was achieved. Thirty years ago, few would have thought that the Soviet bloc would crumble, thanks in part to the persistence of individuals from Havel to Lech Wałesa and Andrei Sakharov, who voiced prophetic truths despite all costs. Few would have thought that South Africa would become a democracy, with Nelson Mandela its president. Few would have imagined that women throughout the world would begin to insist on shaping their own destiny. Major victories for human dignity rarely come easily or quickly. But they do come.

"When nothing seems to help," said the early twentieth-century reformer Jacob Riis, "I go and look at a stonecutter hammering away at his rock perhaps a hundred times without as much as a crack showing in it. Yet at the hundred and first blow it will split in two, and I know it was not that blow that did it—but all that had gone before."

If we want a more humane society, we'll need to risk partial steps, failed experiments, and ambiguous results. We work and work, then "once in a lifetime," as the poet Seamus Heaney writes, "the longed-for tidal wave of justice can rise up, and hope and history rhyme." "How often in this century," writes Howard Zinn, "we have been *surprised*. By the sudden emergence of a people's movement, the sudden overthrow of a tyranny, the sudden coming to life of a flame we thought extinguished. We are surprised because we have not taken notice of the quiet simmerings of indignation, of the first faint sounds of protest, of the scattered signs of resistance that, in the midst of our despair, portend the excitement of change."

RADICAL PATIENCE

For most of human existence, the world changed at a glacial pace. People were born, grew up, worked, loved, died much as their parents and grandparents had before them. They believed that society was governed by external forces. The purpose of life was to fulfill tradition, not overturn it.

Now, circumstances are almost the opposite; we suffer from an overload of change. Our society makes speed an ultimate virtue, as if simply by moving faster we can overcome all obstacles, including our own mortality. Yet, as Milan Kundera writes, "there is a secret bond between slowness and memory, between speed and forgetting." We need to challenge the all-leveling pace of vast institutions, global markets especially, so as to give human communities time to sort through what is wise and unwise in the cornucopia of new choices. We also need to slow down our lives enough to determine what we want to fight for in the first place. This means taking time to reflect and listen closely. It means finding what T. S. Eliot called "a still point in a turning world," and returning to a slower rhythm of life that might even presage the kind of future we'd like to fight for. It means developing radical patience.

Writing from a Christian social activist tradition, Jim Wallis explains the need for meditative respite: "Action without reflection can easily become barren and even bitter," he says. "Without the space for self-examination and the capacity for rejuvenation, the danger of exhaustion and despair is too great. At an even deeper level, contemplation confronts us with the questions of our identity and power. Who are we: To whom do we belong? Is there a power that is greater than ours? How can we know it?"

But too often we don't pause to reflect. Writing in the *Whole Earth* magazine, poet Anne Herbert examines the cycle of frenetic motion and rapid burnout so common among activists, and asks how our choices might differ if we cultivated the view that we have a hundred years to change the world, instead of constantly scrambling to stave off imminent collapse. She describes experiences with "organizations, campaigns, whole movements, [all run with] everybody feeling behind, feeling there isn't enough time, feeling important because every little thing is urgent because it hasn't been well planned."

In this regard, I sometimes think of the physician Helen Caldicott, who in the early 1980s inspired more people to challenge the nuclear arms race than any other individual I can think of. The crisis she addressed was indeed urgent, with our missiles and those of the Soviets both set on hair-trigger launch, and Reagan administration officials discussing the idea of winnable nuclear war. Yet Caldicott let herself be so overwhelmed by her foreshortened sense of time and the possibility of annihilation that she quickly grew brittle. Her talks grew more and more apocalyptic. She began to give her audiences the impression that unless they acted that very instant, and acted almost perfectly, whatever they could do might be too late. Before the 1984 election, she pronounced that there was "a mathematical certainty" of nuclear war if Reagan were reelected to office. Shortly afterward Caldicott withdrew from active involvement, and remained silent concerning peace and environmental issues for nearly a decade.

Those who are able to sustain their activism for a lifetime know how to pace themselves and maintain their moral reserves. Longtime civil rights activist Ysaye Barnwell, of the singing group Sweet Honey in the Rock, has compared social involvement to the process of making music. In both, she says, you can't rush things. "Music has its rhythm and pace. You have to keep up with it and not go too slow or too fast, or the song won't work. You need to take all the time you need. You want to breathe, savor each note, feel the spaces between the words that you sing."

Granted, the crises we face often demand immediate attention. And some efforts, like electoral campaigns or union organizing drives, face finite deadlines, which we need to respect. But even then, we work best when we're calm and deliberate rather than harried and desperate. Finding the right pace is easier if we bear in mind that it's going to take time to produce the social changes we desire, so activism has to be a lifelong endeavor. As Billie Holiday sings, "The difficult—I'll do right now. The impossible—will take a little while."

It may seem odd to advocate patience when homeless families sleep on our streets, laws passed by Congress increase the number of children who will go hungry, and management decisions of giant timber companies doom thousand-year-old trees. But by "patience" I don't mean tolerance or acceptance of human destructiveness. As Martin Luther King, Jr. said, we need "to be saved from that patience that makes us patient with anything less than freedom and justice."

Activists who practice radical patience continually address urgent issues, but they do so mindful of the larger cultural and political context within which these issues arise, and out of which other critical issues will arise in the future. They understand that success depends not only on changing specific policies but also on broadening the stream of activist engagement, building new relationships, initiating new dialogue, and opening up new opportunities for citizens to take a stand. If we work well and wisely, our efforts will help regardless of the short-term outcome of particular battles. Jim Forest, of the international religious pacifist group Fellowship of Reconciliation, compares the labors of social activists to those of the artisans who built the great medieval cathedrals, working generation after generation on projects whose completion most would never live to see.

Not getting too attached to the results of our actions isn't only a strategy to avoid burnout, then. It's also the approach that's most likely to yield significant social change. "There are moments when things go well and one feels encouraged," writes Danilo Dolci, the great Italian pacifist who challenged the Mafia in Sicily and helped empower poor peasant communities. "There are difficult moments and one feels overwhelmed. But it's senseless to speak of optimism or pessimism. The only important thing is to know that if one works well in a potato field, the potatoes will grow. If one works well among men, they will grow—that's reality. The rest is smoke. It's important to know that words don't move mountains. Work, exacting work, moves mountains."

Savoring the Journey

Another way of saying this is that if we're going to keep working to create a better world, we must find ways to savor the work itself, and the everyday richness of life. Approached in desperation, social activism can erode our souls, can cause us to treat the world as nothing more than a vehicle for our causes. Activists who endure know this. That's why they balance their demanding work with pursuits that nourish their souls and bring joy into their lives. When Hazel Wolf visited the Soviet Union in her mid-eighties, she stayed up half the night dancing and drinking. Dan Ellsberg's son once described watching him bodysurf at a beach in northern California. "It was a clear, beautiful day. The water was cold. On that afternoon, he seemed like he didn't have a political thought in his mind. He just kept riding the waves. He probably spends more time thinking about the awful things in the world and how to stop them than anyone else I know. But that day I was so glad he was just doing something he enjoyed."

I remember the Catholic peace activist Philip Berrigan drinking red wine and talking passionately with an old friend about Sophia Loren's beauty and prowess as an actress. Berrigan's willingness to spend much of his life in jail for protesting war stemmed directly from his profound gratitude, from how much he prized the richness of God's gifts, including Loren's abundant talent.

Among the riches that deserve savoring are life's absurdities. As I've mentioned, humor can be a powerful way to reach out to others. It also helps us stay the course, preventing us from taking ourselves too seriously, helping us put life's bruises in perspective, enlarging our vision. Humor gives us ways to come to terms with pain, loss, and failure, yet also look beyond it.

Because of the Chinese occupation of Tibet, the Dalai Lama has experienced years of exile, the deaths of many close friends, and the systematic ravaging of his culture. He has every logical reason to despair. Yet whenever I've heard him talk, he's been mischievous and playful. Giving a scarf to Seattle's mayor, he joked, "It's made in China." When someone asked about the occupation, he said, "The fourteenth Dalai Lama is very popular. Without the Chinese, he probably wouldn't be." When asked what he did for fun, he flapped his hands like chattering mouths and said with a giggle, "I gossip."

The Dalai Lama clearly savors life, in all of its delight and all of its sorrow. In *Zen and the Art of Motorcycle Maintenance,* Robert Pirsig writes, "Mountains should be climbed with as little effort as possible and without desire. . . . Then, when you're no longer thinking ahead, each footstep isn't just a means to an end but a unique event in itself. . . . To live only for some future goal is shallow. It's the sides of the mountain which sustain life, not the top. Here's where things grow." Those most committed to their communities value their journey as well as their destination. For all the obstacles they face, they derive satisfaction from the people they meet, the challenges they engage, the lessons they learn, and the knowledge that they're staying true to their beliefs.

"There's always something to do, no matter what [your] age, as long as you can get up and walk and talk," Jessie de la Cruz, a seventy-four-year-old farmworker organizer, told Studs Terkel. "There's always hope. We have a saying: 'La esperanza muere al ultimo.' Hope dies last. Hope for whatever you want to do. If you can't do it today, there's always tomorrow or the next year."

Those who work most steadfastly for justice relish the struggle, even as they look beyond it to the world they'd like to help create. At her Columbia, South Carolina, house, eighty-four-year-old African American activist Modjesca Simkins pointed out the dining room table where a young NAACP lawyer named Thurgood Marshall had composed his early briefs. Modjesca cofounded her state NAACP in 1939, and the two worked together for years. She showed me a faded handbill from the late 1950s, at the top of which were the following words: "Main Street in Columbia Is Off Limits To Seekers After Freedom." The flier advised black participants in an Easter boycott to trade with friendly merchants or "wear old clothes in real dignity," rather than patronize Woolworth's, McCrory's, and other stores "where you are most welcome to stand on your 'dogs' and gnaw on a Hot Dog while a simple request for a 'SITTING DOWN' lunch will mean insults and arrest."

Modjesca helped win that fight, just as she helped break the state's all-white Democratic primary and desegregate South Carolina's public schools. Though the movement won much, she said, the poor were still poor, the powerful and wealthy still on top. People needed to keep their eyes on the light, she said, for "the betterment of mankind," and "not let the chintzy things get in the way." Faith came from "exposure to suffering," and if you had as much faith as you could put in a mustard seed, she believed you could move the world.

Along with her civil rights involvements, Modjesca also took stands on issues like the environment. She thought most blacks felt that "the white man got the world messed up. Let him straighten it out himself." The black community, used to being excluded from public decision-making, was fatalistic even about getting holes in the streets fixed. Like most Americans, Modjesca said, they had "a disease where they run along like a feather in the breeze till they come up against something they didn't see." But if the nearby

Savannah River atomic complex ever blew, they'd "be pinched up just like pork skins, along with everyone else."

It was hard raising these questions, Modjesca went on, because most people cared only about "what song's on the radio or what they're going to buy, not about what kind of world they're going to leave for their children." But Modjesca persevered. The Saturday after my last visit to her house, she planned to get up at five-thirty A.M. and drive 170 miles in her battered tan Chevy to address an environmental rally in Savannah, Georgia. "I never turn down requests from young people," she said. "So as the song says, I'm 'gonna put on my high-heeled sneakers,' and go. Take two of my friends who like things like that. I hope I can get some good fish down there on the wharf."

THE POWER OF STUBBORNNESS

As I've suggested throughout this book, the journey of involvement is hard, but immensely fruitful. Let me talk about the qualities that allow individuals to persist, whatever the times they live in, throughout their lives.

I've mentioned the need to be patient and to savor the journey as we go. Less obvious, perhaps, is the virtue of sheer stubbornness, placed in service of higher ideals. We need to be open to learning, to change, and to compromise. But sometimes we just have to dig in our heels and resist the fine-sounding rationalizations that would appease our conscience and silence our voice. Because if we don't, we'll forget what we wanted to fight for in the first place.

Modjesca embodied this kind of stubbornness throughout her life. Besides her obvious passion, fiery spirit, and strong sense of humor, she simply refused to give up. When I think about people who continue their involvements for years, whatever the odds, they remind me of farmers who keep replanting when hail destroys their crops. They keep on because there's work that needs to be done.

If sometimes this work is frustrating, that's part of the bargain. Besides, as John Kenneth Galbraith writes, "There is something personally satisfying about being disagreeable by advancing the truth."

The longtime Minnesota activist Marv Davidov tells the story of Bob Zellner, an Alabama organizer whose father was a Klansman and a preacher. Zellner eventually became the first white field secretary of the Student Nonviolent Coordinating Committee (SNCC). When a Klan mob tried to lynch him, Zellner wrapped his arms around a tree, holding on with all his strength. It took so many men to pry him off that at last a Klan leader looked down and said, "Anybody who wants to live this much, we're going to let you." Zellner inspired Marv to fight for what's right with the same dogged determination.

Such stubbornness gives us that extra measure of strength we sometimes need to resist the morally intolerable but potentially overwhelming forces of our time. A friend of Pete Knutson's was crewing on a boat through a treacherous passage in Canada's Queen Charlotte Sound when they entered a fog bank. All around, the waves pounded the rocks. People couldn't see past their faces. The skipper panicked, abandoned the helm, and exclaimed, "It's all over, boys. We're done for." Then he went below to lie down on his bunk, smoke a cigarette, and wait for the boat to hit the rocks. "Well, you may be done for," said Pete's friend and the other crew members, "but we're not." And they steered themselves through the passage and out of danger.

Pete likes to tell this story. Those at the helm of our society may well have given up on creating a just world. If we follow their lead, we may founder on cynicism and despair. But that doesn't mean we're powerless. It's in our hands to steer society toward a better outcome, no matter how thick the fog or how dark the night.

Pete feels far better, he says, trying to change things, even if doing so means taking on powerful interests. "They're not going to get rid of me," he says with a smile. "They're not going to shut me up. I take some perverse satisfaction in giving them grief."

"We could have given up during 640," he explains, "when the aluminum industry, the timber companies, and the sport fishing interests all came after us. We could have said, 'It's all over, boys.' But we managed to translate what was important about saving the commercial fishing economy to people who cared about the environment. You never know if you're going to win or not, but if you don't sell out to expediency, it's amazing what a handful of people can do.

"We often underestimate our power," Pete believes. "We fall into a trap of intellectually convincing ourselves that there's no way we can change things. We get paralyzed by the enormity of the problems and the apparent strength of our opponents. But in a weird way, that magnifies our helplessness. We think of ourselves as beleaguered and isolated. Yet lots of other people share our sentiments about the difference between greed and human respect. We need to help give them a voice."

Maybe, Pete wonders, the forces we challenge recognize the power of an engaged citizenry better than those of us who are involved. "When the major industrial interests behind Initiative 640 were meeting, they had a copy of the article I wrote for the local Sierra Club newsletter opposing it, and exposing their environmental duplicity. They read it aloud, and were just livid. They referred to me as 'the eco-gillnetter.' You just have to laugh when you realize that you're some multibillion-dollar corporation's worst nightmare. It's like Nixon being totally obsessed by the antiwar movement, while he denied he was even paying attention. We just can't predict the impact we'll have."

We can't predict our impact, which is why we should persist. We can view the stubbornness that Pete exemplifies as the deepest kind of patriotism, standing up for the well-being of the planet and saying in effect, "We aren't just visiting. We live here. And we intend to pass on a better world."

I saw this attitude in a seventy-eight-year-old grandmother, Ruth Youngdahl Nelson. A brother of hers had been a two-term Minnesota governor, another a congressman. Ruth herself was a nationally prominent Lutheran laywoman who'd been named National Mother of the Year. Ruth had always charted her own path: meeting her minister husband after defeating him in a three-mile swimming race; helping integrate their Washington, D.C., church at a time when that seemed unthinkable; consistently speaking her mind. But her life remained relatively respectable until the early 1980s, when her minister son, Jon, committed civil disobedience at the Seattle-area Trident submarine base.

Ruth visited Jon in jail. Later, he made plans to participate in a small-boat blockade of the first Trident submarine. Ruth announced that she would join in—because, she felt, sometimes you had to draw a line. Jon tried to dissuade her. "You might be almost ninety by the time you get out of jail," he reminded her: The government was threatening ten-year jail sentences. "Let me do it," he said. "I'm younger." Though Ruth loved her son, she wasn't going to be talked out of her convictions. "I think it's very obnoxious," she responded, "that we should threaten to obliterate thousands of people who we've never even met. I have to say no to what this submarine represents."

On the day of the Trident's arrival, the Coast Guard brought in an armada. They used high-powered water cannon to scatter the protestors' small boats and dump their occupants in the water. Then a young sailor aimed his cannon at the motorboat containing Jon, Ruth, a suburban nurse, a former priest, and a Lutheran deaconess. Ruth mustered up all her prairie-bred courage and integrity, and in her most grandmotherly style shook her finger at him.

"No, no, young man," she commanded, kindly but firmly. "Not in my America. Please. You wouldn't do that." The young sailor looked at her, froze, and backed down.

SLOW-BURNING FIRE

Like Pete Knutson outraged by the destruction of Northwest salmon runs and Ruth Nelson by the "very obnoxious" nuclear weapons, we often become involved because we get angry. We see lives and hopes damaged by distant institutional powers. We see the gap between the world that is and the world that should be. Watching particular human beings turned into expendable abstractions, we feel we have to do something.

Mastered and honed, such anger can help us keep going for the long haul. Without "a capacity for anger," argues Reverend William Sloane Coffin, we begin "to tolerate the intolerable. . . . If you are not angry, you are probably a cynic. And if you lower your quotient of anger at oppression, you lower your quotient of compassion for the oppressed. I see anger and love as very related."

Yet political anger can also devour us. Anyone who's been around social movements has met people so consumed by their fury that they scarcely remember what they're fighting for. Some of these activists are fueled by personal resentments, using their causes as an outlet for their every complaint against family, friends, and a world that fails to appreciate their gifts. Others have adopted the stereotype of the shouting protester as a political tactic, on the assumption that only the greatest militancy can force the powers that be to pay heed. For most of us, however, the danger lies in being overwhelmed by the gravity of the injustices we see yet feel inadequate to address. We point out that children are suffering and dying, but no one wants to know. We talk of the despoliation of the earth, and the pillaging goes on as usual. Images of suffering and destruction become our sole focus, our obsession. Necessary indignation turns into rage. We give up in frustration or lose sight of the world we'd like to create.

How do we transmute our anger so that, in Gandhi's words, "as heat conserved is transmuted into energy," it becomes "a power that can move the world"? How do we use this volatile fuel to help us challenge injustice without succumbing to it ourselves?

First, we can remember the sense of human connection that underpins our commitment. Second, we can practice radical patience. When the old woman in her neighborhood died in the cold, remembers Virginia Ramirez, "I didn't know what to do. It was very hard to control my anger. I'd kept it quiet for so many years that when I began to let it out, it consumed me. When I first spoke out, I bit people's heads off. I had to do role-playing to learn how to have an impact without attacking people. You lose control when you feel there's nothing you can do. When you feel you can stop these bad situations, you do it in a different way. I'll always be angry about the situation of my community. But if I can work for the long run, I'll have better results."

"I had to turn my anger into a slow-burning fire instead of a consuming fire," explains Myles Horton. (Horton founded the Highlander Center, where Rosa Parks attended workshops before her epochal protest.) "You don't want the fire to go out—you never let it go out—and if it ever gets weak, you stoke it. But you don't want it to burn you up. It keeps you going, but you subdue it because you don't want to be destroyed by it."

In a document called "Tent of the Presence," the Industrial Areas Foundation's Black Caucus echoes these sentiments: "Anger sits precariously between two dangerous extremes. One extreme is hatred, the breeding ground of violence. The other extreme is passivity and apathy, the breeding ground of despair and living death." The caucus endorses anger that's "focused and deep and rooted in grief."

Meditation teacher Steven Levine, who's done powerful work with prison kids and the dying, agrees that we may need to be angry in the process of working for change. He urges, however, that we accompany this anger "with a soft belly," so we stay rooted, flexible, and receptive, and don't tie ourselves in knots. Beneath our anger, Levine says, lies "an ocean of sadness," which we need to acknowledge if we're to act effectively. We can't do that if we're clenched in blind fury.

We can also look beyond our anger to the visions we'd like to fight for. This means valuing moments of courage and compassion, celebrating the everyday grace of life, and focusing not only on what's wrong, but on what we believe in.

MOMENTS THAT INSPIRE US

Sometimes we have to search far and wide for signs of political progress. Other times, they're obvious. When I asked Alison Smith what sustains her, she was riding so high from helping pass Maine's pioneering campaign reform that the question seemed almost moot. Her state might set a national precedent. They'd radically changed their local electoral system. They'd pressured their Republican senators and Democratic congressmen to support serious national reform. "Life's lots more fun," Alison says, "if you feel like there's hope."

By that point, she'd learned so much about campaign reform that she helped monitor the state legislature as it implemented what the voters had passed. She was also working to get citizens to participate in the new income tax checkoff, and encouraging candidates to run under the Clean Election option. "I've been meeting with electoral reform activists around the country," she says, "and they all know about our coalitions and strategies. They're trying to follow our path. I always felt we were doing good work. But it's amazing to realize that people are watching us and getting inspired. I just got elected to the national board of the League of Women Voters, to help other states work on these issues. I'd like to make this enough of a success so my children can live in a country where regular people feel proud of their democracy, know people running for office, maybe even run for office themselves. But it won't happen unless people participate. The longer I do this work, the harder it feels to stop."

Our successes don't have to play on a grand stage to boost our spirits. When we last talked, Virginia had just returned from a celebration. For forty years people had prodded the city to rebuild an old street that flooded every time it rained. Officials said repeatedly they didn't have the money, though they'd spent plenty on wealthier neighborhoods. Finally COPS mustered the support to pass a bond issue. "The other day the engineers came by to start construction," Virginia said, "and we had a party to celebrate. It will be a real street, with sidewalks and storm drains. People were so excited, talking about how their sidewalks would look and their little yards, and how much they'd take pride in it. It's a small thing, but it gives hope to the community."

One of those celebrating, Virginia said, was a young woman with a three-month-old baby. "My grandmother always wanted to see them fix the street," the woman told Virginia. "She fought so hard to get a bond passed, but they always said it was too expensive, and now she's died. I wish she could have lived to see it."

"But you're here," Virginia responded, "and so's your child. Now when your child walks to school someday, she won't have to walk through all the mud and water. It's for you now, and for her."

"These are the kinds of victories," Virginia told me, "that keep me going."

Even in the face of apparent defeat, we can take heart from the victories of others—examples we might call miracles of hope. Nobel Peace Prize winner José Ramos-Horta has seen his country of East Timor brutalized by Indonesian rule. Since 1975, more than 200,000 people have been killed, including members of his family and many of his closest friends. Yet Ramos-Horta draws hope from those times when the human spirit has triumphed over force, with little help from those in power, like "the practitioners of realpolitik in Washington, London, and Bonn. According to them, Václav Havel should have continued to accept the irreversibility of Soviet rule in Eastern Europe. The Armenians shouldn't have a country. South Africa shouldn't be free. Pinochet should still be ruling Chile. But all this has been changed by human courage."

America is full of citizen efforts that testify to the power of our actions, even in a seemingly inhospitable time. It's tempting to give up on campaign reform—but then people like Alison challenge the cynicism that insists politicians have to be bought and paid for. Urban violence seems inevitable—but then people like David Lewis and Deborah Prothrow-Stith create innovative programs to limit its reach. When commercial nuclear reactors began to proliferate, supporters envisioned them blanketing America—but then a movement including Michael Lowe and countless others blocked their construction, raised basic safety issues, and helped stop the atomic industry dead in its tracks.

The people whose journeys I've described have consistently transformed untapped or long-ignored human potential for change into inspiring social progress. Who could have imagined that Glenn Hening and his circle of friends could mobilize surfers to protect the environment, or that Pete Knutson would do the same with his fellow fishermen? Could anyone anticipate that Virginia and her fellow COPS members would bring a billion dollars of public and private investment into San Antonio's poorest neighborhoods? In a time when unions are being dismissed as anachronisms, people like Jorge Rivera and the Seattle high-tech workers are helping revive them as vital social movements. And in a time when we feel helpless before the power of giant corporations, citizens like Carol McNulty, and efforts like the Gap campaign, are proving that they may be far more responsive to coordinated citizen pressure than we think.

In all these cases, and in many more, individuals acted despite their uncertainties. They didn't have all the answers. Their victories haven't ushered in the ultimate kingdom of justice. But they should give us real hope.

"I feel so privileged," says the Seattle staffer of the Fellowship of Reconciliation. "Every week I get so many wonderful examples of how people are acting, coming across my desk in all these little newsletters. It keeps me encouraged. If you're not involved, you never find out about any of it."

Inspiration can also come from the past. We remember people, stories, injustices that fire our imagination, times when citizen efforts succeeded against impossible odds. This storehouse of memories helps us endure. Sixty years later, Victor Reuther still draws strength from the great Flint sit-down strike of 1936, which helped establish the United Auto Workers, the union his brother Walter would head. "I never saw such bravery and solidarity," he remembers. "When they saw what was happening to their sons and fathers and brothers in the plant, the whole city of Flint turned out, broke through the police lines, and came to their defense. That demonstration has stayed with me all these years and convinced me that inside each of us there is this will to be brother to brother and brother to sister." Now, in his eighties, Reuther works with the reform campaign of Teamsters for a Democratic Union. He still takes heart, he says, from examples like Flint.

CHANGED LIVES

What inspired Reuther was a peak moment of courage and solidarity. I feel my own spirits revived when I hear the kinds of stories I've recounted in this book. The people I've described have their moments of bleakness. They don't win every battle. But they continue, despite the obstacles. And if we take their lives seriously, we'll know that our actions can matter. "You can't help but be inspired," said one longtime activist, "simply knowing people who've been involved all their life and always will be."

Just as we draw hope from unexpected leaps of progress, we can also draw hope from changes in particular lives, as individuals grow stronger, find their voice, and help others do the same. This is why, whenever we work to transform the world, we can make an impact in two ways. If we win our immediate battles, we can reform specific institutions, change specific policies, and open up new possibilities for the future. So we need to act as well as we possibly can, to be efficient with our resources, and to levy our pressure strategically. Yet even if we lose seemingly critical fights, our actions may still help open minds and change hearts. They may inspire people to rethink their values and choices, raise questions they'd kept to themselves, move from silence and accommodation to engagement. Our first priority is institutional change. The stakes are real, in human lives and the future of the earth. But we can also count it as a victory each time we bring new participants into a culture of commitment.

Few things are as heartening as watching this process. "You see this big iceberg out there," says Carol McNulty's husband, Bill. "It's hard to see how to shift its direction. But locally, you see this person on board who wasn't before, this person writing letters, another person who's going to fund-raise. It's progress."

The pioneering gay activist Harry Hay describes the powerful sense of accomplishment he gets when he travels around the country and young men tell him, "Thank you for my life." "Every time," Hay says, "every time, it wipes me out. For me, that's the greatest gift of all."

One change nurtures another. Having toyed with Islam while in prison, David Lewis now makes it a mainstay of his life. He draws strength from going to AA meetings, reading the Koran, and attending a mosque, where, he says, "I can see the power of people gathering, and devoting themselves to God." He also feels inspired by people whose lives he's helped turn around, like an African American man who felt hopeless in prison until he heard David speak, then got out and became Free at Last's lead outreach worker. Another, a Latino man, had swum across the Rio Grande five years before, knowing not a word of English. Now he's graduated from college with honors and helps run the organization's health education efforts.

David recently attended the graduation of Free at Last's women's residential treatment program. "You look in a woman's eyes," he says, "as she's walking out of our facility to an apartment and a job. Six months ago she was standing on the side of a freeway with a sign that said 'I'll do anything for a sandwich.' Those are the kind of things that keep me going. They're sometimes far between. You can go for a while when you don't see any hope, just groan and doom. But then when change happens, all the money in the world can't pay for looking in another human being's eyes and knowing that God gave you the ability to help them change. When I see the uplifting of another human being out of the jaws of destruction and calculated bullshit, it just affects me profoundly."

Growing as a Person

Earlier I noted that effective social activism builds upon existing belief structures, giving us opportunities to apply our innermost notions of justice to new causes and circumstances. Should our commitment continue, these values likely will grow deeper and more complex with time and experience, in the process nourishing our soul.

"When I joined the PTA, I was so timid," says Virginia Ramirez. "All I could do was make the punch and cookies. Then I started being challenged when I joined COPS. I became hungry for learning. I had so many wonderful mentors who taught me, and helped me think through what I believed. They taught me to listen to the pain in our poor community, but also hear the good stuff, because there's lots of that, too. You can learn a lot from the smile of a child, or watching a mother's face. I just went to a graduation of our new job-training program, the one I testified before Congress about. I felt good that I worked on it. After fifteen years, I'm still growing as a person."

Virginia takes particular pride in being able to stand up for her own views. "When I was growing up, women weren't equal. It wasn't nice to talk to another man, except for my husband. When I joined the organization, I saw more equality, and learned to speak when I had an opinion. As a Hispanic woman, that was a very important step, for me to learn to deal with men as an equal."

COPS also constantly helped members evaluate their actions, so they could continue learning. The community group succeeds, she believes, because it stresses developing individual skills. "The issues are important," she says. "But what happens with the people is more important. I was watching one of our new leaders today.

She's forty-eight years old and chairs our committee on streets and drainage. I've seen her grow so much in the past year. Now she's training others and holding all these meetings. It's a wonderful transition."

COPS doesn't lose many battles, Virginia says, but even when it does, the group's emphasis on personal development helps members maintain their commitment. After every campaign, successful or not, they ask themselves how they might have proceeded differently, enlisted more support, conveyed their message more clearly, built a broader coalition. "Even when we lose," Virginia explains, "we still gain something."

When times get hard, Virginia relies on her community. "Sometimes you have to say, 'I've just had enough,'" she says. "You go home and take a week off. But then you see someone, and they say 'Oh, Mrs. Ramirez, I'm so happy to see you. I'm so happy you were out there representing us.' Or they remind me how much fun we had working together. Or you see an injustice and get mad all over again. These are the things that make me go back, and think that whatever's going on, I want to be part of it."

STRAIGHT LINES AND DETOURS

As Virginia says, nothing is more hopeful than watching people grow. But the paths we follow as we develop are rarely fixed or linear. Social activists often shift course, taking on different issues with different approaches, all the while trying to realize a larger vision of justice. In the early 1990s, Alice Walker worked passionately to challenge the global practice of female genital mutilation. But she limited herself to five years of work on the issue: "It was too hard to carry on for longer than that in such an intense way." When the five years ended, she scaled back, confident that she would move on to other equally important causes, and that for now she'd done what she could on that one.

Cornel West talks of African American music as a model for an approach where the path we take evolves continually. "When you look closely at jazz, or the blues, for example, we see a sense of the tragic, a profound sense of the tragic linked to human agency. . . . [The music] does not wallow in a cynicism or a paralyzing pessimism, but it also is realistic enough not to project excessive utopia. It's a matter of responding in an improvisational, undogmatic, creative way to circumstances, in such a way that people still survive and thrive."

Even when our efforts succeed, we may shift our ways of acting in accordance with the rhythms of our lives. This was true of Sonya Vetra Tinsley and her attempts to use music to draw people together. Sonya's project, Serious Fun, had a powerful impact. Promoted by local radio stations, the events it sponsored mixed socially conscious hip-hop, rock, folk, and reggae groups, deliberately drawing together interracial audiences. Each concert also included presentations by community activists. At one event a representative of a welfare mothers' support group gave an address. On other occasions, audiences heard from a homeless people's advocacy group, a project to unionize day laborers, and organizations spearheading efforts to register minority and low-income voters. Concerts were held at various locations so people from diverse neighborhoods would feel a stake in the project and attend its events. Sonya's goal, she says, was "to slowly make people comfortable about going outside their familiar turf. We wanted to bring together diverse communities who'd probably otherwise never meet."

Serious Fun also nurtured an interracial community of local musicians, bringing them into the Atlanta schools to perform and to discuss issues like violence, teen pregnancy, racism, family relationships, and images of women. The organization ran workshops on youth and student organizing, and on the role of the arts, continually linking music with a larger social vision.

But after three successful years, Sonya decided it was time to move on. For a long while, she'd been writing songs that she performed with local musicians in clubs and at political benefits. Now she decided to risk making her own musical career her priority. "I'm not abandoning my core values," she explains, "though I went through lots of soul-searching and guilt about backing away from direct organizing. But I'm twenty-eight now. This isn't the kind of field where you can walk in the door and break in at age forty or fifty, although once you get going, you can perform for the rest of your life. If I didn't give my all to it at some point I'd always wonder." Sonya had lined up an experienced producer and thought she had a shot. She cut a CD of wise, funny songs about life, politics, and love, with a voice between Whitney Houston and Sheryl Crow. She was showing them around to different record labels. Some industry people were already interested. She also had a new job assisting the Atlanta-area director of the Grammys, which gave her lots of time to focus on her music.

"Sometimes your life path isn't a straight line," Sonya says, after some thought. "You can approach the same destination, but with detours. Sometimes you have to go around the back way. I grew up never quite sure if I wanted to be Martin Luther King, Jr. or Tina Turner. When I look at musicians I've most admired, they've combined service and artistic passion and been socially involved. They're people like Bob Geldoff, who went from the Boomtown Rats to organizing Live Aid, or Stevie Wonder, or Sarah McLachlan. When McLachlan was organizing her tour, she wanted Paula Cole to open for her. People discouraged her because they said two women on the same bill wouldn't sell. So she organized the all-women Lilith Fair, which became the top-selling festival last year and raised over seven hundred thousand dollars for women's causes."

When Sonya was a girl, music gave her a sense that "there was more to the world than what I could see in my small town. I listened to Motown, Stax, and old R&B, to Marvin Gaye singing 'What's Going On,' and the Staple Singers doing 'I'll Take You There.' I love people who can say something meaningful in a pop song, like Sting, Tracy Chapman, and Ben Harper. I admire women like Joan Osborne and Sheryl Crow, who can say important things even in a love song. I like the idea that people like myself may end up listening to my records, but also ten-year-old girls who are just beginning to think about how they fit into the world. Music's supposed to help people have fun and feel good, because there's plenty to feel bad about. But my highest respect goes to artists who also find ways to say something that's real, so you don't have to turn off your mind when you turn on the radio."

Sonya hoped her music would inspire people to think about the state of the planet, their community, their neighborhood. She also hoped to establish herself enough to be able to reach out to other musicians and develop common social projects. "Pursuing music feels similar to organizing work. Both efforts are about faith, corny as that may sound. They're about swimming upstream daily, learning how to pace yourself, keeping going when the odds look worse than ridiculous. Following a journey of faith in the arts or organizing is about envisioning a dream and articulating it as best you can. It's about believing in things before they seem possible, and helping people sense what isn't quite there yet. That's why the arts so often inspire people to make change."

FAITH AND HOPE

Working toward seemingly unreachable dreams requires hope. At times, as I've suggested, we gain it from seeing tangible results from our efforts or those of others. More often, hope is a way of viewing the world, which can be strengthened and refined through experience, helping us persevere despite all obstacles. "You have to draw a distinction between hope and optimism," writes Cornel West. "Vaclav Havel put it well when he said 'optimism' is the belief that things are going to turn out as you would like, as opposed to 'hope,' which is when you are thoroughly convinced something is moral and right and therefore you fight regardless of the consequences." Given the meanness of our time, West isn't sure optimism is warranted, that we can necessarily count on a better common future. But his hope won't let him give up.

Hope, in this view, rarely springs from certainty. Instead, it begins and ends in what stirs our hearts, where we place our trust, how we conduct our lives. As the writer Norman Cousins explained: "The case for hope has never rested on provable facts or rational assessment. Hope by its very nature is independent of the apparatus of logic. What gives hope its power is not the accumulation of demonstrable facts, but the release of human energies generated by the longing for something better."

The more we voice our beliefs and speak to these longings, the more hope has a chance to emerge. We talk with new people, hear inspirational stories, build bonds with new communities. We no longer sit passively, immobilized by despair. Jim Wallis captures this self-fulfilling quality when he says, "Hope is believing in spite of the evidence and watching the evidence change."

Those who are hopeful experience as many frustrations and disappointments as anyone else, but they're better equipped to withstand them and thus keep on for the long haul. As the Reverend Carla Berkedal, of Earth Ministry, says, "Hope isn't about the things that we can see—all the problems. It's about the things that we can't see, and having faith in them." Like Berkedal, many of us draw our hope from strong religious traditions. At the core of these traditions is belief in a divine spirit that's always present to support us, and in a promise that acts of courage, faith, and compassion will sooner or later make an impact—that, as Martin Luther King, Jr. said during the Montgomery bus boycott, "the universe bends toward justice." The novelist David Bradley describes this faith as a fundamental trust that "somewhere, never mind exactly where, something good and right and fair is happening which someday, never mind exactly when, will make itself apparent; that in some distant constellation a star has flamed to unaccustomed brilliance, and what we must do is wait for the arrival of the light." Because this light is always and everywhere immanent, ready to reveal itself, our religious traditions remind us that we're never completely alone and forsaken. However much human destructiveness can ravage individual lives, communities, and even ecosystems, it cannot destroy the fundamental source of life and, thus, of hope.

Rosalie Bertell, a Catholic nun with a Ph.D. in mathematics who has become an outspoken expert on radiation and human health, compares our situation with that of the Israelites during their wilderness sojourn. After their exodus from Egypt, the tribes wandered the desert for years; many soon longed for the familiar security of their previous bondage. Even when manna fell from heaven, many held back from accepting it. We need to know how to take in new nourishment, new manna, Bertell says, from the community we can create, and from our sense of faith. It's inevitable, she believes, that sometimes we will long for the comforts of our own familiar bondage, a life of political silence. Inevitably, we'll mistrust the prospects for change. Maybe, like Moses, we will only glimpse the promised land that we seek. But we have to take the first steps to leave Egypt.

Activists like Bertell draw heart from a God who gives strength to the weary and powerless, who comforts the oppressed. "When things go real bad," says Virginia Ramirez, "and sometimes they do, I'll pray. If I'm on the road and I'm having a bad day, like I made a jackass of myself, I'll say, 'Oh Lord, it's been a bad day. Please be with me.' We want to win so things can get better. But if we lose, we lose. It's not going to tear us apart. Even if we lose, God will give us more strength, because then we have to fight even harder."

David Lewis also relies on a spiritual source of support, during good times and bad. "I was in a real low place," he says, "driving from Oregon to California after a workshop. But I had a feeling of this presence next to me, comforting and soothing me, reviving and engaging me. We like to be certain about what we count on. If we can't touch it, see it, kick it in the ass, we don't consider it real. But there's a deeper force that helps me cut through the garbage and remember the truth."

In an essay he wrote in a Nazi prison cell while he was awaiting execution for his participation in a plot to kill Hitler, the Lutheran theologian Dietrich Bonhoeffer explored the link between faith and moral strength. In a world where evil approaches us in "so many respectable and seductive disguises that [our] conscience becomes nervous and vacillating," he wrote, and where we're taught to trust duty, reasonableness, or private virtue, keeping ourselves "pure from the contamination arising from responsible action," we can easily accommodate the worst moral ills. The courage to challenge them, Bonhoeffer said, resides in "the man whose final standard is not his reason, his principles, his conscience, his freedom or his virtue, but who is ready to sacrifice all this when he is called to obedient and responsible action in faith and in exclusive allegiance to God."

Bonhoeffer counsels a highly demanding faith. While we may want to trust the wisdom of the self, he argues, it can't be an isolated self, the one-dimensional creation of a shallow or destructive culture. Instead, we need to listen to that voice of conscience that represents the deeper wisdom of God, and be loyal to it, embracing what he called "the cost of discipleship." Many of Bonhoeffer's writings and speeches, as he worked to organize German churches against Hitler, challenged what he called "religionless Christianity," which adapted far too easily to the terrible crimes being committed in Europe at the time. We challenge injustice, wrote Bonhoeffer, by trying to make our whole life "an answer to the question and call of God."

Most religious traditions consciously address the question of hope, placing it within the larger spiritual framework of our lives. For those of us who don't believe in a transcendent force or being, the ultimate sources of hope aren't always immediately apparent. From my experience, many secular activists take it for granted that issues alone will motivate people to act, that if we promote strong alternative perspectives, and articulate them well, our fellow citizens will necessarily respond. We tend to underestimate or ignore altogether the spiritual and psychological reasons why people take public stands. Yet since the eighteenth-century intellectual movement known as the Enlightenment, citizens who've fought for liberty, justice, and democracy have, I believe, embraced a particular implicit philosophy of hope, rooted in assumptions about historical progress.

Some of these activists viewed their efforts as part of the civic republican tradition that was embodied in people like Thomas Jefferson, and has intellectual roots going back to Aristotle. Others acted on behalf of a vision of economic democracy, as conceived in the labor and socialist traditions. And others staked their reform efforts on the mix of technical invention, economic growth, and modest redistribution of resources at the heart of the post–Second World War social welfare state. In all these cases, people acted in the belief that history is moving toward a time when justice will reign. That future wasn't automatic, but conscientious human effort could help bring it about. Together with people's direct outrage at insults to human dignity, and a more general longing for a better world, their belief in this promise helped them to speak out, take stands, and organize.

Now, for all the reasons I've described, that promise is less certain. People feel themselves at the mercy of unaccountable global forces. The democratic process seems corrupted by wealth. Philosophies of radical change that once inspired millions look like historical dead ends. Ecological limits pose new challenges to the assumption that we can sustain endless growth. Given all this, those of us on the secular side can't take our political hope for granted. We have to actively reclaim it, maybe even cobble it together.

Much of this involves nurturing a sense of larger connection similar to that of the religious activists, though expressed in non-theological terms. One encouraging model comes out of the perspective of environmentalists inspired by the complex majesty of the natural world, a shifting dance of creation that existed long before humans inhabited the earth, and will exist long afterward. As Rabindranath Tagore writes, "The same stream of life that runs through the world runs through my veins night and day and dances in rhythmic measure. It is the same life that shoots in joy through the dust of the earth into numberless blades of grass and breaks into tumultuous waves of flowers."

When I despair of our culture's greed and cravenness, I often go for a walk on my favorite Seattle beach. It's a long, arching cove, with red-barked madrona trees growing on the tall bluffs that rise behind it. Across the water, I see the snowcapped Olympic Mountains. The sun sparkles on the waves. Ferries and freighters go by. After a short time there, I feel calmer, less frenetic, connected with something larger and more enduring. I remember that we inherit a rich and generous planet, which, if we treat it well, should offer enough to sustain us all.

How else can the more secular among us find and sustain hope? Glenn Hening is motivated by a connection with his children. "When you put them to bed at night," he says, "you want to be able to look at yourself and ask, 'What did I do to make the world a better place for them?' You can't depend on anyone else to ask that question for you. You have to take responsibility for the life you brought into the world. You have to decide if you've lived up to your responsibility."

Even if the past holds no guarantees for the future, we can still take heart from previous examples of courage and vision. We can draw hope from those who came before us, to whom we owe so much. We can remember that history unfolds in ways we can never predict, but that again and again bring astounding transformations, often against the longest of odds. Our strength can come, as I've suggested, from a radical stubbornness, from savoring the richness of our journey, and from the victories we win and the lives that we change. We can draw on the community we build.

More than anything, activists religious and secular keep going because participation is essential to their dignity, to their very identity, to the person they see in the mirror. To stay silent, they say, would be self-betrayal, a violation of their soul. Plainly stated, it would feel cheap and tacky. "That's why we were put here on this earth," they stress again and again. "What better thing can you do with your life?" "There'll be nobody like you ever again," says veteran environmentalist David Brower. "Make the most of every molecule you've got, as long as you've got a second to go. That's your charge."

This means responding to the ills of our time with what Rabbi Abraham Heschel once called "a persistent effort to be worthy of the name human." A technical editor who chaired her local Amnesty International chapter felt demeaned just by knowing about incidents of torture. To do something about it helped her recover her spirit. "When you stand in front of the Creator," says Carol McNulty, "you want to say, 'I tried to make a difference.' It isn't going to be what kind of car I had or how big a house. I'd like to think I tried."

Being true to oneself in this fashion doesn't eradicate human destructiveness. We need to live, as Albert Camus suggests, with a "double memory—a memory of the best and the worst." We can't deny the cynicism and callousness of which humans are capable. We also can't deny the courage and compassion that offer us hope. It's our choice which characteristics we'll steer our lives by.

PICKING YOUR TEAM

Cynicism or hope? *That's* the real question, the choice all of us face, as individuals, families, neighborhoods, communities, nations, and members of a species whose continued survival is by no means guaranteed.

Howard Zinn explores the tension between our best and our worst in terms of how we view America's past. "What we choose to emphasize in this complex history," he writes, "will determine our lives. If we only see the worst, it destroys our capacity to do something. If we remember those times and places—and there are so many—where people have behaved magnificently, this gives us the energy to act, and at least the possibility of sending this spin-ning top of a world in a different direction." Zinn continues, "History is full of instances where people, against enormous odds, have come together to struggle for liberty and justice, and have *won*— not often enough, of course, but enough to suggest how much more is possible."

By deciding which side of history we want to be on, we also decide what kind of community we want to be part of. "Every day presents infinite reasons to believe that change can't happen," says Sonya Vetra Tinsley, "infinite reasons to give up. But I always tell myself, 'Sonya, you have to pick your team.' It seems to me that there are two teams in this world. And that you can find evidence to support the arguments of both. The trademark of one team is cynicism. They'll tell you why what you're doing doesn't matter, why nothing is going to change, why no matter how hard you work, you're going to fail. They seem to get satisfaction out of explaining how we'll always have injustice. You can't change human nature, they say. It's foolish to try. From their experience, they might be right."

Then there's another group of people, Sonya believes, "who admit that they don't know how things will turn out, but have decided to work for change. I see Martin Luther King, Jr. on that team, Alice Walker, Howard Zinn. I see my chaplain from college and my activist friends. They're always telling stories of faith being rewarded, of ways things could be different, of how their own lives have changed. They'll give you reasons why you shouldn't give up, testimonials why we've yet to see our full potential as a species. They believe we're partners in God's creation, and that change is really possible.

"There are times when both teams seem right. Both have evidence. We'll never know who's really going to prevail. So I just have to decide which team seems happier, which side I'd rather be on. And for me that means choosing the side of faith. Because on the side of cynicism, even if they're right, who wants to win that argument anyway? If I'm going to stick with somebody, I'd rather stick with people who have a sense of possibility and hope. I just know that's the side I want to be on."

COMMITTED TO EACH OTHER

No one I know has persisted longer or influenced more people than Hazel Wolf. Six hundred and fifty people filled a hall to celebrate her hundredth birthday. Hundreds more were turned away. In characteristic fashion, Wolf used the occasion to establish an endowment for Junior Audubon clubs in middle school classrooms, just as at her ninetieth birthday she'd raised money to send medical aid to a women's and children's hospital in Nicaragua. The event mixed bird-watchers, labor activists, Native American leaders, Communists, environmentalists, a former Washington governor, and an array of ordinary citizens, old and young, all inspired by her life. "Hazel's touched hundreds of people," said the president of Audubon's local chapter. "Thousands," people corrected spontaneously. "Not hundreds. Thousands." The president laughed and agreed.

The ceremony opened with slides of Hazel as an activist in her thirties, with her determined eyes and half-smile, and in her mid-nineties, kayaking on Washington's Puget Sound. People laughed at testimonies to her style of "endless pressure, endlessly applied." A Native American friend drummed and chanted, then offered a prayer for "this beloved elder" who'd walked on the planet and left tracks for others to follow. Someone described how Hazel founded Audubon chapters statewide, and got fired three times for starting unions when she was working for the Roosevelt-era WPA. Ron Allen, president of the National Congress of American Indians, recalled how he scraped through college wondering if he even belonged, but took heart whenever Hazel knocked on the door of his basement apartment "to tell me how I was going to make a difference." McCarthy-era attempts to deport Hazel, joked Earth Day founder Denis Hayes, were all a misunderstanding. She "filled out a form asking if she favored the overthrow of the U.S. government by force, revolution, or violence. She assumed it was a multiple-choice test and circled 'revolution.'"

Now, as Hazel told Hayes, she wakes up each morning and rubs her eyes, delighted to be on "the right side of the grass." Quoting the poet Samuel Ullman, Hayes described Hazel's quality of youth as the presence of courage over timidity, and an appetite for adventure rather than for a life of ease. "People grow old," in Ullman's words, "by deserting their ideals. Years may wrinkle our skin, but to give up our enthusiasm wrinkles the soul." By that standard, said Hayes, no one in the room was younger than Hazel.

People stood and applauded, as they did again and again throughout the ceremony. The applause wasn't perfunctory. For years, Hazel had stirred all of our souls as a model of how to fight with passion and joy. She walked more slowly than she had a decade earlier, talked more slowly as well. But she remained as quick-witted as ever—joking that she'd have to negotiate with the beavers that built five dams in a nearby marsh now bearing her name, "because we all know that dams without fish ladders are a problem." Hazel still savored the world she fought to save.

Near the evening's end, she noticed that no one had taken some fliers that had been left on a table to advertise a book on women environmental pioneers. So she excused herself from the parade of people who were congratulating her, grabbed a sheaf, and moved through the crowd with long-practiced style, greeting old friends and asking each, "Did you get one yet?" She kept talking, joking, and teasing, handing out fliers all the while.

Long runners like Hazel sustain their involvement less through an accumulation of knowledge than through a steady weaving of personal relationships; as time goes by, they become tied to more and more people who are struggling for justice. "I was describing to someone the solidarity we felt in trying to change Inland Steel," says Scharlene Hurston. "It was like war buddies, pulling people out of the trenches, and knowing you'll be friends for life. There were moments when we were tired or felt defeated. But we energized each other. When one person was tired, others picked them up. We were committed not just to the cause, but to each other."

Sonya Vetra Tinsley finds the same camaraderie with the activists she works with. As she says, "The relationships you build are so important. Rarely does everyone lose faith at the same time. It's nice that it works that way. I've come to realize that faith is not what you have because everything's going well. It's what keeps you going when you continue to believe and persist even when things are hard."

We inspire each other simply through our participation. We lift our coworkers' morale by showing up and sharing our humor, passion, and desire to act together for a common cause. We do this most easily when we have specific organizational structures to plug into—unions, churches, COPS, the Sierra Club, the League of Women Voters. And when those organizations nurture the kinds of approaches that help keep people involved: visions that link long- and short-term goals; opportunities for citizens to make various commitments of time and energy; a willingness to listen and learn; forgiveness of our own shortcomings and the shortcomings of others, and a recognition that the most important fruits of our labors may not be evident for years. But whether through formal or informal communities, we're more likely to continue when working with people whose company we enjoy and whose lifelong commitment helps strengthen our resolve.

As Howard Zinn writes, "The reward for participating in a movement for social justice is not the prospect of future victory. It is the exhilaration of standing together with other people, taking risks together, enjoying small triumphs and enduring disheartening setbacks—together.

"These years," writes Zinn, "when I attend reunions of SNCC people, and we sing and talk, everyone says, in various ways, the same thing: how awful they were, those days in the South, in the movement, and how they were the greatest days of our lives." This isn't nostalgia, so long as those who look back remain engaged in the present. But it recognizes the unique satisfaction of fighting together for what's right.

Even temporary communities can nurture our spirits. David Lewis draws day-to-day strength from his colleagues in Free at Last. But he also felt inspired by the Million Man March. "People can say what they want to about Louis Farrakhan, but it was a profound feeling I've never equaled in my life," he recalled. "I looked out on that Mall in Washington, D.C., and saw a million other black men from around the country, with not one can of beer, no joints, no crack pipes, no one cussing at each other. I saw black men quit their jobs after their boss said, 'If you go to that march, don't come back.' The friend I stayed with in New York worked for Goldman Sachs and was too scared even to go. But then I saw other black men saying, 'Don't worry, I have a company you can work with.' I saw black women who gave people they didn't even know their sons to take on the train to the march, then waited and picked them up when they returned. I saw older African Americans with everything to lose and young men with nothing to lose. It gave me so much enthusiasm to do what I need to do."

Engaged community builds a sense of loyalty to others similarly struggling for a better world, and to all who've moved democracy forward in the past. Virginia Ramirez often recalls her sixty-eight-year-old fellow COPS activist who spoke no English but so inspired her that "whenever I got tired, and began to say, 'This is too much,' I'd think, 'If she can do it, what's holding me back?' "

"I've thought about quitting," says a young Nebraska activist who organizes his fellow small farmers, "especially at times when I don't see results. But I've seen so many people in harder situations who keep on and don't give up. A friend of mine who works with the League of Rural Voters had a tornado hit their farm. He was injured with his wife in an auto accident. He has the responsibilities of two kids. But he's kept on staying active throughout."

Our communities don't have to be rooted in a specific time and place. They can extend to all those who fight for human dignity. José Ramos-Horta talks of being sustained by people who'd worked for justice before he began to. He singles out the Dalai Lama and Chinese human rights activist Harry Wu; Nelson Mandela, sitting in jail for over twenty-five years; Aristedes Mendes, the Portuguese consul-general in Bordeaux, France, who issued false Portuguese passports during World War II and thus saved thousands of Jewish lives. "If those people had the courage to do what they did," says Ramos-Horta, "how can I give up? If I give in because of the difficulties, and simply sit back, I'm betraying all those who have died, all those who are fighting or in prison." He feels emboldened, he says, by all these acts of courage.

THE FULLNESS OF TIME

No matter how dedicated we are, social change never happens overnight. "Lots of people believe that it does," Virginia Ramirez told me, "but it always takes time. You get a few scars in the process. You never make these kinds of changes in one day." Think of my friend Lisa Peattie, who helped prompt famed baby doctor Benjamin Spock to speak out for peace—just by marching with her kids in the rain, ragged, wet, and holding her sign. Think of the Columbia University students whom Desmond Tutu thanked for helping to end apartheid. Think of the thousands inspired by Hazel Wolf. "All you can do," says Sonya Vetra Tinsley, "is keep on the best you can, and stay ready for the possibilities that come. The picture's always going to be bigger than you can see."

The poet Rainer Maria Rilke said much the same thing in the following eloquent lines:

My eyes already touch the sunny hill,
going far ahead of the road I have begun.
So we are grasped by what we cannot grasp;
it has its inner light, even from a distance—

and changes us, even if we do not reach it,
into something else, which, hardly sensing it, we already are;

As Rilke seems to be suggesting, although the future is unknowable, it nonetheless pulls us forward, toward what we might become. Whether citizen activists are just starting out or have been involved for years, those who persist learn to view this as a contingent world, whose future depends on the choices we make today. The Berlin Wall didn't fall by itself; people dismantled it, politically and physically. Lyndon Johnson didn't desegregate the South; it took the courage of those who risked their lives in Selma, Nashville, Greenville, Birmingham, and hundreds of places that never made the headlines. Similarly, our current social crises won't be solved unless far more of us participate. James Baldwin put it this way: "Everything now, we must assume, is in our hands. We have no right to assume otherwise." We are grasped, as Rilke says, by what we cannot grasp.

You may recall psychiatrist Robert Jay Lifton's concept of the "broken connection," the severed link between our convictions and our conduct. One way to repair this breach is to cultivate a sense of history. If we see our political efforts as isolated acts, we're almost certainly going to grow desperate and disheartened. By contrast, viewing them as part of an ongoing historical narrative helps us feel we have all the time we need to act, even given the urgencies of the moment. It lets us concentrate on the work we have at hand, and trust that if we follow our most generous impulses, our labors will bear fruit. It shifts us from thinking solely about current crises, to asking how our efforts can best shape the world for generations to come.

However we work for what Jesse Jackson calls "the ancient and ageless cause" of human dignity, we need this perspective. Perhaps we need it more than ever in a time of cynicism and dashed hopes. Think of some of the diverse events that inspired the civil rights movement and helped make it possible: Gandhi's nonviolent protests in India; the anticolonial rebellions in Africa; the labor struggles that led to the formation of supportive unions from the United Auto Workers to the Brotherhood of Sleeping Car Porters; the long and patient work of people like Modjesca Simkins and of groups such as local NAACP chapters. Brought about by a tremendous upswelling of courage, vision, and commitment, the triumphs of the civil rights movement came later. But like all advances for freedom and justice, they would have been impossible without a rich legacy of struggle and resistance.

Remember Winston Willis, who joined Columbia University's pivotal anti-apartheid campaigns and later became the head of the Black Students Association. After Winston left Columbia, he taught eighth grade in Harlem, then returned to school to get a doctorate in history from Atlanta's once all-white Emory University. In a talk to black students at Emory, he explained that he'd followed the example of his parents (who were active in the civil rights movement) and of the black student leaders who'd preceded him at Columbia. "We're here not just because we're good students, or on our intrinsic merits," Winston said. "We're literally here by the blood of our people."

"I'm only twenty-seven," he told me, "but I'm beginning to come to grips with the reality that I probably won't see the fundamental changes I want when I'm still around. It helps to know there are many folks before us—and many more who will follow."

As Winston says, each of us builds on the work of others. We can take the stories of people who've struggled for justice in the past as a challenge to do the same. Others have risked and persevered. Now it's our turn. As Rabbi Tarfon wrote, nineteen hundred years ago, "It is not up to you to complete the task. Nonetheless, you are not free to desist from it."

The cynics will continue to smirk, insisting that our efforts are futile. But we're never truly alone when we act with courage and vision. And we never know what we might create if we try. To fail to realize the power of our actions is to reduce the potential of our soul. It's to diminish the spark that burns within us.

We all have our own distinct gifts, strengths, and opportunities to make our lives count. We all have our particular fears, flaws, and constraints. But no one kind of person is responsible for healing all the wounds of the world. That has to be a common task. The challenge is to ask what we want to stand for, and to do our best to act on our beliefs. For our choices will create the world that we pass on.

I began this book by quoting Rabbi Hillel: "If I am not for myself, who will be for me? And if I am only for myself, what am I?" Hillel asks a final question: "If not now, when?" I take his words to mean the moment of commitment cannot be deferred. It must become a lifelong process, one that links our lives to the lives of others, our souls to the souls of others, in a chain of being that reaches both backward and forward, connecting us with all that makes us human.

Resource Guide

BOOKS AND ARTICLES

Alinsky, Saul. *Rules for Radicals*. New York: Vintage Books, 1989.
Alperovitz, Gar. "Distributing Our Technological Inheritance." *Technology Review*, October. 1994.
Andrews, Molly. *Lifetimes of Commitment*. Cambridge: Cambridge UP, 1991.
Arendt, Hannah. *Eichmann in Jerusalem*. New York: Penguin, 1977.
Aronson, Ronald. *After Marxism*. New York: Guilford Press, 1995.
Barber, Benjamin. *Jihad vs. McWorld*. New York: Times Books, 1995.
Barlett, Donald and James B. Steele. *America: What Went Wrong?* Kansas City: Andrews & McMeel, 1992.
Bateson, Gregory. *Towards an Ecology of Mind*. New York: Ballantine, 1972.
Bateson, Mary Catherine. *Composing a Life*. New York: Plume, 1990.
Bell, Derrick. *Confronting Authority*. Boston: Beacon Press, 1994.
Bellah, Robert, et al. *Habits of the Heart*. New York: Harper & Row, 1986.
Berry, Thomas. *The Dream of the Earth*. San Francisco: Sierra Club Books, 1988.
Berry, Wendell. "Solving for Pattern." *The Gift of Good Land*. San Fransisco: North Point, 1981.
Bly, Carol. *Changing the Bully Who Rules the World*. Minneapolis: Milkweed Editions, 1996.
Boal, Augusto. *The Rainbow of Desire*. New York: Routledge, 1995.
Bobo, Kim, Jackie Kendall and Steve Max. *Organizing for Social Change*. Washington, DC: Seven Locks Press, 1991.
Bollier, David. *Aiming Higher*. New York: AMACOM, 1996.
Bonhoeffer, Dietrich. *Letters & Papers from Prison*. New York: Macmillan, 1979.
Boyte, Harry. *Commonwealth*. New York: Free Press, 1989.
Branch, Taylor. *Parting the Waters*. New York: Simon & Schuster, 1988.
Brower, David. *Let the Mountains Talk, Let the Rivers Run*. New York: HarperCollins, 1995.
Buber, Martin. *Paths in Utopia*. Boston: Beacon Press, 1958.
Campell, Will. *Forty Acres and a Goat*. Atlanta: Peachtree Publishers, 1986.
Camus, Albert. *The Rebel*. New York: Vintage Books, 1956.
Cobb, John B. *Sustaining the Common Good*. Cleveland: Pilgrim Press, 1994.
Coles, Robert. *The Call of Stories*. Boston: Houghton Mifflin, 1989.
—*The Moral Life of Children*. Boston: Houghton Mifflin, 1986.

Covey, Stephen. *The 7 Habits of Highly Effective People.* New York: Simon & Schuster, 1990.
Daloz, Laurent Parks, et al. *Common Fire.* Boston: Beacon Press, 1996.
Daly, Herman and Jonathan Cobb. *For the Common Good.* Boston: Beacon Press, 1989.
Dass, Ram and Paul Gorman. *How Can I Help?* New York: Knopf, 1985.
Day, Dorothy. *The Long Loneliness.* San Francisco: HarperCollins, 1997.
Deikman, William. "The Spiritual Heart of Service." *Noetic Sciences Review,* Winter 1997.
Denby, David. "Buried Alive." *The New Yorker,* July 15, 1996.
Diamond, Irene. *Fertile Ground.* Boston: Beacon Press, 1994.
Dionne, E. J. *Why Americans Hate Politics.* New York: Simon & Schuster, 1991.
Dominguez, Joe and Vicki Robin. *Your Money or Your Life.* New York: Penguin, 1993.
Donnelly, Doris. *Forgiveness and Peacemaking.* Erie, PA: Benet Press, 1993.
Edelman, Marian Wright. *The Measure of Our Success.* Boston: Beacon Press, 1992.
Edelman, Peter. "The Worst Thing Bill Clinton Has Done." *Atlantic Monthly,* March 1997.
Ehrenreich, Barbara. *Fear of Falling.* New York: Pantheon: 1989.
Ericsson, Stephanie. *Companion Through the Darkness.* New York: HarperCollins, 1993.
Everett, Melissa. *Making a Living While Making a Difference.* New York: Bantam, 1995.
Flacks, Richard. *Making History.* New York: Columbia UP, 1988.
Fox, Matthew. *Wrestling with the Prophets.* San Francisco: HarperCollins, 1995.
Friere, Paolo. *Education for Critical Consciousness.* New York: Continuum, 1973.
—*Pedagogy of the Oppressed* New York: Continuum, 1970.
Gandhi, M. K. *Nonviolent Resistance.* New York: Shocken Books, 1951.
Gaventa, John. *Power and Powerlessness.* Champaign-Urbana: University of Illinois Press, 1980.
Geoghegan, Tom. *Which Side Are You On?* New York: Plume, 1991.
Gerber, Lane. "We Must Hear Each Other's Cry." *Genocide, War & Human Survival.* ed. Charles Strozier and Flynn Michael. Lanham, MD: Roman & Littlefield, 1996.
Gerzon, Mark. *A House Divided.* New York: Tarcher/Putnam, 1996.
Gilligan, Carol. *In a Different Voice.* Boston: Harvard UP, 1982.
Ginzburg, Natalia. *The Little Virtues.* New York: Scaver Books, 1986.
Gitlin, Todd. *The Twilight of Common Dreams.* New York: Owl Books, 1995.
Goleman, Daniel. *Emotional Intelligence.* New York: Bantam Books, 1995.
Greenleaf, Robert. *Servant Leadership.* Mahwah, NJ: Paulist Press, 1977.
Greider, William. *Who Will Tell the People.* New York: Simon & Schuster, 1993.
Griffin, Susan. *The Eros of Everyday Life.* New York: Anchor Books, 1996.
Gutierrez, Gustavo. *A Theology of Liberation.* Maryknoll, NY: Orbis Press, 1973.
Halberstam, David. *The Children.* New York: Random House, 1998.
Hanh, Thich Nhat. *Being Peace.* Berkeley: Parallax Press, 1987.
Harding, Vincent. *Hope and History.* Maryknoll, NY: Orbis Press, 1990.
Harrington, Michael. *The Long-Distance Runner.* New York: Henry Holt, 1988.
Havel, Václav. *Disturbing the Peace.* New York: Vintage Books, 1990.
Hawken, Paul, et al. *Natural Capitalism.* Boston: Little Brown, 1999.
Heschel, Abraham, et al. *Moral Grandeur and Spiritual Audacity.* New York: Noonday Press, 1997.
Hillman, James. *The Soul's Code.* New York: Random House, 1996.
Hirschman, Albert O. *The Rhetoric of Reaction.* Boston: Harvard UP, 1991.
Hooks, bell and Cornell West. *Breaking Bread.* Boston: South End Press, 1991.

Houston, Jean. *A Mythic Life*. New York: HarperCollins, 1996.
Hyde, Lewis. "Alcohol & Poetry: John Berryman and the Booze Talking." *American Poetry Review*, reprinted in *Pushcart Prize Anthology*, New York: Penguin Books, 1987.
Isaac, Catherine. *Civics for Democracy*. Washington, DC: Essential Books, 1992.
Johnson, George. *Beyond Guilt and Powerlessness*. Minneapolis: Fortress Press, 1989.
Jordan, June. *Naming Our Destiny*. New York: Thunders Mouth Press, 1989.
Kabat-Zinn, Myla and Jon Kabat-Zinn. *Everyday Blessings*. New York: Hyperion, 1997.
Kohlberg, Lawrence. *The Philosophy of Moral Development*. New York: Harper & Row, 1981.
Kozol, Jonathan. *Savage Inequalities*. New York: Harper Collins, 1992.
Lappé, Frances Moore and Paul Martin Du Bois. *The Quickening of America*. San Francisco: Jossey-Bass, 1994.
Lasch, Christopher. *The Minimal Self*. New York: W. W. Norton, 1984.
Lemann, Nicholas. "Kicking in Groups." *Atlantic Monthly*, April 1996.
Lerner, Michael. *The Politics of Meaning*. Reading, MA: Addison-Wesley, 1996.
Lifton, Robert Jay. *The Broken Connection*. New York: Basic Books, 1983.
Loeb, Paul. *Generation at the Crossroads*. New Brunswick, NJ: Rutgers UP, 1994.
—*Hope in Hard Times*. Lexington, MA: Lexington Books, 1987.
—*Nuclear Culture*. Philadelphia: New Society Publishers, 1986.
Lorde, Audre. *Undersong*. New York: W. W. Norton, 1992.
Luks, Allan with Peggy Payne. *The Healing Power of Doing Good*. New York: Ballantine Books, 1991.
MacIntyre, Alasdair. *After Virtue*. Notre Dame: Notre Dame UP, 1984.
Macy, Joanna Rogers and Molly Young Brown. *Coming Back to Life*. Blaine, WA: New Society Publishers, 1998. *www.newsociety.com*
Macy, Joanna and Thich Nhat Hanh. *World as Lover, World as Self*. Berkeley: Parallax Press, 1991.
McCann, Lisa and Laurie Anne Pearlman. *Psychological Trauma and the Adult Survivor*. Levittown, PA: Brunner/Mazel, 1990.
Merton, Thomas. *New Seeds of Contemplation*. New York: W. W. Norton, 1974.
—*Raids on the Unspeakable*. New York: New Directions, 1964.
Miller, Alice. *For Your Own Good*. London: Virago, 1987.
Mishel, Lawrence et al. *The State of Working America*. Ithaca, NY: Cornell UP, 1999.
Moore, Thomas. *Care of the Soul*. New York: HarperCollins, 1992.
Morrison, Roy. *We Build the Road as We Travel*. Warner, NH: Essential Book Publishers, 1997.
Morrison, Toni. *Beloved*. New York: Plume, 1988.
Nicarthy, Ginny. *Getting Free*. Seattle: Seal Press, 1997.
Nouwen, Henri et al. *Compassion*. New York: Doubleday Image, 1983.
O'Gorman, Angie, ed. *The Universe Bends Toward Justice*. Philadelphia: New Society Publishers, 1990.
Oliver, Mary. *New and Selected Poems*. Boston: Beacon Press: 1993.
Orwell, George. *Homage to Catalonia*. New York: Harcourt Brace, 1987.
Palmer, Parker. "The Heart of Knowing." *Shambala Sun*, Sept. 1997.
Peck, M. Scott. *The Different Drum*. New York: Simon & Schuster, 1987.
—*The Road Less Traveled*. New York: Simon & Schuster, 1978.
Pipher, Mary. *Reviving Ophelia*. New York: Putnam, 1994.
—*The Shelter of Each Other*. New York: Ballantine, 1997.
Prejean, Sister Helen. *Dead Man Walking*. New York: Vintage Books, 1993.
Prochaska, James. *Changing for Good*. New York: Avon Books, 1995.

Prothrow-Stith, Deborah and Michaele Weissman. *Deadly Consequences*. New York: HarperCollins, 1991.

Putnam, Robert. "Bowling Alone." *Journal of Democracy*, January 1995.

Remen, Rachel Naomi. *Kitchen Table Wisdom*. New York: Riverhead Books, 1996.

Rich, Adrienne. *The Will to Change*. New York: W. W. Norton, 1971.

Rilke, Ranier Maria, translated by Robert Bly. *Selected Poems of Ranier Maria Rilke*. New York: HarperCollins, 1981.

Rodriguez, Luis. *Always Running*. New York: Touchstone Books, 1994.

Rorty, Richard. *Contingency, Irony and Solidarity*. Cambridge: Cambridge UP, 1989.

Roszak, Theodore. *The Voice of the Earth*. New York: Simon & Schuster, 1992.

Rubin, Lillian. *Worlds of Pain*. New York: Basic Books, 1992.

Sanders, Scott Russell. "The Most Human Art." *Utne Reader*, Sept.–Oct. 1997, special section on the lessons of stories.

Schaef, Anne Wilson. *When Society Becomes an Addict*. New York: Harper & Row, 1988.

Schor, Juliet. *A Sustainable Economy*. New Party Pamphlet available from 1-800-200-1294.

—*The Overworked American*. New York: Basic Books, 1992.

Seligman, Martin. *Learned Optimism*. New York: Random House, 1990.

Sharp, Gene. *The Politics of Nonviolent Action*. Boston: Porter Sargent, 1973.

Shaw, Randy. *The Activist's Handbook*. Berkeley: Univ of California Press, 1996.

Snyder, Gary. *Turtle Island*. New York: New Directions, 1975.

Solomon, Norman. *The Habits of Highly Deceptive Media: Decoding Spin and Lies*. Monroe, ME: Common Courage Press, 1999.

Staub, Ervin. *The Roots of Evil*. Cambridge: Cambridge UP, 1989.

Steinem, Gloria. *Revolution from Within*. Boston: Little Brown, 1993.

Stout, Jeffrey. *Ethics After Babel*. Boston: Beacon Press, 1988.

Stout, Linda. *Bridging the Class Divide and Other Lessons for Grassroots Organizing*. Boston: Beacon Press, 1997.

Terkel, Studs. *American Dreams: Lost and Found*. New York: Ballantine Books, 1981.

—*Coming of Age*. New York: The New Press, 1995.

Trueheart, Charles. "Welcome to the Next Church." *Atlantic Monthly*, August 1996.

Tutu, Desmond. *The Rainbow People of God*. New York: Doubleday, 1994.

Vernier, Phillipe. From Phillipe and Dorothy Berkeley, *The Choice Is Always Ours*. San Francisco: HarperCollins, 1989.

Walker, Alice. *Living By the Word*. New York: Harcourt Brace, 1989.

Wallis, Jim. *The Soul of Politics*. New York: Orbis Press/The New Press, 1994.

Washington James, ed. *A Testament of Hope: The Essential Writings and Speeches of Martin Luther King, Jr*. New York: HarperCollins, 1986.

Weiskel, Timothy. "Some Notes from Belshaz'zar's Feast." *The Greening of Faith*. Hanover, NH: UP of New England, 1997.

Werbach, Adam. *Act Now, Apologize Later*. New York: HarperCollins, 1998.

Weschler, Lawrence. *Soilidarity*. New York: Simon & Schuster, 1982.

West, Cornel. *Race Matters*. New York: Vintage Books, 1994.

Whalen, Jack and Richard Flacks. *Beyond the Barricades*. Philadelphia: Temple UP, 1989.

Wiesel, Elie. The Refugee, from MacEoin, Gary, ed., *Sanctuary*. New York: Harper & Row, 1985.

Williams, Patricia. *The Alchemy of Race and Rights*. Cambridge: Harvard UP, 1980.

Williams, William Appleman. *Empire as a Way of Life*. New York: Oxford UP, 1980.

Williamson, Marianne. *A Return to Love*. New York: HarperCollins, 1992.
— *The Healing of America*. New York: Simon & Schuster, 1997.
Wink, Walter. *Engaging the Powers*. Minneapolis: Fortress Press, 1992.
Wu, Harry with George Vecsey. *Troublemaker*. New York: Times Books, 1996.
Wuthnow, Robert. *Acts of Compassion*. Princeton, NJ: Princeton UP, 1991.
Zinn, Howard. *A People's History of the United States*. New York: HarperCollins, 1980.
— *You Can't Be Neutral on a Moving Train*. Boston: Beacon Press, 1994.

MAGAZINES

Hope magazine, P.O. Box 52242, Boulder, CO 80323 (800) 513-0869 www.hopemag.com

In These Times, 2040 N. Milwaukee Ave., Chicago, IL 60647 (800) 827-0270 www.inthesetimes.com

Mother Jones, P.O. Box 469024, Escondido, CA 94046 (800) 334-8152 www.motherjones.com

Ms. magazine, 20 Exchange Pl., 22nd floor, New York, NY 10005 (212) 509-2095

The Nation, 72 Fifth Ave., New York, NY 10011 (212) 242-8400 www.thenation.com

National Catholic Reporter, Box 419281, Kansas City, MO 64141 (800) 444-8910 www.natcath.com

Noetic Sciences Review, 475 Gate Five Rd., Suite 300, Sausalito, CA 94965 (800) 383-1586 www.noetic.org

The Other Side, 300 W Apsley St., Philadelphia, PA 19144 (215) 849-2178 www.theotherside.org

The Progressive, 409 East Main St., Madison, WI 53703 (608) 257-4626 www.progressive.org

Sojourners, 2401 15th St. NW, Washington, DC 20009 (800) 714-7474 www.sojourners.com

Teaching Tolerance, Southern Poverty Law Center, 400 Washington Ave., Montgomery, AL 36104 (334) 264-0286 www.splcenter.org/teachingtolerance.htm

Tikkun, 26 Fell St., San Francisco, CA, 94102 (800) 395-7753 www.tikkun.org

Utne Reader, P.O. Box 7460, Red Oak, IA 51591 (800) 736-8863 www.utne.com

Whole Earth magazine, 1408 Mission Ave., San Rafael, CA 94901 (415) 256-2800 www.wholeearthmag.com

Z magazine, 116 St. Botolph St., Boston, MA 02115 (617) 266-0629 www.lbbs.org

ORGANIZATIONS AND WEB SITES

Alternative Press Center www.altpress.org/newdir.htm (Comprehensive listing of progressive magazines and zines)

American Civil Liberties Union, 125 Broad St., 18th Floor, New York, NY 10004 (212) 549-2500; www.aclu.org

American Newspeak: www.scn.org/news/newspeak/ (Best political satire on the Net)

Americans Talk Issues, PO Box 5190, St. Augustine, FL, 32084. www.publicinterestpolling.com. (Innovative approaches to public interest polling, detailed in their book, *Locating Consensus for Democracy*)

Center for Living Democracy, RR #1 Black Fox Rd., Brattleboro, VT 05301 (802) 254-1234 www.livingdemocracy.org (Information on innovative local projects)

Citizens for Tax Justice, 1311 L St. NW, Washington, DC 20005 (202) 626-3780 www.ctj.org (Best available analysis of federal and state taxation patterns, including more progressive alternatives)

Economic Policy Institute, 1660 L St. NW, Suite 1200, Washington, DC 20036 (202) 775-8810 www.epinet.org (Best source on economic trends and inequality)

Electronic Policy Network www.epn.org (Diverse links on current policy issues)

Environmental Working Group www.ewg.org (Core information source on environmental issues)

Fairness and Accuracy in Reporting, 130 W. 25 St., New York, NY 10001 (800) 847-3993 www.fair.org (National media-watch group with some local chapters. They also put out an excellent magazine called *Extra*)

Giraffe Project, PO Box 759, Langley, WA 98260 (360) 221-7989 www.whidbey.com/giraffe (Publicizes people who "stick their necks out" through resource material)

Institute for Public Accuracy www.accuracy.org (Expert alternative perspectives on breaking news stories)

New Dimensions, PO Box 569, Ukiah, CA 95482 (800) 935-8273 www.newdimensions.org (Excellent syndicated radio show on spirituality and social transformation, also produces a magazine)

Oneworld www.oneworld.org (Gateway to global political and environmental groups and issues)

Webactive www.webactive.com (Huge collection of organizational links and RealAudio interviews, with weekly radio commentaries by progressive figures like Jim Hightower)

WAYS TO GET INVOLVED

ACORN (Association of Community Organizations for Reform Now) 737 8th St. SE, Washington, DC 20003 (202) 547-9292 (National low-income community group)

AFL-CIO 815 16th St. NW, Washington, DC 20006 (202) 639-5000 www.aflcio.org/home.htm (Comprehensive links on labor organizations and issues)

American Friends Service Committee, 1501 Cherry St., Philadelphia, PA 19102 (215) 241-7000 www.afsc.org (Veteran Quaker peace and justice group with regional offices)

American Renaissance Alliance, 4410 Massachusetts Ave., Suite 409, Washington, DC 20006 (202) 544-1219 www.renaissancealliance.org (New organization, founded by Marianne Williamson, to bridge spiritual and social change efforts)

Amnesty International, 322 8th Ave., New York, NY 10001 (212) 807-8400 www.amnesty.org

Catholic Worker, 36 E. 1st St., New York, NY 10003 (212) 254-1640 (Organization founded by Dorothy Day to link service, spirit, and social change, with local Catholic Worker houses and a national newspaper)

Center for Campus Organizing, 165 Friend St., #1, Boston, MA 02114 (617) 725-2886 www.cco.org (Major national student organizing group)

Children's Defense Fund, 25 E St. NW, Washington, DC 20001 (202) 628-8787 www.childrensdefense.org

Democratic Socialists of America, 180 Varick St., 12th Floor, New York NY 10014 (212) 727-8610 www.dsausa.org (Counterpart to European socialist parties, puts out excellent magazine and has local chapters)

Fellowship of Reconciliation, P.O. Box 271, Nyack, NY 10960 (914) 358-4601 (Veteran ecumenical religious peace group with national magazine and local chapters)

Greenpeace, 1436 U St. NE, Washington, DC 20009 (800) 326-0959 www.greenpeaceusa.org
Habitat for Humanity, 121 Habitat St., Americus, GA 31709 (800) 422-4828 www.habitat.org
Idealist www.idealist.org (Global gateway site on volunteer and nonprofit opportunities, searchable by issue, country, and organization name)
Industrial Areas Foundation (IAF), 220 West Kinzie St., Fifth floor, Chicago, IL 60610 (312) 245-9211 (Parent organization of COPS, with regional affiliates)
Infact, 256 Hanover St., 3d floor, Boston, MA 02113 (617) 742-4583 www.infact.org (Coordinates grassroots boycotts)
Institute for Global Communications www.igc.org (One of the best progressive gateway sites, with alternative news stories and links to organizations and publications)
Jobs With Justice, 501 Third St. NW, Washington, DC 20001 (202) 434-1106 www.jwj.org (National network to support local labor organizing)
League of Women Voters, 1730 M St. NW, Washington, DC 20036 (202) 429-1965 www.lwv.org
NAACP (National Association for the Advancement of Colored People), 4805 Mount Hope Dr., Baltimore, MD 21215 (410) 358-8900 www.naacp.org
National Labor Committee, 15 Union Square West, New York, NY 10003 (212) 242-0700 www.nlcnet.org (Coordinates anti-sweatshop campaigns like the Gap boycott)
New Party, 88 Third Ave., Suite 313, Brooklyn, NY 11217 (800) 200-1294 www.newparty.org (Best of the national third-party alternatives, focusing on winnable local races)
NOW (National Organization for Women), 1000 16th St. NW, Suite 700, Washington, DC 20036 (202) 331-0066 www.now.org
Parents for Public Schools, 1520 N. State St., Jackson, MS 39202 (601) 353-1335 www.parents4publicschools.com
Pax Christi, 532 W. 8th St., Erie, PA 16502 (814) 453-4955 www.nonviolence.org/pcusa (International Catholic peace group)
Peace Action, 1819 H St. NW, Suite 420, Washington, DC 20006 (202) 862-9740 www.peace-action.org
Progressive People Links www.people-link.com (Links to an eclectic selection of social change groups)
Public Campaign, 1320 19th St. NW, Suite M1, Washington, DC 20036 (202) 293-0222 www.publicampaign.org (Major coordinator of clean elections campaigns)
Public Citizen, 1600 20th St. NW, Washington DC 20009 (800) 289-3787 www.citizen.org (Research and advocacy group, founded by Ralph Nader, on consumer, health, and environmental issues)
Public Interest Research Groups (PIRGs), 218 D St. SE, Washington, DC 20003 (202) 546-9707 www.pirg.org/uspirg (Campus and community-based group originally founded by Ralph Nader)
Rainforest Action Network, 221 Pine St., Suite 500, San Francisco, CA 94104 (415) 398-4404 www.ran.org
Servenet, Youth Service America, 1101 15th St., Suite 200, Washington, DC, 20005 (202) 296-2992 www.servenet.org (Online database of volunteer opportunities, searchable by zip code for any region of the country)
Sierra Club, 85 Second St., 2nd floor, San Francisco, CA 94105 (415) 977-5500 www.sierraclub.org
Student Environmental Action Coalition (SEAC), P.O. Box 31909, Philadelphia, PA 19104 (215) 222-4711 www.seac.org
Surfrider Foundation, 122 S. El Camino Real, Suite #67, San Clemente, CA 92672 (949) 492-8170 www.surfrider.org

Volunteermatch, www.volunteermatch.org (Interactive site on U.S. volunteer
    opportunities, searchable by zip code and kind of involvement)
War Resisters League, 339 Lafayette St., New York, NY 10012 (212) 228-0450
    www.nonviolence.org (Veteran pacifist group, with local chapters and
    magazine)
IfNotNow.com www.ifnotnow.com (Site created by major environmental and
    social justice groups to let ordinary citizens easily coordinate letters to
    Congress)

Acknowledgments

It takes a village to write a book, at least in my case. *Soul of a Citizen* would have been impossible without a larger community that offered intellectual brainstorming, financial support, emotional sustenance, places to stay, and a wealth of other kinds of assistance.

Thank you Larry Agran, Nancy and Buster Alvord, Architects of Travel, Allison Barlow, Harriet Barlow, Jim Becker, Rabbi Leonard Beerman (who's inspired my journey from the beginning), David Bergholz, Mark and Sharon Bloome, the Body & Soul Conference, Brainerd Foundation, Leslie Brockelbank, Elizabeth Clementson, Barbara Cohn, Compton Foundation, Craig Comstock, Sue Cook, Cook Brothers Educational Fund, Midge Cowley, Rebecca Dare, Lenny Dee, John Deklewa, Jonathan Dolger, Gary Dreiblatt and Nancy Sinkoff, Jim Driscoll, Wendy Emrich, Marge Fasman, Gary Ferdman, Ellen Ferguson, Carol Ferry, Lila Garrett, the Giraffe Project, Wade Greene, the George Gund Foundation, Adrienne Hall, Bill Harris, Jane Hatfield, Bill Hess, Ann Hirschi and Kraig Schwartz, Tresa Hughes, Pamela Johnson, Anis and Julie Karam, Alan Kay, Corrine Dee Kelly, Jeana Kimball, Kongsgaard-Goldman Foundation, Albert A. List Foundation, Rodney Loeb and Carol Summer, Shirley Magidson, Suzy and Wally Marks, Nan McMurray, Charley Meconis and Robbie Sherman, Ken Mountcastle, Josephine Murray, Hing Lau Ng, Joan Palevsky, Bill Patz, Ruth Pelz, Puffin Foundation, Alan and Andrea Rabinowitz, Virginia Ramirez, Samuel Rubin Foundation, Barbara Schinzinger,

Stanley Sheinbaum, Alan Sieroty, John and Janet McKee Silard, Alan Slifka, Alison Smith, Norman Solomon, Paul and Ann Sperry, Jerry Starr, Larry Swanson, the Tibet House's Peacemaking Conference, Tides Foundation, Sonya Vetra Tinsley, Peter Titcomb, Bill and Betsy Elich Vandercook, Fred Waingrow, Joan Warburg, Cora Weiss, Jaki and the late Ron Williams, and Bob and Blaikie Worth.

I also drew on the skills and resources of some good institutions: the Economic Policy Institute for studies of recent economic shifts, the media activist group FAIR, the Pew Center for the People & the Press for their continuing studies of contemporary American values, and the wonderful and ever-patient staff of the Seattle Public Library.

Thanks for providing my institutional base to the Center for Ethical Leadership, in particular Bill Grace and Dale Neinow, and to the Western States Center's Dan Petegorsky and Liz Deuker. Thanks to Abby Brown of Public Relations Services and Rochelle Lefkowitz and Hildy Karp of ProMedia for lining up more print and broadcast interviews than I could possibly imagine. George Greenfield of Lecture Literary Management and Jodi Solomon and Bill Fargo of Jodi Solomon Speakers helped create the financial base for my labors of writing by arranging my lectures at colleges and conferences. My Seattle local of the National Writers Union offered friendship, business acumen, and mutual aid. Thanks to my St. Martin's support group of Matt Baldacci, Elaine Bleakney, John Cunningham, Miranda Ford, Andrew Miller, John Murphy, Sally Richardson, Patti Rosati, and copyeditor Jolanta Benal.

Soul of a Citizen has also benefited from the comments of Ron Aronson, Elaine Bernard, Kim Fellner, Dick Flacks, Jorge Garcia, Glen Gersmehl, Jean Houston, Pete Knutson, Joanna Macy, Peggy Taylor, Sam Tucker, Magda Waingrow (my eagle-eyed mother), and Howard Zinn. Wayne Grytting gave excellent feedback and has also designed my Website: www.soulofacitizen.org. Wayne's own site, American Newspeak, www.scn.org/news/newspeak/, has been rightly called the best political satire on the Net by nearly every major reviewer. Lane Gerber connected me with key psychological research and made sure I got it right. Harvey McKinnon guided me down the paths of ecophilosophy. And Mark Powelson—editor and publisher turned lay theologian—helped me give questions of faith the weight they deserved.

Some key individuals were so closely woven with the genesis and fruition of this book, it's hard to imagine it without them. Jean Tarbox gave me the original idea for this project, and JoAnn Miller then pushed it further. John Weeks cracked the whip to get me writing. My agent, Geri Thoma, of Elaine Markson Agency, has been an invaluable guide, not only in the marketplace, but also on everything related to the book. Liz Gjelten cut and reorganized my initial drafts until their logic worked in every way. Edwin Dobb then helped me hone every sentence and word. And Becky Koh of St. Martin's not only edited the final draft, but bought the book in the first place and then convinced her colleagues to take it seriously enough to give it a shot.

My wonderful stepson, William Martin, reminded me what real life is all about and found just the right Gary Larson cartoons when I needed to cite them in the text. My wife, Rebecca Hughes, brought her tremendous caring into my life and made me happier than I've ever been. That she also strengthened the manuscript in immeasurable ways is the least of my blessings.

About the Author

Paul Loeb, an associated scholar at Seattle's Center for Ethical Leadership, has spent thirty years researching and writing about citizen responsibility and empowerment—asking what makes some people choose lives of social commitment, while others abstain. He has written three highly praised books: *Generation at the Crossroads: Apathy and Action on the American Campus*; *Hope in Hard Times: America's Peace Movement and the Reagan Era*; and *Nuclear Culture: Living and Working in the World's Largest Atomic Complex*. He's written for a wide range of publications including *The New York Times*, *Washington Post*, *Los Angeles Times*, *St. Louis Post-Dispatch*, *Baltimore Sun*, *Psychology Today*, *Salon*, *Utne Reader*, *Village Voice*, *Mother Jones*, *Technology Review*, *New Age Journal*, *National Catholic Reporter*, and *International Herald-Tribune*.

Loeb has also appeared repeatedly on national TV and radio, including appearances on such TV networks as CNN, PBS, and C-SPAN, the *NBC Nightly News* with Tom Brokaw, National Public Radio, the ABC, NBC, and CBS radio networks, and national German, Australian, and Canadian radio.

Loeb attended Stanford University and New York's New School for Social Research, then edited *Liberation* magazine. He lives in Seattle with his wife, writer Rebecca Hughes, and stepson, budding humorist William Martin. Loeb has lectured to enthusiastic responses at two hundred colleges and universities around the country—including Harvard, Stanford, Dartmouth, Chicago, Michigan,

MIT, Yale, Cornell, Brown, Wisconsin, and Columbia. He has key-noted many conferences including the American Society on Aging, the National Conference on Race and Ethnicity in American Higher Education, the National Association of Student Personnel Administrators, the all-company meeting of Patagonia Corporation, and the Unitarian General Assembly.

Paul Loeb is currently lecturing throughout the United States and is available for speaking engagements and workshops. For further information, contact him through the Center for Ethical Leadership, 3232 41st Ave SW, Seattle, WA 98116, at (206) 935-9132, at paulloeb@bigfoot.com, or on the Website www.soulofacitizen.org.